W9-DBU-047

SOME MODERN NOVELISTS

SOME MODERN NOVELISTS

APPRECIATIONS AND ESTIMATES

BY

HELEN THOMAS FOLLETT

AND

WILSON FOLLETT

"What is a novel if not a conviction of our fellowmen's existence strong enough to take upon itself a form of imagined life clearer than reality?"

NEW YORK

HENRY HOLT AND COMPANY

Published January, 1918

THE QUINN & BODEN CO. PRESS
RAHWAY, N. J.

PREFACE

Of the dozen appreciations and estimates gathered here, several have appeared in *The Atlantic Monthly* and one in *The Yale Review*, to the editors of which magazines we make grateful acknowledgment for permission to revise and reprint about half of the material in this book.

We hope that, in and underlying the group of essays, the reader may find a unity of intention expressed in neither the title nor the form of the volume. Each of these seemingly detached papers is conceived as a footnote to a tendency: the modern tendency of fiction—and, for that matter, of all humane thinking and living—toward a fuller sense of the continuity in things, in the world and in man's collective life.

This sense of continuity—call it "living in the whole," the social conscience, or simply the will to brotherhood—is of course no new thing, either in the world or in literature. The discovery by Adam and Eve that there was a certain rewarding solidarity even in the sharing of sin and fear must have been a comparatively recent development of the social intuition. Yet that intuition has entered, it seems to us, upon a definably new phase, not dating indeed from any single event or even from any single decade, but growing without cessation ever since that memorable yesterday when our English-speaking world was suddenly made the richer by three great works of the imagination called *Adam Bede*, *The Ordeal of Richard Feverel*, and *The Origin of Species*.

This new phase is characterized, as we understand it, by the union of the old and universal dream of brotherhood with the new scientific curiosity about the nature and the bases of society. The change is from emotional or philanthropic appreciation—that is, humanitarianism—to intellectual and impersonal appreciation. This new force has become, at its worst, sociologic muck-raking and, at its best, a new humanism. It was given scope and momentum, obviously, by the break-up of the old theology, the perception of organic unity in material creation, the rise of the social sciences, and the generally increased feeling of our joint responsibility to each other and to the whole.

In fiction the principal effect of this force has been a shifting of emphasis from the exceptional to the typical, from the special to the general. Naturally the novel has still to deal with individuals; but it deals with them not, as once, for the diversion they provide so much as for the truth they represent. In short, the novel specializes in the relations of the individual, and its emphasis works from him outward to larger and larger units—his family, his class, his community, his race, mankind. He exists, then, for a crucially representative testing of social institutions and ideas. However interesting he may be for himself alone, he does not exist for himself alone: his excuse for existence is in his social implications.

This general change in the purpose and direction of the novel is what we have tried to study in a number of authors, each of whom is a more or less specialized manifestation of the drift of modern life and thought toward the social, the communal. That drift amounts in itself to an insistent and searching new canon of criticism, the whole rationale of which is still largely an unwritten story. We attempt that story here only in a series of marginalia. Yet, lest the reader forget what absorbing and tremendous development it is we wish to annotate, we have thought it well not to let the general principle go quite unstated. This is the excuse for a short Introduction, "The War and the Reader," a sincere if possibly too sententious effort to describe the ministry of the renewed social conscience of art to the private conscience of the reader, and more especially the great quickening of both kinds of conscience in these years of blood and terror; years which impose an added necessity of moral self-justification upon everything thought, known, and done—and not least upon the artist, his public, his critic, and his critic's public.

It ought to be added that we try here, not to present a synoptic account of each author as a whole, or even to discuss every one of his important works, but to identify each author by what is central and essential in him—to locate his center of gravity.

H. T. F.
W. F.

CONTENTS

INTRODUCTION

THE WAR AND THE READER

THE WAR AND THE READER

I

George Meredith, who is commonly thought of as having written his novels for a very small audience and missed all but a fraction of even that, has begun to have his belated day. His public grows; and it may be said that, to an intellectual majority of readers, he has proved himself among the great intellectual necessities. If we subtract the faddist Meredithians, the professional disciples and idolaters, it will still be true that Meredith, in the years after he stopped writing and yet more fully in the years after his death, had from the world's appreciation that which he had sought from it, first patiently and at last impatiently, during his forty years of work.

This Meredith of the small but growing audience, the Meredith who wrote poems that read like epigrams and epigrams that read like poems, stands, then, close and ever closer to us. And yet not so mysteriously close as another Meredith whose history is just the opposite. While the author of *Richard Feverel* and *The Amazing Marriage* seeks a public which, to this day, must be reckoned more in brains than in numbers, it is odd and strange to us to recall that George Meredith once served an enormous and heterogeneous public which no longer exists. It is an important fact to recall at this time, for that forgotten popular Meredith of long ago adds a cubit to the stature of the whole man; and, not as an artist perhaps but as a moral symbol, the forgotten Meredith speaks to us more insistently than the remembered.

It was over fifty years ago, in the year after the close of our American Civil War, that Meredith, then in his thirty-eighth year, laid down his pen of novelist for his other of war correspondent of a great London journal. Hurrying to the Austro-Italian battle-front in northern Italy, he began his series of letters to the *Post*. That battle-ground by the Po was near enough to the one where at this moment the armies of the same two nations, the sons and grandsons of the same men, face each other—so near that time closes before us like a revolving door, and we feel queerly the sense that those same forces must always have confronted each other just so, eternally deadlocked over the same desperate issues.

That war of '66 was not Meredith's war, but he made it his own through an indestructible and passionate imaginative sympathy for any sort of human struggle toward any sort of liberty, by whomever waged, on whatever soil. The extent, the fierce intensity of that emotion he proved in the work which remains as the permanent fruit of his short Italian campaign, the stirring historical pageant *Vittoria*. "In the end," he says, "a country true to itself and determined to claim God's gift to brave men will overmatch a mere army, however solid its force."

Now we are in the midst of a war that is Meredith's

in the nearest, most intimate of all possible senses; and it is doubly certain that if his living personal presence were still part of the English world he would once more desert his great affair of the mind and answer somehow the strong human call to action. It is more than likely too that his irony would find a rebuke for those of us who can go on behaving as though nothing had happened to the world. And especially his lash would reach those who write books, and books about books, with no very exacting sense of what books are for; those who can look on our study, our literature, our art, our criticism, as though they were in themselves of the first importance. He would see a target for cold scorn in the spectacle of some persons with pens in their hands, and some others with books in their hands, trying irresponsibly to enjoy the fine fruits of his heritage of race, language, and tradition, just when the whole tree that bore those fruits is being all but uprooted. To Meredith the fruits of art meant less than nothing apart from the tree on which they grew and the soil of civilization in which the tree must be planted. "All right use of life, and the one secret of life," he said, "is to pave ways for the firmer footing of those who succeed us; as to my works, I know them faulty, think them of worth only when they point and aid to that end."

What strikes us, then, through this symbol of the two Merediths is the unconscious cynicism of attempting to phrase the meaning of art in terms of anything other than its service to life. How can we continue now to look upon art, life's second self, without a qualm or a question, as though in itself it greatly mattered? Whatever we choose to interpret literature, and more particularly the novel, as meaning or as being worth, it is quite sure that some small pettifogging ways of interpreting it are swept away for the present, perhaps for always, in the same flood that carries off so much other wreckage of our cluttered modern world—the flood of history at the full, broken over its dikes and raging, the so terribly renewed and still renewing bath of blood. If our whole consciousness is not drenched with that; if we have the heart in the midst of it, and in a world grown so small that what threatens one of us threatens every one, to sit in our comparatively safe place apart with a detached, an idly curious glance for the red tide that rises; if we feel no insistent demand to revise the standards and values we have lived by, to ask in a new way what is the worth of the things we do and whether there is any solid ground under our interest in them; if in short we can still go the old placid ways—then we are indeed "little folk of little souls." For our part we are unable to imagine a writer or a lecturer about the fine arts as sitting down at his desk or mounting his platform without the sense of futility, of self-distrust —of something amounting to a challenge to his self-respect. And that is why this series of papers about some writers of books must begin with a consideration more fundamental than any that concerns books alone. It must present literature, not as a thing aloof, self-regarding and self-justifying, but as part of the very mesh or web or broken pattern of life itself, life in the largest sense—a thing of relations, interpenetrations, contacts, and hence perhaps not the smallest item of the infinite whole.

II

We speak of certain small ways of regarding literature and of defining it: let us be more particular as to some of them. Suppose we subscribe, either by words or by consenting silence, to the old, old basic doctrine of all æsthetics, that the ultimate purpose of art is to give pleasure. How can we make peace with our consciences on these terms, except by giving "pleasure" a much more sweeping definition than it has been accustomed to bear? Suppose we hold by the other old worn formula of "Art for Art's sake": how shall we retain our self-respect unless by giving "Art" a meaning so broad that we might as well shift the formula at once to "Art for Life's sake"? How can we for an instant put up with the notion of literature as simply an escape from the actual, a cloister of quiet and release? How, especially, can we find anything but a mockery in the sentimentalism that infests so much of our English literature, and nearly all of our American fiction—that sentimentalism which, as Meredith pointed out, is but the opposite face of pruriency, and which may be defined as the childish and spoiled desire to have our cake and eat it too? In this latter respect, our sentimentalism, we are a cynical people. In business, in politics, we are always droning about the need to be practical, to "face the hard facts of life"—whereas in our education, our religion, our novels and dramas and paintings, those facts are precisely what no consideration could hire us to face.

All these fashions of sundering art from life are fashions of belittling both—how cynically, it takes a decade and a war like the present completely to disclose to us. Every age reduces itself somehow to a catch-word. That of the eighteenth century was "reason" or "restraint" or "the golden mean"; that of the nineteenth was "liberation"; that of the early twentieth may be read by the future as "efficiency," which is a working translation of "cynicism." Efficiency means a place for each thing and each thing in its place—work while you work, play while you play, read while you read, make war while you make war, and above all keep things in separate sealed compartments; don't let these separate things interpenetrate lest they interfere with one another. This species of cynicism, so far as it concerns letters, has flowered in a phrase that heads we don't know how many columns of literary chit-chat: "The World of Books."

Now, it is into that detached and irresponsible world, that place of pure "unmoral" decorativeness and diversion, that criticism has no longer any heart to invite the reader. It is into that world that Meredith never wished to entice anybody—and in that sense Meredith is no more than a synonym for high moral decency. "The World of Books" is a synonym for the opposite thing, moral irresponsibility and immaturity. To see the world as somehow one, to reduce its paradoxes and cross-purposes to some sort of synthetic unity, to discover in the whole mixed scheme some value great enough to include and interpret every lesser—this is the distinguishing necessity of a real intellect. It is that necessity which demands of us that we discard now, if we have never done so before, the idea of literature as existing for idle pleasure, or for the delight of our decorative sense, or for an avenue of romantic escape; it is that which breaks down for us the walls of our little make-believe prison-world of books.

The plain truth is that this war has taken the pen out of the hand of the individual critic and put it into the hand of the multitude. The only fiction which remains tolerable at all is that which speaks in a clear voice to some direct human needs created or re-emphasized by the war; the only standard of criticism worth raising is the sum of those very needs. Art must be, as never before, a ministry to need; criticism must be, as never before, the quick response of need ministered to, the indifferent silence of need ignored or travestied. Thus the war becomes a critic, and the only critic of enough scope and candor to meet the requirements of the hour.

War is the great satirist, the great cynic: more than ever now, in a world so shrunken that we must all live at the center of it. However the future may judge of the war as creator, the least prophetic can hardly have escaped seeing it as supreme and universal critic. A destroyer, this war, and a leveler; a teacher of unfaith, a testing scourge for men and movements, for ideas and creeds. Many things we shall never countenance again on the old terms; many other things have dropped quite out of mind, as not worth even the glance of retrospect—illusions that could only quail and shrivel in the glare of war the critic. Nothing can seem quite the same thing; nothing can survive except by multiplying its claims and paying a higher price for survival.

To say that we are impatient with this and that thing which might have pleased us three years ago is not enough, though it is something. To say that we have welcomed this and that thing which could not have pleased us three years ago is not enough, though it is much. To this extent at least we have all submitted to war's destructive criticism of our former selves. But the criticism is constructive too; for the war, indiscriminately wrecking, has taught us to discriminate. Some things, more precious than we had known, we must cling to the more fondly because they are threatened. We have been forced to prove how few were the things we really wanted, how many the incumbrances we merely thought we wanted. Strong indeed must be the moorings of any collective faith which is not swept away now; full indeed of inward light must be the ideal which can still seem to shine for any great number of eyes, while the shadow of these black condor wings is passing over it. Whatever appears beautiful now *is* beautiful, has something of the eternal in it.

To revert to our symbol, Meredith gives us in the singer Vittoria his parable of art paying the increased cost, crowned and consummated by service to life, to noble aspiration, to liberty and fraternity. Vittoria is introduced by the Chief into his circle of patriot conspirators and liberators. To him she is "a noble virgin; the Vestal's fire burns straight." In such lies his hope for the future of Italy—and Meredith's for the future of mankind. But Ugo Corte resents Vittoria's intrusion into real affairs. "Are we to have women in a conference?" he asks sarcastically; and when he finds that Vittoria is an artist, "a cantatrice about to appear upon the boards," his scorn is redoubled. "'Ah! that completes it. . . . We require to be refreshed with quavers and crescendos and trillets! Who ever knew a singer that cared an inch of flesh for her country? . . . These singers have no country.'" This is exactly the common attitude of the world of affairs toward the artist. But Vittoria makes of song itself a cry for liberty, an instrument to fire the will and unite oppressed people against oppression. "'If they shoot me I shall be satisfied to know that I have sung a song that cannot be forgotten.'" And the song that she sang, the message of her art, was

"Italia, Italia shall be free!"

The answer of the artist in her to her country's need is like the answer of the artist in Meredith to the world's need. After all the two Merediths are one in mind and purpose. We have heard the Meredith of the novels say that "all right use of life . . . is to pave ways for the firmer footing of those who succeed us": hear him add, of his own art, "Close knowledge of our fellows, discernment of the laws of existence, these lead to great civilization. I have supposed that the novel, exposing and illustrating the natural history of man, may help us to such sustaining roadside gifts."

III

If the novel does not and cannot decently exist for us in any one of the inferior ways just named—to refresh us with "quavers and crescendos and trillets" —we have of course instantly to face the question of what it does exist for, and of how we can define it so as to salve our self-respect and exalt our few hours of study to the level of true spiritual adventure—the level, let us say, represented by Meredith putting aside everything else for his Italian battle-front. Let it be said at once that, for such an adventure, no definition can be made to answer except the largest available or thinkable.

Every man who thinks about life—that is to say, every man who in any vital or valid sense *lives*—sees or tries to see in life something, some ideal or concept, perhaps near at hand and triumphantly possessed, perhaps intangible or remote, which is for him more important than anything else in the world; something, at all events, for which he must exist, by which he must evaluate everything else; some meaning that he draws, by pain and labor and unremitting effort of the will, out of the muddle of the world-purpose. To

St. Paul this something was the Charity which is love; to Shelley it was ideal or intellectual beauty; to Matthew Arnold it was the spirit of criticism, a definite striving toward the sum of all best things thought and known; to Henry James it was that intuition of our fellows which can all but take the place of conscience; to Mr. H. G. Wells it is, or lately was, the austere beauty of science, of impersonal order; to Mr. Joseph Conrad it is Fidelity, Solidarity. To Meredith it was the still small voice of Nature speaking to man, and the unconscious response of the nature in man. Whatever that greatest thing is to you, however you interpret it, wherever you find or by whatever name you call it, it is what you must see in every page that is worth your reading. Nothing else will do at all. Anything less is the most miserable of makeshifts. When the greatest in imaginative literature strikes with a sure touch the chord of the greatest in you, imaginative literature has won its rare, its priceless success; missing that contact, it has woefully and wastefully failed.

How shall we characterize this greatest reality except by saying that it is your *faith?* We are told by some that among the fruits of the present war must be a quickening of religious faith—faith in dogmas, in forms, in the church, in prayer. It may be—though it would almost seem that the world has gone too far from ritualism, and the church too far from Christianity, to leave much probability of the return. But even the least mystical of us must create or renew somehow a faith in the remission of the world's sins by the shedding of blood—if only because so much blood has been shed that unless remission of some sort comes, there will be nothing left for faith to cling to. Wherever our instinctive sympathies lie, however we interpret the issues fought about, each of us has something which he wants to see come out of the struggle, some triumph of principle, some kind of order or brotherhood, that must be worth what is being paid for it, since it is not to be had on less ghastly terms. That reality, even if we dare not hope to see it come immediately to pass, is our hope, our greatest thing. We must believe in it, and in ourselves as obscurely working for it, in order to keep on tolerating ourselves.

We see every struggle as only one aspect of that greater struggle. Whatever we covet for the world is what gives life its meaning to us. We see it as explaining every form of effort—experiments of the inventor's laboratory, play of brush and chisel in the studio, schemes of the social philosopher for reform, gropings of the teacher in the classroom among the thousand petty drudgeries of that routine, the reachings-out of history for contacts with man's former strivings, the drenching of a continent with blood of a million youths—and, it may be, even our moments of rustling over the leaves of a dead writer's living books. Whatever we call the essence that gives meaning to any one of these, it is the same that gives meaning to them all. We want one thing so much that we must accept or refuse everything else for the sake of it. And if we cannot accept our books too for the sake of it, then not to refuse them is cynicism and blasphemy.

This is what we mean by insisting that the novel must be defined spaciously enough to include the whole instinctive sense of community with practical living. We must spare ourselves every risk of seeming to station life and letters in two separate enclosures, to the belittlement of each. That is the task reserved for our cynical and sterile but still very prevalent modern æstheticism—with which, we may add incidentally, Meredith has, of all writers, least to do.

IV

We have still not come to the specific problem of what is required of fiction: we have dealt only with what the reader ought to require of himself as he undertakes to consider fiction—the attitude by which he can dignify his consideration of it. Yet we have constantly implied the nature of the thing to be sought. Among all our various actual and possible ideals, there is obviously one element in common: call it the sense of community, the social conscience, human solidarity. It is the thing that craves some form of human understanding, that will be always trying to cross or break down the innumerable barriers of race, of creed, of class, to increase the feeling of kinship among all the members and groups of the human guild. It gives us our democracy, our sociology, our general disposition to abolish the misunderstandings that keep the weak degraded, the powerful haughty.

It underlies such pieces of literature as Caxton's Bible, Paine's *Rights of Man*, Carlyle's *Past and Present*, Ruskin's *Fors Clavigera*. It runs like a golden thread through the whole fabric of the mid-century "novel of protest" as written by Dickens, Disraeli, Kingsley, Mrs. Gaskell, and others. It turns the sentences of an archaic document such as Milton's *Areopagitica* into massive blocks heaped one on another to the building of a new temple of liberty. It underlies too our modern unrest, our agitation for reforms momentous and trivial, from World Federation down to communal kitchens.

If there is a special glory that we can ascribe to fiction in English during the fifty years past, it is the intensification of this feeling of solidarity and of its significance; of this perception that, despite our various artifices of creed and class, we are after all a worldful of creatures in the same boat, fleeing the same storm, and certainly doomed unless we pull together. We have been taught to cherish the thing that seeks brotherhood and hates war, which is the temporary failure of brotherhood. Against it stands everything that makes war inevitable, everything that makes labor hate capital, or sex distrust sex—all the prides and prejudices and sentimentalisms. It is the face of the future beheld in glimpses, in visions, lost perhaps sometimes in cannon-smoke but always watching over the battle; it is the one beautiful and permanent reality. And it is the characteristic note of our modern fiction, especially the Russian and the English, where the vibration of it is the very pitch of truth itself. It is what we must try, too, to keep vibrating as the fundamental of all that we can have to say in these pages.

Not that we are debarred from considering the "style" or the "art" in fiction: those too we must weigh, but only as the artist's necessary means of adapting his largest general purpose to our attention, our receptivity. They are the humble agents of a design without which they would be meaningless. Neither is it proposed that we seek out primarily the didactic element, the preachment, in fiction. If we find it there, we find it where, by definition almost, it does not belong. The novelist must not preach at us, if only for the reason that no valid argument about moral truth can conceivably rest on invented premises. No: it is the artist's choice of a certain kind of truth that teaches us, that criticizes life, as we say; his fundamental selecting and excluding process, not his moralizing.

Not the æsthetic, not the didactic, then, is our affair: rather the whole set of means and expedients judged in the light of the ultimate end they serve, and with heed to the service rendered, by means and end together, to the indestructible and universal craving for the knowledge that is brotherhood. There is no finer summary of all objections to the arid and academic view of the novel, and no finer general definition of the novel itself, than this phrase of Mr. Joseph Conrad: " . . . *a conviction of our fellow men's existence strong enough to take upon itself a form of imagined life clearer than reality.*" The novel's beauty as a thing clearer than reality is, if you like, its art; but its justifying power, by which first of all the humanist must undertake to judge it, is the power to enforce the conviction of our fellow men's existence. Art is valuable, in short, because it is a negation of all the prides and prejudices and hates; because it is socializing. And the art of fiction is justified by nothing less than this: that it is one of many weapons, one of many promises of eventual triumph, in the contest to which every other is subordinate and ephemeral—the struggle for union, the war against war.

The moral beginning and the moral end of art so conceived are all in one cadence of Vittoria's song:

> "For all Humanity doth owe a debt
> To all Humanity, until the end."

NOVELISTS OF YESTERDAY

The Will to Believe and the Will to Doubt

GEORGE MEREDITH
GEORGE GISSING

I

GEORGE MEREDITH

I

It is partly because Meredith so abundantly realized the spirit of solidarity, which we may describe as the breath and essence of modernism, that he seems much nearer to us than George Eliot, who only groped for it among the débris of her world of rationalistic skepticism. The more obvious reason is that he wrote so much longer, and lived so long beyond the end of his writing. His last novel, *The Amazing Marriage,* was published in 1895, and he died in 1909, within a month of the death of his friend and severe critic Swinburne. But the former reason, the one which defies chronology, is the more significant. If *The Amazing Marriage* of 1895 strikes us as a more modern book than *Daniel Deronda,* George Eliot's last novel, it has surely every right to do so; but there is nothing in dates to explain why *The Ordeal of Richard Feverel* and *Adam Bede,* both of 1859, should bridge a gap equally wide.

The difference they mark is roughly that between doubt and faith:—by which it is meant not that Meredith clung to an old orthodoxy which George Eliot had the courage to discard, but rather that he found his way through doubt to a new faith, of a sort to supersede the formulas of his time; so that even in the one book which most resembles the early novels of George Eliot, his *Rhoda Fleming*, he seems more of our generation than of hers.

This sort of contrast between contemporaneous authors is one reason why the history of literature is not always to be read by the strict logic of the calendar. As a fact, even the seasoned and inured reader of novels has a special difficulty in adjusting *Richard Feverel* to the year where chronology puts it. In some important points of technique alone it went on from where Dickens left off, and did it ten years before Dickens had left off; and it has little of the Victorian diffuseness of Trollope, whose major career was then but just begun. Technically, it stands nearer to us than any English novel between itself and Jane Austen; in thought and substance, it stands nearer to us than Mrs. Humphry Ward's *Robert Elsmere,* a book, comparatively, of the day before yesterday—and one which Meredith found time to praise because it expressed with frankness a great deal that he had for thirty years so calmly assumed that he found no need to express it at all. The first importance of Meredith, then, is that he was the first figure of great eminence in English fiction to have got through the jungle of scientific rationalism to a new faith that is exempt from the challenges of science.

We need to inquire in some detail what this faith was, because it is what places Meredith nearest us, and also because there is absolute concord between his reading of the world and his reading of man's special destiny. Mr. Chesterton introduces us at a stroke to both when he says: "Meredith was perhaps the only man in the modern world who has almost had the high honor of rising out of the low estate of a Pantheist into the high estate of a Pagan. A Pagan is a person who can do what hardly any person for the last two thousand years could do: a person who can take nature naturally. It is due to Meredith to say that no one outside a few of the great Greeks has ever taken nature so naturally as he did."

Such a way of taking nature involves, of course, an exuberant appreciation of beauty in the physical world, and that assuredly Meredith has. His possession and use of it appear about equally in his first great novel and in his last, to draw the line by naming the two extreme points of it. But to note so much is to touch only the surface of Meredith's world. His interpretation of nature goes far deeper than, for example, that of Scott, to whom nature is a glowing frame for the human drama. To Meredith, all things are one in the sense that nature is quite literally the creator, the benign mother, of man; man is her "great venture," and, regarding her, he regards the whole of which he is a part, and whose destiny is his. It is idle for men to ask whether the world is good or evil, friendly or hostile; it is as irrelevant as though a rainbow should ask such questions of its parent cloud.

In this matter Meredith stands at the opposite extreme from George Eliot, who is always conscious of the duality of things—of man coping with natural forces, trying to wrest them to his purpose, and often having to submit to their ironic destructiveness. Meredith writes from the sick-room, as one of the last familiar utterances of his life: "There is no irony in Nature." He is aware of man's apparent strife against nature: only he believes that nature herself has implanted in man the thing that strives blindly against her; implanted it for her own purpose, and for man's good. Out of man's struggle, out of his skepticism and his despair, come all the triumphs and the faiths that nature means him to attain to; and even the things he evolves against her will, she draws back into herself for sustenance. Of this fact Meredith finds a symbol in the serenity with which earth receives the discarded books of man's sick philosophies, turning them to earth again.

A belief in something amounting to human perfectibility is the natural outcome of such a "reading of earth." Meredith views the progress of man in a succession of stages, the last of which lies in the future. First, nature is simply the wrapping of man in his chrysalis stage. Presently he comes into animate existence, but with the brute physical self uppermost. Next, he learns the lessons of Sense and Self, wars with his brother atoms, hardly knowing them for brothers; he becomes a creature of pride, cupidity, lust, and the manifestations of "blind self"—in fine, of egoism. This is the stage in which man wastes the most precious of his powers. But even through the mist of man's tragic life of the present, there emerge and shine the promises of the ultimate stage which optimism pictures: man with mind enthroned over sense, reason mounted on the lower faculties and driving them according to nature's intent. Nature exacts of man "order, high discourse, and decency," "the lyre of language clear"; and presently he shall satisfy her, when he has "burst the chrysalis of the blind," shaken off "his distempered devil of self."

> When fire has passed him vapor to the sun,
> And sun relumed,
> Then shall the horrid pall
> Be lifted, and a spirit nigh divine,
> "Live in thy offspring as I live in mine,"
> Will hear her call.

And then man shall understand his own toil and his pangs of creation. He shall look "on a land whereon his labor is a carven page," and "naught writ on sand." He shall understand at last all his "fables of the Above," the sword and the crown, heaven and hell; hate, love—"the bright wing, the black hoof"—all the makeshifts nature has compelled him to invent expressly that he may develop himself to her appointed end of normality and harmony.

All this, presented here in greatly reduced paraphrase of such poems as "Earth and Man" and "Earth's Preference," may be called the authentic or positive optimism. We use the word "optimism" too loosely, to denote the temperament that makes the best of a bad matter. Meredith makes it mean, as it ought, the will and the courage to make the best of a good matter—the infinite and eternal whole of things.

Clearly this aspect of his belief has something to do with the laughter and the perpetual youthful zest of the man and of his work. There is in him to thc last line no weariness, no questioning, no abatement of the furnace heat that fused the forms of his experience into truth and beauty, which he saw as one. In abundance, in dash and gaiety, the incessant will to explore and conquer, he is, as some one has said, the last of the Elizabethans. One manifestation of this abundance is his occasional extravagance of language, a frenzy of the imagination that laughs at time, circumstance, and probability. Phrases such as "wild cloud-mountains that drag the hills along," and the comparison of an enraged sea to "ramping hosts of warrior horse," claim kinship with Marlowe and Shakspere. This sort of thing, executed in cold blood, is literary conceit merely. Melted in the heat of an unquenchable creative energy such as Meredith's, it speaks to the emotions direct, and laughs at analysis. In the presence of it, we hardly need Mr. Chesterton to tell us that Meredith died with half his stories untold, for lack of the time and the bodily energy to tell them all.

The optimism which underlies this sustained rapture we have illustrated from the poems because there it stands written most clearly, and because in the novels Meredith is in the main too truly an artist to preach his philosophy except through his characters and his scene. But the same sense of cosmic unity is present in the novels; everything else is an embroidery upon it; and to miss it is to have lost the whole of Meredith among the parts. No one who has read him with any care can have failed to notice the frequency of the passages where he finds a notation for the harmony between the best in nature and the best in man, the one answering the call of the other.

An example from the first important novel and another from the last may be allowed to stand for a score of like instances. In *Feverel*, the chapter called "Nature Speaks" recounts Richard's solitary walk in the Black Forest, through night and storm into serene sunlight, on the night when he learns of the birth of his child. It is a thing not of nature's counsel that has kept him away from Lucy—a morbid pride of humility, the sentimental persistence in useless self-abasement and self-loathing. Through this pall not of nature's weaving pierces with terrible sweetness the summons of nature to the father in him. He has found, shivering in the path, a tiny leveret, and put it in his breast. "He was next musing on a strange sensation he experienced. It ran up one arm with an indescribable thrill, but communicated nothing to his heart. It was purely physical, ceased for a time, and recommenced, till he had it all through his blood, wonderfully thrilling. He grew aware that the little thing he carried was licking his hand there. The small rough tongue going over and over the palm of his hand produced the strange sensation he felt. Now that he knew the cause, the marvel ended; but now that he knew the cause, his heart was touched and made more of it. The gentle scraping continued without intermission as on he walked. What did it say to him? Human tongue could not have said so much just then."

The other instance, from *The Amazing Marriage*, is in the inimitable account of the prize-fight, "A Taste of Old England." In the midst of the recital of that exhibition of Brawn and Sense uninformed by mind, Meredith turns aside to point out its clash with nature's design: "The clouds went their way; the hills were solid, but like a blue smoke; the scene here made them very distant and strange. Those two men were still hitting, not hating one another; only to gratify a number of unintelligible people and win a success. But the earth and sky seemed to say, What is the glory? They were insensible to it, as they are not—they are never insensible to noble grounds of strife. They bless the spot, they light lamps on it; they put it into books of history, make it holy, if the cause was a noble one or a good one." Thus all men, so far as they are swayed by the best in themselves, are drawn by nature into one, into a solidarity of bestness. Wherever they are not responsive to her call, they fly apart into social anarchy and hatred. For to Meredith there is no solidarity except that of bestness. The analyst's task becomes then to find out what is the will of nature, and to pick his way through whatever falsity in human affairs runs counter to it.

II

A single step takes us to the heart of Meredith's pagan idealism. Drawing no division between nature and human nature, finding in the one a reflection and fulfilment of the other, he feels the same joy in the presence of each. He takes nature, we have seen, naturally; he takes not less naturally the other cosmos in man's heart, the working of natural law in man's tangled life of flesh and soul. By this it is not meant that his attitude is akin to the brutal naturalism of Zola or of the earlier George Moore: we have already heard him propose spirit, the ideal faculty, as the ultimate purpose of nature wrought out in man's life, and we have seen him looking forward to a time when it shall surmount and subdue the animal. What Meredith declares war against is not law, or even convention, but whatever forces interfere with the harmonious working together of animal and spiritual. He denies neither flesh nor soul. Always and consistently he affirms their interdependence, the necessity of their becoming ideally one. "Our battle is ever between flesh and spirit," he makes Diana write. "*Spirit must brand the flesh, that it may live.*" In "The Three Singers to Young Blood" he makes youth hear successively the voice of nature, a lark's carol; that of man's reason or counsel, a jangling caw; and that of passion, a nightingale's rapture—

> Liquid first, and then the caw,
> Then the cry that knows not law.

But—

> Hark to the three. Chimed they in one
> Life were music of the sun.

And Meredith does really anticipate the time when these three notes shall chime. Indeed, he does discover and reveal, in scenes where he touches upon the ultimate perfection in human intercourse, the complete accord. The final understanding of Diana and

Redworth, the profound gaiety of the spiritual adjustment between Clara Middleton and Vernon Whitford, the mystical union of Weyburn and Lord Ormont's Aminta in the astounding chapter called "A Marine Duet";—these are instances where reason and nature and passion coincide—"the senses pouring their live sap, and the minds companioned, and the spirits made one by the whole-natured conjunction."

Conversely, *Richard Feverel* presents the tragedy of the jangling discord. Nature calls Richard with a sweet insistence that promises felicity; Reason, in the guise of Sir Austin's well-intentioned "System," thwarts his response to the first call; and that mischance makes it possible in turn for passion, "the cry that knows not law," to solicit him into still another path, and to his destruction. Tragedy in Meredith is always based on some such cross-purpose as this: it is the failure of the ideal accord among all the faculties implanted by nature in man. Love, Meredith calls "a finer shoot of the tree"; but it is "planted in good gross earth." Not to see its fineness is to be blind to nature; not to see the good gross earth from which it springs is equal blindness.

Whence Meredith's life-long battle against the two extremes which he hated: grossness and sentimentalism, the pretence that man is all animal and the pretence that man is not animal at all. Meredith has a name for each of these repugnant extremes: the gross naturalism that discerns only the beast in man is "dirty-drab," the parlor sentimentalism that denies the beast is "rose-pink." Life, he says, is neither;

and from the first word to the last he wages uncompromising war on both. How he hated the dirty-drab, whether in living or in letters, may be shown by this characteristic piece of Meredithian Billingsgate, from a personal letter: "I have gone through the horrible book of Mendès, with the sensation of passing down the ventre de Paris and out at anus into the rat-rioting sewers, twisted, whirled, tumbled amid the frothing filth, the deadly stench, the reek and roar of the damned. Cloacina sits on such productions; Dementia, born of the nameless, dissects them. . . . It is the monsterization of Zolaism. O what a nocturient, cacaturient crew has issued of the lens of the Sun of the mind on the lower facts of life!—on sheer Realism, breeder at best of the dung-fly!"

Yet Meredith does not stop at the hatred of foulness: even of such Realism, he is moved to add, "Yet has that Realism been a corrective of the more corruptingly vaporous with its tickling hints at sensuality." And from this point Meredith goes on to show what is not too commonly perceived: that sentimentalism and grossness are really the two faces of the same foe, contradictory aspects of the one unnatural outlook on life. Sentimental people, according to one of the finest of Diana's aphorisms, "fiddle harmonics on the strings of sensualism." The sentimentalist is a sneaking counterpart of the voluptuary, just as the epicure is a glutton with a little more subtlety. Freedom from the appetites is neither for the man in whom they riot nor for the man who regards them with horror and plumes himself on his resistance: it is only for the natural man who takes them for granted without letting them become an end, and to whom they are neither morbidly seductive nor morbidly repellent.

Now, of these two imperfectly natural beings, it is to be noted that the sentimentalist is the more dangerous, because he is more insidiously subtle than the voluptuary. His disguise is so impenetrable that it deceives even himself. This is undoubtedly why Meredith's most frequent attack is against sentimentalism, the mask of grossness. He is always talking about self-deception, about "the vices of the world's nobler half . . . half-conceptions of wisdom, hysterical goodness, an impatient charity"—such impatient charity as that of the philanthropist who must set the world right at once. These nobler vices, Meredith insists, are "the sickness and writhings of our egoism." Normality always does hate foulness as a matter of course; but it takes a social comedist of Meredith's acuteness to dissect the anatomy of egoism.

III

It has proved impossible to proceed even so far without some references to Meredith's theory and treatment of love. It is of course in his account of the sexes that he does most to affirm the necessity of harmonious accord between flesh and spirit, and his hostility to whatever unnatural thing draws veils of pretence over the relations of men and women. And it is at this point that we come to the greatest single implication of his hatred of sham. If he is to make in practical terms any sufficient answer to the sentimentalism of prudery and the realism of foulness, if he is to provide any real substitute for the rose-pink and the dirty-drab, then he must invent his answer and his substitute in terms of womanhood. The reason is simply that, of both foulness and sentimentalism, women are the principal victims. Sex is the one reality most hooded in hypocrisy and self-deception. It is, then, as the creator of shining and celestial women, come to be only a little lower than the angels and infinitely more real than they, that Meredith gives us his greatest.

His women overthrow sentimentalism because they have the flush and the frankness of absolute health, mental and physical self-knowledge. They overthrow foulness, because they see that the body's beauty is the beauty of a temple. "True poets and true women," Meredith says, "have the nature sense of the divineness of what the world deems gross material substance." He is, by this definition of his own, the true poet; and the crown of his poetizing passion is in the radiance that has gathered round such names as Rhoda and Dahlia and Clara and Diana and Lucy and Aminta and Carinthia Jane. These are above the flattery of men; nor shall we be adding one ray to their luster when we echo the common saying that these women have their elder, not greater, sisters in Portia and Rosalind and Imogen and Desdemona.

One must take time at least to suggest the sense in which Meredith is a "feminist." Certainly he is not blind to the temptations and individual shortcomings of the sex. He cordially detests the masculine woman, the woman who, after "a probationary term" in the character of a woman, decides to become a man. He has no use for the faddish woman, the woman who, at a certain time of life, "relapses upon religion and little dogs." Nor does he contend that woman is generically either greater or better than man. But in all his stories we do find an undercurrent of suggestion that in the greatest women there is something of divinity which the greatest men can only worship.

And there remains this important truth, partly a paradox: that, creating women of the grandest stature, loving as he does to lavish wit and beauty upon them, to surround them with glamour, even to clothe them worthily, he nevertheless creates them primarily for the education and chastisement of men. It is to men always that the spoken or unspoken message is addressed. It is to men that he says: "You have to teach your imagination of the feminine image you have set up to bend your civilized knees to, that it must temper its fastidiousness, shun the grossness of the overdainty. Or, to speak in the philosophic tongue, you must turn on *yourself*, resolutely track and seize that burrower, and scrub and cleanse him; by which process, during the course of it, you will arrive at the conception of the right heroical woman for *you* to worship: and if you prove to be of some spiritual stature, you may reach to an ideal of the heroical feminine type for the worship of mankind, an image as yet in poetic outline only, on our upper skies."

Men, he sees, have not succeeded in shunning "the grossness of the overdainty." "They desire to have a still woman, who can make a constant society of her pins and needles." "They create by stoppage a volcano, and are amazed at its eruptiveness." "Men do not so much fear to lose the hearts of thoughtful women as their strict attention to their graces." There is plenty of such evidence that Meredith sees in woman a special saving grace, a regenerative and cleansing power, of which the world is sooner or later to look for the chief impulse of its betterment. He creates his score of women as his protest against the something in man that dreads the liberation of woman, that is all for preserving "the present market." The Meredithian name for that something is Egoism, and *The Egoist* is its epic. Sir Willoughby Patterne is the man who struts and poses before the mirror of his own vanity, and requires that his women-folk be always holding up the mirror before him in subtle flattery. He does not want them to expand or change, lest they see *him* in some new compromising light, or become less accessible, or demand more in return. Of this sentimental egoism, Meredith has a dozen representatives. Mr. Chesterton has protested against Meredith's epigram, "I expect that woman will be the last thing civilized by man." But it is not Meredith's epigram: it is Sir Austin Feverel's, and Sir Austin is a cynic self-confessed, an exponent of the cage-and-chain philosophy of sex. The Meredithian answer to his epigram is precisely that man must be one of the first things civilized by woman.

Indeed, Meredith's characteristic theme—one might almost say his only serious theme—is the subjugation of egoism, sentimentalism, or pruriency in men by such women as we have named. At the outset the man may hold the woman lightly; in the end she becomes to him a lost heaven. How many of the love stories in Meredith end with the spoken or unspoken words "Too late"!—that of Carinthia Jane and Fleetwood, the sullen sentimentalist; that of Sandra and Wilfrid Pole, the irresponsible sentimentalist, the man who could "pledge himself to eternity" but could not keep an appointment "for eleven o'clock of the morrow morning"; that of Lucy and Richard Feverel, the remorseful sentimentalist; that of Aminta and Lord Ormont, the sentimentalist in love with his own prestige; that of Dahlia and Edward Blancove, the cowardly sentimentalist. These are not all. It is in *The Egoist* alone that there is neither redemption nor hope of redemption: Sir Willoughby is the impregnable citadel of egoism. In each of the other instances, the great woman, by being supremely and naturally herself, draws the man toward truth even while his neglect or his stupidity is repelling her love; and in the end, when he knows the full extent of his loss, he has at least begun to be purged of his baseness. This is the one story that Meredith told again and again. It seems to us that no one since Shakspere has told it so well.

IV

In the novels, if not as yet in the human comedy at large, the three members of Meredith's trinity do actually chime as one; so that, in passing from these generalities about nature and passion to reason or counsel, we have to do still with an unbroken unity. In other words, we can follow the continuity of Meredith through his general ideas about life to the intellectual formulas of his own literary art, and find him still the same Meredith in his peculiar rationale of composition.

If there is any single matter to impede us, it is the notorious "obscurity" of his style. He explains the existence of that quality—one may take exception to the common name for it—when he says: "Thought is tough, and dealing with thought produces toughness." The difficulty for the reader follows, not from eccentricity or mannerism, but simply from the unparalleled condensation or close packing of the thought. Meredith's style may be contrasted in different ways with that of Browning, whose process is obscure because it is an affair of leaps and lapses and elisions, where the reader must fill in the sense; with that of Henry James, whose verbal manner was an embroidery upon his thought, and who persistently played with ideas and images; and with that of Trollope, who provided so many breathing spaces for the reader's attention to catch up that the alert eye can slip or slide down the page, and understand the whole from half the words that compose it. Meredith weaves a much finer, firmer verbal mesh than we can find in any one of his forerunners in the novel. Every word carries its burden. Miss a word and you lose a sentence; a sentence, and you lose the paragraph. His play is almost never with a thought or a metaphor: it is with a character or a situation, in the treatment of which the thoughts succeed one another with incredible and breathless rapidity, flashing back and forth, crossing and recrossing, with the vivid skill of expert sword-play. There is tremendous terseness and discipline of phrase, with absolutely no diffusion. Meredith's style is one of the most difficult there is—and one of the most rewarding. For this reason, it is good sense to read him at first slowly, leaving nothing unmastered behind one. A single book really mastered halves the difficulty of the second; a course of reading Meredith renders almost anything else in English prose easy reading. With the rejection of Meredith because of the amount of effort that must be brought to the acceptance of him, it is not necessary to be very patient. Those who gnash their teeth over his vocabulary and his formation of sentences need only be referred to the master of one of the grandest styles ever written, and certainly one of the most difficult—Shakspere.

One can hardly leave this subject of Meredith's compactness with no word of the innumerable nuggets of thought and expression, the epigrams, in which his pages abound. Wit is not the essence of Meredith: it is the excess, the last handful on a measure pressed down and running over. There is no need to illustrate extensively: to read almost any chapter is to discover one's own illustrations. Remember that Diana said of her own epigrams that they had "the value of chalk-eggs, which lure the thinker to sit." Remember how she phrased Meredith's faith in the soul, in spite of hostile winds that blow upon it: "The light of every soul burns upward. Let us allow for atmospheric disturbance." Remember that a snore is poetized as "the elfin trumpet of silence"; that a moonlit eve is "not night, but veiled day"; that a dark patch of rippling waters is "like a pool of snakes"; that a man who maintains an angry self-control is "grinding his passion into powder for future explosions." The complete Meredithian can cite perhaps a hundred such felicities without opening a book; but this is not quite the region in which we wish to leave our emphasis.

We must, however, add that such concentrated deposits of thought and expression have often a purely rhythmical beauty not excelled by their neatness. By a quite simple typographic arrangement, Professor John Livingston Lowes has proved, in an ingenious and diverting article called "An Unacknowledged Imagist," that many of Meredith's sentences possess all the distinctions claimed by the best contemporary *vers libres* of the "imagist" mode. Thus—

A pillar
Of dim silver rain
Fronted the moon
On the hills.

. . . .

Over the flowering hawthorn
The moon
Stood like a wind-blown
White rose
Of the heavens.

. . . .

Edged moments,
When life is poised
As a crystal pitcher on the head,
In peril of a step.

This whimsical contribution to the criticism of Meredith's style lends some indirect sanction to a theory that has long seemed to us to denote something of significance: that the great increase in pointedness and epigrammatic quality in Meredith's prose, especially after 1880, is best accounted for by remembering that Meredith was becoming a more and more specialized kind of poet. The qualities which most distinguish his prose after the period of *The Egoist* are the same which appear to excess in his poetry of the same years.

V

But all this is a parenthesis which does not bring us to the intellectual center of Meredith's handling of his material—which lies in his conception and use of Comedy. The Comic Spirit is to him the "Sword of Common Sense." It is his principal weapon against the sentimentalism and the grossness of life. If it seem anomalous to speak of Comedy as primarily intellectual,—and historically it is by no means anomalous,—we can but assert that it remained for Meredith to re-create and restore the analytical function of Comedy. We have had, in English fiction before him, plentiful quantities of the droll, the facetious, the side-splitting, and the ironic; but his comedy has always behind it, above any since that of his favorite Molière, the design of analysis—such analysis as the intellect must first searchingly perform, before the artistic or fashioning instinct can seize on the material.

Meredith's laughter is truth; an assertion, not a surrender, of the mind. It is the intellect itself turned to mirth. For an account of the rôle comedy plays in his conception of art, and of its essential differences from humor, irony, and satire, one reads his *Essay on the Idea of Comedy and of the Uses of the Comic Spirit;* also his "Ode to the Comic Spirit" and the prefatory chapter of *The Egoist.* These deny with proof what there is time here to deny only by assertion: that Meredith is primarily the ironist or satirist. There is a remark, somewhere quoted by Henry James from Turgenev, to the effect that the ultimate novelist will be a person "purged of sarcasm." With this remark Meredith would have agreed. Comedy differs from humor in that it does not patronize its object; from irony and satire in that the object of the ridicule is not "chilled" by it. It is a fashion not so much of poking fun at a person as of letting him poke fun at himself. In both the process and the purpose, the intellectual element predominates. "Philosopher and comic poet are of a cousinship in the eye they cast on life."

Comedy means, then, in Meredith, the effect without the sting of satire. "In Comedy is the singular scene of charity issuing of disdain under the stroke of honorable laughter." He uses the Comic Spirit to trip up and unmask pretences—and pretences are exhibitions of the sentimental, whether they occur in politics, in learning, in business, or in social intercourse. Wherever Meredith sees the negative vice of pretence, of fine words without the meaning or the feeling to match them, he shows the pretender with the sly Muse peeping over a shoulder, and straightway the pretender's dignity is undone. "You may love, and warmly love, so long as you are honest. Do not offend reason. A lover pretending too much by one foot's length of pretence, will have that foot caught in her [Comedy's] trap." Comedy, although "not opposed to romance," "watches over sentimentalism with a birch rod." It is our "means of reading swiftly and comprehensively"; it can condense "whole sections of the Book in a sentence, volumes in a character, so that a fair part of a book outstripping thousands of leagues when unrolled, may be compassed in one comic sitting." Conversely, lack of the comic sense, a solemn literalness, is the cause of our present epidemic of "the vasty and the noisy, out of which, as from an undrained fen, streams the malady of sameness, our modern malady." Comedy it is who "proposes the correcting of pretentiousness, of inflation, of dullness, and of the vestiges of rawness and grossness to be found among us. She is the ultimate civilizer, the polisher, a sweet cook."

Incidentally it is to be noted that Comedy such as this depends for its reception, as Meredith calls to our notice, on a cultivated society, with something approaching equality of the sexes, with a certain amount of cooling leisure, and above all with the capacity for a reciprocal play of intellect between artist and public. The lack of such a society has clearly something to do with Meredith's own failure to command wide popularity. It is that lack, rather than either his own inherent complexity or (as has been charged) his want of democracy, that leaves his permanence to be guarded by discriminating minorities, at least until such time as the whole lump shall have been leavened.

The more closely we inspect Meredith's doctrine of comedy, the more phases of his success and his failure we find explained by it. It explains, partly, his feminism. Only where the sexes are equal and free can comedy profit by a flourishing demand. "Where the veil is thrown over women's faces, you cannot have society, without which the senses are barbarous and the Comic Spirit is driven to the gutters of grossness to slake its thirst."

More aptly still, his doctrine explains the technique of his art of the novel. "The Comic Spirit," he wrote, "conceives a definite situation for a number of characters, and rejects all accessories in the exclusive pursuit of them and their speech. For, being a spirit, he hunts the spirit in men; vision and ardor constitute his merit." Whence Meredith's care for analysis, dissection of character and of "internal history." "Brain-stuff is not lean stuff." "To suppose it dull is the profoundest of errors." Whence too the striking fact about Meredith's development: that he was impelled to the attainment of his comic end with fewer and fewer, less and less cumbersome means—fewer characters, places, scenes, less involved machinery. *Feverel* is comparatively rich in characters, in supernumeraries especially, and also in background. There are ten personæ of great importance, and the plot is a rather complex organization, with simultaneous events in different scenes. But there grows upon Meredith from year to year, under the influence of his feeling that comedy "rejects all accessories," a profound intensiveness of workmanship that reaches perhaps its final stage in *Lord Ormont and His Aminta*, where the number of characters of great importance is reduced to the three of the eternal triangle.

With this change in technique there grows upon Meredith too a sense of the solitariness of human lives, or, let us say rather, of the great moments, the perfect understandings, at the summits of human lives. And his ideal becomes to take the soul and study it in the overmastering experiences that disentangle it from the massed disordered spectacle of life, to set it apart on a pinnacle or in a wilderness—the pinnacle it may be of love, which is the remotest thing in the world, or the wilderness of pride. Not that he lost touch with the realities of man's life as a social animal: but he used smaller and smaller segments of that life, and compressed more and more of meaning into the single exhibition, revealing his people in the intense phases into which they put all they were or could be. Always after 1880 he was trying to find the perfect or pivotal hour in which alone his protagonist most fully lived; and in the light of that hour he was interpreting every other aspect of the given history. We can express nearly the full measure of this growth by saying that in Meredith the comic spirit finally achieves what tragedy alone achieves elsewhere in the novel and the drama. Tragedy too is a way of condensing whole volumes of the Book of Life into the stress of some great moment of fiery ordeal; it is a way of isolating characters temporarily from the complex and showing all the world's complex of forces operative in them alone; it thrusts a whole mass of life, good and evil mixed, into a fiery incandescence in which the dross shrivels and the mass is purified. These functions Meredith performs by his elevation of comedy to the tragic altitude. On the technical side this development is the greatest aspect of his success.

Finally, we look to the same quarter for an explanation of Meredith's failure; his failure not only to make his work commonly understood, but even to make his basic intentions understood. The saddest outcome of his career,—it might almost be called his tragedy,—was that all the great democratic realities of his intention have been lost among the aristocratic appearances of his performance. His ideal was the diffusion of humaneness; and it is clear that he had the vision of a sort of official State comedy, comedy as an accredited national institution, toward the fulfilment of which vision he would gladly have played his part. But there was neither the society for audience nor the society for subject; and therefore he must write *for* the few readers who had his own democratizing intuition, and *about* the few infinitesimal societies which embodied his dream of what intercourse could be. His aim was to democratize an ideal—and the democrat still looks askance, as at one whose shabby aim was to idealize an aristocracy.

We make out forlornly from this distance that it was bound to be so. Yet if Meredith was right about the future, the comic spirit which presides inscrutably over all destinies can be trusted to accord him the same discerning justice that his own comic sense apportions to the multitude of characters, great and small, who move back and forth across his own narrow and carefully prepared scene.

VI

Whatever criticism has to say on a score of minor points, its final emphasis must return to the point of departure: Meredith's proclamation of the unity in things, his service of life, his unalterable conviction of the brotherhood of all men and of the interlocking of all destinies. It is heartening to us to remember how, with all his zest of life and huge enjoyment of his own wit, his varied and brilliant gifts,—surely the most brilliant that have ever been brought to focus in the novel,—he nevertheless humbly valued his own achievement as a service rendered, a straightening of the way for other and still grander enterprises. It is this noble humility that counts for immortality; only those who are content to die live forever.

As a fact, there are external and historical considerations that should go far to dispel any timid misgivings about the deathlessness of Meredith. He is too integral and momentous a part of the English tradition of genius not to live on. The strongest link between our time and that of George Eliot, he is at once the last of the great irrepressible comic creators of our literature, and the first of our restrained and intellectualized modern craftsmen. But the transcendent proof of his immortality is in his own fullness of life—a vital immediacy which submits to no proof precisely because it is something to be *felt*. Barrie felt it when he wrote his exquisite little fantasy called "Neither Dorking Nor the Abbey," based on the contention whether Meredith's ashes should be buried in Westminster Abbey or in the village cemetery at Dorking. And Mr. Thomas Hardy felt it when he placed his tribute at the end of the volume called *Time's Laughing-Stocks*, a collection of the dead loves, the faded flowers of life—all the things which time has turned at length to dust and ridicule. For Meredith alone, of all subjects there treated, reverses the irony and the ridicule, and makes a laughing-stock of Time itself.

II

GEORGE GISSING

I

It is easy to see now that George Gissing had more to do with the modern sociologic novel's coming of age than any British writer of his generation. Because that is so, and because he did something to the novel beyond what his time had cleared the ground for, criticism has tended to overrate him by assuming that his books are intrinsically as great as their influence. Appreciation of Gissing has had a perverse history. He was undervalued before his death because his themes seemed shabby to the popular idealism of his time. Since his death he has been overpraised because the popular idealism of his time seems shabby to us, and because he was the first to treat themes in which everybody is now interested. Rejected by his contemporary public because he was ahead of his time, accepted by posterity for exactly the same reason, he has been but little considered on his merits as an artist; and one foresees that, when such consideration comes, he will have to go through another period of depreciation before occupying his rightful and permanent place.

It seems to us we shall have kept the balance true

between his historical importance and his obvious artistic limitations when we have said that a great part of his influence was made possible precisely because he had those particular limitations, and because he remained to the end a lone example of the artist thwarted and unfulfilled. If he had been somewhat more of an imaginative creator, if he had even been completely free to be himself, we should have had little, or less, or even perhaps nothing, to remember him by. The task that fell to him was for a realist in the narrow sense; by which we mean a copyist. A creative imagination would completely have overleaped that task. Gissing, if his life had been free, might not have been a novelist at all, and certainly would not have known what the task required him to know. The place that he fills requires, then, just his combination of inward deficiencies with outward accidents.

Does the paradox require some amplification in historical terms? Gissing's work fell in a period when, as Mr. Bernard Shaw has pointed out, the man with thirty shillings a week was so pryingly curious about the man with thirty pounds a week that almost any reasonably facile scribbler could make an enviable income writing about "society." And it was just beginning to be true that the man with the thirty pounds felt a similar curiosity about how the other nine-tenths lived; a curiosity, often partly morbid and nearly always irresponsible, that sometimes went thinly disguised as philanthropy or humanitarianism. To such a period, Gissing gave, and kept giving, a fiction that treated with minute and sustained realism the life of that vast underworld as yet unpenetrated by the classes which supported the six-shilling novel. As was said of him twenty years ago, near the end of his work: "He reeks with the savour, he is bowed beneath the fruits, of contact with the lower, with the lowest middle-class, and that is sufficient to make him an authority—*the* authority in fact—on a region vast and unexplored."

To the curiosity of his public Gissing owed a large fraction of the little momentary success he won. If curiosity had been all he appealed to, his success might have been prodigious. But Gissing was anything but irresponsible; and whoever read one of his early novels in the mood of a sight-seer in the slums was not likely to repeat the mistake. He did his work for those who were willing to feel and to carry on their own consciences something of the burden that he was literally carrying on his own shoulders, "the burden of futile lives." Responsibility was the beginning, middle, and end of his moral attitude; it took with him the shape of facing squarely all that was intolerable in the facts; and if it was shattering and deadly to the curiosity that gluts itself unmorally on morbid details, it was equally so to the sentimental optimism that formulates glib and specious remedies. His realism was honest in motive and unpretentious in its claims—and it is our present point that in the 1880's this was both the most and the least that a sociologic realism could profitably undertake to be. If it were less sincere, it would not belong to literature at all; if it were more ambitious for constructive remedies, it would defeat itself through prematurity.

The real strength of this unfashionable restraint of Gissing is most evident when contrasted with the weakness of its fashionable counterpart, the sentimental and flippant sociologizing of, say, Walter Besant. The ambitious attempt of the Besant school of fiction was to name a panacea for all the ills of industrial society, and to do it before any one, even the professional sociologist, had an adequate comprehension of how intricate the problems were. What we see in *All Sorts and Conditions of Men* is the spectacle of a good-humored, mild-mannered British aristocrat proposing to reform the whole life and outlook of the British artisan by setting before him off-hand a few æsthetic and vocational advantages which he had neither time nor inclination to profit by, and which, if he could have profited by them, would simply have annihilated him *as* an artisan. The very prematurity of this brand of uneconomic humanitarianism explains its passing success. The world had not yet discovered how hard it is to find out what is the matter with it, and Besant, who pretended that understanding and reform asked nothing more than good intentions, made a powerful and popular appeal. Twenty years later, *All Sorts and Conditions of Men* would have taken its natural place in the sub-reputable stratum of popular sugared romance. In the '80's it built the East London People's Palace.

The fact was that the time had not arrived for discussing any definite propaganda of social amelioration. There can be no adequate reform without a general apprehension of the conditions that call for it. Gissing, in his earlier novels, shows his full awareness of the difficulty. In one of them, for example, a clergyman who refuses to commit himself for or against socialism says, "I have nothing to do with economic doctrines, only with Christianity"—and his parishioners take the phrase "economic doctrines" as a polite euphemism for something unmentionably dark and diabolical. All the novelist could validly do at such a time, unless he chose to remain, with Meredith and Hardy, apart from matters directly sociologic, was to report the existence of certain problems, the direction of certain tendencies, and the impossibility of any improvised solution whatever. The task was primarily one for realism—the realism which heaps up and documents great masses of facts not commonly perceived, and which is guarded from oversanguine conclusions by an innate tendency toward skepticism and discouragement. Such a discouraged realist the time, and a series of personal mischances, furnished in the person of Gissing, after Hardy and Meredith the most significant Late Victorian novelist of English birth, and a writer as sharply unlike either as they are unlike each other.

II

So much for the impersonal side of Gissing's relation to his time. But it is one of the singularities of literature that the first English novelist who saw the problems of classes in the scientific way was also a man who had felt those problems in the most personal way. Harsh experience may be an efficacious teacher, but it is not commonly a teacher of the temperate and unbiased outlook. Search out a sensitive young English lad who has thrust himself beyond the social pale by committing a petty quixotic crime that good may come of it; feel his despair under the censure of society, in the tangible form which the law gives that censure; examine the wreck of his future of a scholar and humanist; follow him across the Atlantic, go with him from city to city; live with him for days at a time on peanuts and a rather limited imagination; try everything that he tries, from poetry to plumbing; see him, a boy of twenty, squeezing his brain dry in the effort to write acceptable stories of English life for a Chicago newspaper; then go back with him to a London life of outward squalor in garrets of queer, unkempt houses in mean streets; understand what it costs him to write three and four long novels a year, to be invariably underpaid by publishers and sometimes cheated; bear in mind all the while that he is above everything a hedonist, loathing poverty as a disease, shrinking from harsh contacts, knowing all his affinities to be with a social stratum which has become inaccessible—and then ask yourself whether you have not been studying a candidate for enlistment under the red flag. It is such an accumulation of personal disasters that generates class hatred and poisonous theories, ranting fury and dynamite.

This is only the crude material half of what George Gissing underwent, if we are to believe the story so queerly and indirectly told in *The Private Life of Henry Maitland;* and yet the outcome is balance and detachment, a poised curiosity and a dry-eyed pity. Gissing contemplates the things that have happened to him, and he sees the degree in which they may be called inevitable. He looks at others whose outward fortunes are his fortunes: they are mostly people whom he does not like, but he does not blame *them* because life has made them unlikeable, and he asks what is going to be done with them. He faces the whole tangled scheme of things, the waste and the thwarted possibilities, with no remedy to advertise, with only the question, What can be done to lift or lighten the burden of futility? Many of the words that fall from his pen are new ones; still more are brave ones; and nearly all have the bravery of absolute factual truth. Yet, while his books were in pawnshops and his deal table was bare of all but the three or four volumes he could not exist without, he remained a man whose ruling passion was the prosody of Greek classical verse. This is the ultimate pathos of his personal story.

Gissing seems never to have spoken of Greek meters with detachment and restraint: a cool, not to say languid, novelist, he was a passionate archeologist, as we find him in *By the Ionian Sea* and in the unfinished *Veranilda.* Forced into daily intimacy with what he cared least about, he presents the odd combination of a hedonist thwarted in one direction to make a stoic in another; and to this fact, as we have said, he owes a great part of his effectiveness as a novelist. The time had gone for the quasi-sociologic novel of burning protest: there could hardly be another *Mary Barton*, another *Sybil*, or another *Yeast*. The time had not quite come for fiction based on a broad interpretative theory of society, its nature and movements. The only remaining thing was simple documentation of the facts themselves. Gissing was shielded by his limitations from both the past and the future. He was insured against the anachronism of mere protest because his natural loves and hates were elsewhere than in what he was forced to write about; and because his experience deadened part of him, he was also saved from becoming a passionate theorist before the time had furnished the theories. Audacity was numbed in him; and for this very reason he succeeded in doing what could be done. If ever the uninspired code of realism was justified, it was justified in Gissing, whom it saved from romanticism, from sentimentalism, and from sociological guesswork.

To be made a historically important novelist thus, by force of adverse circumstances and without the compulsion of one's own temperament, means of course to be a novelist without being primarily an artist. The purely artistic deficiences of Gissing's work are readily stated; if, without meaning to, we make too much of them, it is partly because most criticism has made little or nothing.

First of all, nowhere does Gissing exhibit that flexile ease which every great story-teller has, either by endowment, like Wilkie Collins, or by laborious mastery, like Flaubert. Even in the short sketches of *The*

House of Cobwebs and *Human Odds and Ends,* where Gissing the story-teller is least constrained, his mechanism is not the lubricated and noiseless contrivance which the best-schooled modern workmanship knows how to assemble. Some axioms of proportion and accent Gissing never mastered at all. Important links between episodes submit without a struggle to the natural tendency of such passages, the tendency to become dull. Whole chapters of Gissing read not so much like a story as like a synopsis. Transitions that could be implied in a sentence occupy long pages of a journeyman expository style. On the other hand, events at which we ought to be present, with our attention keyed to a certain emotional pitch, are reported simply as having happened. Not even *The Whirlpool* gives the impression of telling itself. We feel, behind the work, the industry and the discomfort of the workman.

Henry James, in one of the short London Notes of 1897, shot a keen critical arrow to the very central defect of Gissing's method: the prodigious excess of dialogue. Dialogue by itself completely fails to convey the sense of time elapsed, because everything "appears . . . to occur simply at the occasion of a few conversations about it." Moreover, it is impossible to make people talk all the time and talk "with the needful differences. The thing . . . is simply too hard." Conversation "is singularly suicidal from the moment it is not directly illustrative of something given us by another method, something constituted and presented." It is true that Gissing's fondness for direct discourse, combined with his fumbling treatment of most else, quite undermines the reader's sense of "the stretch of the years in which developments really take place." It is also true that many of the conversations themselves go with a wearisome archaic dullness approaching pedantry. Partly because of this drawback, Gissing never acquired anything of Henry James's skill in handling the small social group and creating its atmosphere. He does no justice to a garden party, a musicale, a tea, a cluster of Sunday idlers in the park; he does little justice to the solitary individual. He is at his best with scenes of two or three people only, or, at the other extreme, with great shouting, surging, inarticulate masses of the populace, the sinister and impersonal mob.

III

Well—as even the fastidiousness of Henry James could grant, "we must take what we can get, and Mr. Gissing has a way of his own." It was part of his way, and indeed the part that brings him nearest us, to turn all the old general problems into specific terms, and all the old specific problems into still more specific terms. He had an ear to the ground for what were as yet hardly more economic and sociological rumblings; and these he made the commonplaces of his fiction. Disraeli and Mrs. Gaskell had written of the mob oppressed and wretched: in *Demos* Gissing wrote of the mob unchained, half-organized, and brandishing its fists at the oppressor. The novel since Dickens had been filled with poor old women: in *The Odd*

Women Gissing filled it with poor old maids. And he let them demand for themselves, not only decent occupations, but very specific occupations and rights: he was thinking not only of professional dignity for women, but also of professional stenography for women and, actually, of votes for women. Every one had been concerned about free speech: in *Thyrza* Gissing was concerned about free libraries. Meredith and Henry James had written novels about novelists: in *The New Grub Street* Gissing almost wrote a novel about novels. Alcoholism and social settlement work hob-nob in his pages; civic improvement and communal kitchens are there together; concessions to Labor and the servant question strike up an acquaintanceship. Gissing was the first to express in such detail the outward aspects of his day—which have not yet quite ceased to be the aspects of our day. In all this he was decidedly more than abreast of his period and its novelists.

The wonder is that he could have been so ready for the facts and so little eager to draw extravagant conclusions from them. Instead of being excited by the symptomatic changes in society, he kept his head and his discouraged sense of the gap that must be spanned if any change of real importance were to come about. He is the aristocrat forced to descend bodily to his material, yet remaining spiritually aloof to analyze rather than gesticulate. Besant offered his solution without stating the problems, and his solution is one of time's laughing-stocks. Gissing stated the problems with no particular hope of a solution—and

Gissing and his problems are still with us. In Besant, the coöperative industrial scheme pays its way and the free libraries are patronized until the slums are a sort of Age of Pericles. In Gissing's *Demos* the coöperative enterprise has to be abandoned, and in *Thyrza* the free reading room for workingmen has to be closed because the workingmen's culture grows as cold as the Laodiceans' piety. Gissing saw no vision; but that very fact is what saves him from being a futile and discredited sort of visionary.

Never did Gissing greatly change in his attitude toward the democracy. His later discouragement, as expressed in the fairly well-known *Private Papers of Henry Ryecroft*, is duplicated in the much earlier *Demos*—a book worth some attention because it exhibits both his fairness to the working class and his entire failure to see in them any force of social regeneration.

For his hero in *Demos* he takes the best workingman he can find. Richard Mutimer is a mechanic of a thrifty family, alert, honest, intelligent, well-read in propagandist literature; a lecturer and maker of speeches, regarding himself as the apostle of a better future. By an accident to a will, he becomes the owner of a great provincial iron-works, with land and houses and an income. He forms a socialist committee to administer the great industry; he builds clean tenements for his workers; he establishes a coöperative store and a free lecture hall; and he plans to use the surplus earnings of the enterprise in propaganda and reform. But almost at the outset pride enters to make him ashamed of his betrothed, whom in his heart he contrasts unfavorably with the daughter of a gentile family into which he has ingratiated himself. And cruelty follows pride. He shows himself susceptible to adroit flattery from an unscrupulous journalist who is looking for profit. He suddenly discovers that his sister is too good for the artisan who has been courting her, and that the really effective way of amalgamating the classes is to marry as far as possible *above* one's self. He shows himself intolerant toward laborers who want to think for themselves, and quite forgets that his altruism had originally set out to better workingmen economically, not to make them swallow his opinions. A good servant, he proves himself to be a hopelessly bad master.

The analysis of Mutimer's moral disintegration is especially shrewd at the point where he allows himself to be drawn into a candidacy for Parliament, not as a Socialist, but as a Radical: by this time he has discovered that a mere name does not matter, and that he can serve his cause as well in one party as in another. At the end of a long series of disappointments and calamities he topples to his ruin under the weight of his own weaknesses. And in the hour of ruin he loses the fickle and ignoble crowd of his supporters —the people who are ready to feed at any trough. Mutimer is the man who tries to be a socialist in a capitalistic world; the mob is a grim destructive force which he tries to use as his instrument. The man becomes a capitalist himself without realizing it; the crowd first applauds and then rends him, according to what it gets from him or fails to get.

In this book there is a quite visible identity between the man and the crowd: it is obvious that Mutimer himself is meant for Demos, a synthesis of all the traits that render the artisan, according to Gissing's pessimism, unfit for power. Gissing would have us remember that the mob is only a collection of men; and he shows us, for the crucial test-case, a man who is only the mob.

IV

Fundamentally, a great deal of Gissing's work, like *Demos,* records an individualist's rejection of democracy and the common man. The individualist values fine sensibilities, and the common man has them not: so at least Gissing seems to say. We have seen that the hero of *Demos* is a compendium of the mob of common men. One of the most characteristic facts about him is his entire lack of moral fineness in dealing with women: in some passages the analysis of his egoism, his unconscious brutality, is almost too cruelly inexorable. Every careful reader of Gissing will remember a great number of passages where unimaginative contempt of women is the mark of men coarsened by a low environment; such contempt might almost be called Gissing's favorite badge of the democrat, were it not that he rather frequently portrays the woman herself coarsened, as he does in *The Odd Women, Demos* itself, and *In the Year of Jubilee.* Generally speaking, his individualism represents a hard and brutal egoism as chief of the common stock of democratic traits.

There is an artistic sense, as we have said, in which

his books are duller than he intended them to be; but the great majority of his characters, most of whom are very common people indeed, are dull *because* he intended them to be. It was no part of his purpose to beautify the side of life that he knew. He treated it dully because to him it was dull. One of his principal points was that poverty is degrading; and he proved that point to his own satisfaction by showing poor people as degraded. He looked at the man with shabby clothes on his back, and he put shabby thoughts into that man's head and shabby words into his mouth. Gissing contemplated the London mob making holiday, and he said that it was like "some huge beast purring to itself in stupid contentment"; contentment being the stupidity of the poor. He contemplated an estranged wife in her mortal sickness, and he made her write to her husband: "For myself I ask nothing. I don't think I shall live. If I do, I will consent to anything you propose. I only ask you to behave without any pretence; if you cannot forgive me, do not make a show of it. Say what your will is, and that shall be enough." This open-eyed resignation is the intelligence of the poor. Hopelessness is the logical goal; hope and happiness are only illusions that increase the bitterness of despair when it supervenes. This is the core of Gissing's pessimism about the lower classes, and it is the reason why his characters are often so expressionless. It is also one reason why he is so expressionless about them. It seemed to him that the pressure of poverty makes all men sickeningly alike.

Of course the answer to Gissing's theory is that it simply is not true. It is only to the enlightened aristocrat that humble folk are unbearably sodden: they are not so to themselves. In real life the extremes of hope and despair never lie so close together that there is no room left for either tragedy or triumph. Gissing himself could leap for joy when he found sixpence in the street. It is strange that he should have portrayed characters to whom the finding of a fortune could make no difference. Most of us are romantics. What we wait for may never come—but then, we wait for it, and that is the important thing. All existence is given its color by things that never happen. When every other reliance is lost, we fall back on our own souls, the mystery of our suffering and of our being able to bear so much. Gissing's people never discover themselves in this way; when the outward circumstances are hopeless, all is hopeless. Gissing knew all there was to know about harsh facts, and faced the knowledge with fortitude; but there was something about the elasticity of the human soul that he never knew, extraordinarily as his own life illustrated it. One is almost tempted to say that he tried to show something about life with characters who did not have life—even enough life to commit suicide.

To be a democrat is to be part of a great paradox in which Gissing never really believed: the paradox that dull circumstances do *not* make dull people, that rather dullness in the surroundings gives quite common people their chance to shine with unearthly luster.

Of democracy in this sense Dickens is, of course, the great exponent. Dickens saw in human nature something that will never give in to the strain of deprivation and misery, something that does not know how to be sordid. You could take away prosperity, but not laughter. You could take away the roof from a poor man's head, but so long as you left him enough of a body to house his soul you could not take away his identity. Lowly circumstances and hard work do not force men into the same shape: wealth and laziness can do enough in that direction. The sixteen hundred folk of Dickens are incurably different—and, broadly speaking, Dickens with all his caricature tells the truth about humanity. But if Gissing had seen all the poor people in all the Dickens novels reveling at the Crystal Palace on a holiday, he would have put them into *The Nether World* in just the phrases he used:

"On the whole how respectable they are, how sober, how deadly dull! See how worn-out the poor girls are becoming, how they gape, what listless eyes most of them have! The stoop in the shoulders so universal among them merely means overtoil in the work-room. Not one in a thousand shows the elements of taste in dress; vulgarity and worse glares in all but every costume. Observe the middle-aged women"—middle-aged women are one of the unfading glories of Dickens—"it would be small surprise that their good-looks had vanished, but whence comes it that they are animal, repulsive, absolutely vicious in ugliness? Mark the men in their turn; four in every six have visages so deformed by ill-health that they excite disgust."

Such a description represents the most forlorn tragedy of the aristocratic mind. Gissing is the conscious aristocrat, consciously thinking down to the level of the people from an intellectual stratum far above theirs, even while compelled into a miserable intimacy with all the paraphernalia of their lives. He lived a great part of his life in the next street to the heaven of the poor; but all he knew was that he was living in hell.

In a sense, all this is to reiterate that Gissing was only half an artist, and that there was nothing in his native temper that would ever have compelled him to write a novel at all. He was, so to speak, a university don and a scholar by birth; and the fortune of his life made him into some one else. Because he was some one else, he took it for granted that he was indistinguishably like a horde of other thwarted people; whereas he was not only an individualist, but in the most profound sense an individual, one of the most strangely different men who ever lived. He thought of the real George Gissing as a person who had died at seventeen; the George Gissing who wrote three novels a year was only a plaything of fate. It is strange that he never saw how completely the man who could write three novels a year without having been intended by nature to do it, was making fate *his* plaything. But Gissing never did see anything half so exciting as that. And the perpetual wonder is, not that work proceeding from such anomalous conditions and from such an attitude should contain some obvious defects, but that it should display any conspicuous merit at all.

V

This aristocratic limitation of Gissing is central and integral, but it is not the whole man. After all, he was human; and being so he did not always have quite the courage of his one inhuman conviction. He might believe that the efforts of degraded men were futile, and that their attempts to rise were only a prolongation of suffering such as complete lucidity would not try to endure: but somehow or other he showed them trying to rise. This is the one respect in which his personæ do attain the stature of real life. They have, as Mr. Paul Elmer More says in one of the *Shelburne Essays*, the *will to live*, to survive, to prove themselves of the strong, to be different. They have the will to live even when they lack the hope. This will, even if you call it only the reflex twitching of a dead organism, does exist, is a force; and those who have it desire life even if they do not attain life.

It is this force that helps us see nearly all of Gissing's characters in one particular light. They are a varied company: clerks, seamstresses, toughs, aged and aging women, men of business wearied or brutalized, sots, degenerates, nouveaux-riches, flashy and loud youths, Madonnas of the slums: but in one trait they are all brothers and sisters. However and wherever we find them, in the rare moments of triumph or the frequent long hours of failure; saddened, calloused, stolid, vulgar, sensitive, or silly, they are always longing for something they cannot define, something they might not care for if they had it; they are always *climbing;*—turning again to the ascent just when they are most hopelessly beaten down, mounting upward perhaps without direction and without reason, without knowing indeed what they mount toward, keeping on because the motion itself is a drug to the senses. Climbing . . . and never getting anywhere.

It is not strange that this part of Gissing, in his early work inhibited and numbed, should have found release as he attained comparative prosperity, at the period of *Henry Ryecroft* and just before that of *Veranilda.* It is a matter of temperament, not of judgment: that Gissing's judgment of the crowd never changed, he makes clear beyond mistake in *Ryecroft.* But his feeling for life changed as he made terms with life; and in *The Whirlpool,* which of all his longer stories reads with the most smoothness, this tenacity of will reaches its maximum. In technique alone, in finish of detail, in concentration and intensity, this book excels *The New Grub Street, Will Warburton,* and *The Odd Women;* it far excels *In the Year of Jubilee* or *The Nether World.* It is also remarkable as Gissing's one successful attempt to apply his realism to lives materially much more prosperous than his own. But it seems chiefly important as the belated disclosure of Gissing's own temperament reaching its full play. A critic who has noted that Gissing's scenes are all painted in black and white and gray might further have pointed out that in *The*

Whirlpool he begins unconsciously to paint in colors —the more remarkably because he is dealing still with London, the "Whirlpool" of his title, which had been to him hitherto all fog and factory smoke. This release of pent colors, however trivial in itself, is really indicative of what was happening to the man.

Of all his books, this is fullest of a certain beat and rhythm: the dull and muffled rhythm of feet that climb; of weary feet that climb incessantly over thorny trails without end. Alma Frothingham is a holiday climber; she starts out to brave the heights in a muslin dress and high-heeled slippers; we do not need the outcome to tell us that she is too dainty and too fragile for such work; it is written between the lines from the beginning that we shall presently see her bedraggled, bruised, her complexion spoiled by sun and wind, her courage gone. An empty prettiness is all her equipment; she was never meant for the heights. Harvey Rolfe too starts out in a holiday mood. He strikes an easy gait; he will stroll for the first part of the way—there is plenty of time before dark. But the way is steeper than he thought. Suddenly he finds that he is lost, and the daylight is going; it will need all his energy and courage to reach a safe shelter. Unlike Alma, he *has* energy and courage. He throws aside the useless weights that have held him back; he struggles on; and if he does not reach the point a more vigorous start would have brought him to, at least his steps have not been all wasted.

The story of these two and of their fellow climbers is the English counterpart of our later American epic of the social climber, *The House of Mirth.* Many of the same narrative elements are here: the part played by financial entanglements in the world of smart ambitions; the woman who means to "arrive" at any cost; the other woman who, in dealing with men, always implies a promise of more than she means to give, who adopts in her different milieu Mrs. Warren's formula of "being good to some man who can afford to be good to her"; the man who, through jealous love, is betrayed into a tragic mistake by appearances worse than the reality; the end with a rising inflection and a question mark—oddly, in either case, following a narcotic overdose, to be interpreted however one's own sense of fitness dictates. Mrs. Wharton's story is much the better known; perhaps, as the work of a more single-minded and ruthless artist, it well deserves to be. But in one respect at least Gissing's story is the greater, though his Alma Frothingham is a pallid figure beside Lily Bart. He faces the ruin his characters have wrought, and shows whatever meager elements of well-being they are able to preserve out of the wreck. The will to live, to ascend, is unconquerable in them; exhausted and drained, with hardly a hope or a destination, but with the climbing instinct surging through despair and a mysterious dazzle of sunshine in their eyes, they are up and off once more.

Cosmopolitan and Provincial

HENRY JAMES

WILLIAM DEAN HOWELLS

III

HENRY JAMES

(March, 1916)

I

To suggest what is felt by those of us who never had the honor of so much as a glimpse of Henry James the man, it is necessary only to say that Henry James the craftsman has become, by the sharp physical finality of death, at last wholly and securely ours. A living author is the more or less prized property of his age, to be cuffed or caressed, or both, as the caprice of the age wills: a dead author is the undisputed possession of the many or few who duly love him. The genius of Henry James, that has for twenty years past expressed itself both as a ripened historical influence and as a series of vivid and commanding appeals to the renewed contemporary appreciation, has attained its rounded completion, not by any possibility to be added to; and this very lamentable fact of the last page blackened over, the last word dictated, has the effect of making over his genius bodily to us as a sum-total, the most lavish gift surely of our time. We have found our title to the gift confirmed in the obituary columns of all manner of dailies and weeklies and their several supplements—columns that have seemed to slam a door on our treasure room of the past and, with a parting twist of the rusted key, crunchingly to lock it; which sovereign gesture of dismissal we need only interpret as a surrender of the key to whatever fortunate comer knows how to turn it, in order to get at the full volume of our inheritance. Such at least will be the attitude of those for whom a new and complete Henry James begins just where the frayed and fragmentary subject of journalism has lately ended; those who feel his death as a summons to the calm privilege of considering his worth and of trying to measure the full extent of what he has come to mean to them.

How much there has been to interfere with the serenity and solid comfort of our possession of him, those can appreciate whose helpless solicitude has followed him, on his more or less annual "appearances," through the rough gauntlet of criticisms, reviews, notices, parodies—the tumult of jeers mostly echoed and therefore meaningless, meaningless and therefore unanswerable except by *his* answer of silence. We have not had, happily for ourselves, the distress of seeing him mind what the heedless said of him: he bore everything as though it had not existed, and to the practical purpose of convincing us eventually that for him it really did not exist. In that, he was like a slender and shrinking youth of incredible unsophistication, caught in some barroom medley of lewd songs meant to confuse him and obscene jokes at his expense, not only not knowing in his innocence what it could all possibly mean, but—wondrously and beautifully—quite making out through his amazement that they didn't know either, those others of the song and the jest, his irresponsible tormentors, who would neither like him nor let him alone, who would do neither more nor less than senselessly bawl at him.

Only we, the shamed outraged by-standers in the crowd, could hardly feel our neighbors' discourtesy the less because he, our lovable stripling, appeared not to feel it at all; the very perfection of his poise being in fact, to our tortured helplessness, the last "turn of the screw." If he had given the least sign of needing us, for defense, for intervention, for anything that could have set us between him and the rabble—. But one couldn't remonstrate without seeming to inform him that one thought of him as being affronted. And if he actually did not know, if it had never occurred to him that he could be exposed to affront, why then, heaven prosper his innocence, we must not set ourselves so near the rabble as to squabble with them over how they ought to treat him. To squabble over the terms of Henry James's reception was, we felt, the great unworthiness, second only to the ignorant derision. It was our affair just to deserve him by prizing what he prized, ignoring what he ignored, and meeting him at his own level, in the Great Good Place his kindly solicitude had made for us. If it was not in his vocabulary to say anything to the criticism of derision, we did best not to have anything to say to it. Only we could not *quite* ignore what he ignored, being of coarser clay; we could not help suffering for him, even if he obviously knew nothing about how to suffer for himself. And then, the shame we felt for our coevals, the vague sense of responsibility for the profane laughter that we could not explicitly disclaim, since we dared not seem to be aware of it—these too were insurgent instincts, not too easily put down.

But now all that is done with, at least nearly enough so that the quiet voice, the accent of appreciation and of faith, hasn't to be a shriek to get itself pitched above the babbling ribaldry. This is the atonement we draw out of our very loss: that, because the resistance is so suddenly withdrawn, appreciation can operate more naturally, with less self-consciousness, than ever before. This is the auspicious time for it to set in earnest about its task of rescue and extrication, grateful that it can begin to disentangle from the old confusion those matters which it feels to be of the first importance.

II

To come at once to the most minutely specific matter of all is to begin where discussion has too often unfortunately ended. We mean, of course, the matter of Henry James's personal style, in the narrower sense of verbal and phrasal quality, the contour and color of sentences. That style is the most intense vibration, certainly, of the personal note, the last inch of the development of expression toward the individual. In its task of fitting Henry James and what he had to say, it dropped more and more into certain persistent mannerisms; so that it is no matter for surprise if the larger significance of his manner seemed to have got lost among them.

The manner of Henry James, as distinguished from any and all mannerisms, is essentially the Henry James sentence. If his phrase-vocabulary is sometimes so idiomatic that it is a species of refined slang of polite society, it must not be overlooked that his characteristic sentence is so beautifully cadenced that it is English of the purest. The rhythm and fluid beauty of prose were obvious and necessary tenets of his artistic faith. The Henry James sentence is a way of modifying everything and of obeying the stern injunction, never elsewhere more than half obeyed, to put modifiers with what they modify. The result is like a tree that has put forth, on one side and the other, so thick a succession of twigs and off-shoots, and so luxuriantly covered their irregularities with massed foliage, that the main trunk is quite obscured. Or it is as though the author had set down his thought, embroidered it in every conceivable way, and then erased all but the embroidery. The meaning seems rather sketched than written; sketched with the finest pencil, in all desirable sharpness, but without hardness, of line.

That soft accuracy of touch appears at its best wherever a situation makes the liveliest appeal to the author's kindly eager solicitude for his characters. For example, Herbert Dodd, a forlorn clerk whom life has "scraped bare," as he sat on his seaward-facing "bench of desolation," "might in these sessions, with his eyes on the gray-green sea, have been counting again and still recounting the beads, almost worn smooth, of his rosary of pain—which had for the fingers of memory and the recurrences of wonder the same felt break of the smaller ones by the larger that would have aided a pious mumble in some dusky altar-chapel." It is in such contexts, where the question is of insight or sympathy, that Henry James is most himself, his touch unique and unapproachable.

In dealing with physical objects and the externals of personality, he often reminds one of the later and less periodic manner of Pater—as, for example, in rendering this interior of a French dining-room: "The little waxed *salle-à-manger* was sallow and sociable; François, dancing over it, all smiles, was a man and a brother; the high-shouldered patronne, with her high-held, much-rubbed hands, seemed always assenting exuberantly to something unsaid; the Paris evening, in short, was, for Strether, in the very taste of the soup, in the goodness, as he was innocently pleased to think it, of the wine, in the pleasant coarse texture of the napkin and the crunch of the thick-crusted bread."

In all such passages—and our offered pair strictly and fairly represent the later and latest manner, the very upshot of the long adventure of Henry James's style—there is the nicest possible care for the music of prose, the chime of sounds in combination, the word fitly spoken that is like "apples of gold in pictures of silver."

So far we make no explicit account of Henry James's extraordinary felicity of phrase, a point in which he strikes one as nothing short of Meredithian.

The impact of his wit is the more forcible because one has it to reckon with almost from the beginning,—indeed, from before the beginning, in the works of his little known, little read father,—whereas so many of his later characteristics grew upon him by slow accretions, from imperceptible beginnings. Nothing in his later work could be better than the description of Mr. Tristram in *The American* (1877) as " large, smooth, and pink, with the air of a successfully potted plant." This is of one substance with his description of Jim Pocock in *The Ambassadors* (1903) as " small and fat and constantly facetious, straw-colored and destitute of marks "; he " would have been practically indisguishable had not his constant preference for light gray clothes, for white hats, for very big cigars and very little stories done what it could for his identity." This is the swift summarizing touch applied to individuals whose reality far exceeds their importance to the story. Another instance of the same felicity, the socially indispensable Miss Banker was " stout red rich mature universal—a massive much-fingered volume, alphabetical wonderful indexed, that opened of itself at the right place." Later, bristling with new items of gossip, she has " filled in gaps and become, as it were, revised and enlarged." Mrs. Assingham, " the most luminous of wives," dazes her somewhat lumpish husband with the dexterity of her analysis of a situation: " Whereupon, breaking short off, to ascend to her room, she presented her highly decorated back —in which, in odd places, controlling the complications of its aspect, the ruby or the garnet, the turquoise and the topaz, gleamed like faint symbols of the wit that pinned together the satin patches of her argument"—and, one is constrained to add, like faint symbols of the wit that describes her, the Henry James wit that pins together the variously textured patches of his prose style from *Roderick Hudson* to the last critiques and prefaces.

III

To the reader who finds in all this only bafflement, one must admit that the process of Henry James does largely consist in amassing subtleties. He flutes overtones instead of sounding the fundamental; and if the whole suggestive series of harmonics turns out not to suffice, as it confessedly does turn out for those who like the full organ of style and its emotional blare of brass, why then nothing is proved except that some persons like the more raucous instrumentation. If this final and non-debatable preference exists on adequate trial, one must make a virtue of accepting it as the *non disputandum* of æsthetics. But practically everything else in Henry James, the whole array of artistic devices and expedients, will be found enormously to count for simplification of the novel and of its machinery.

The principle of his basic simplicity is of course to be sought in his one inclusive interest, which has never for an instant shifted: his interest in the two interdependent fruits of civilization, of breeding, of the human horticulture at its most exquisite. The first of those fruits is perfection of environment, of scene—the spirit or "genius" of place, if place be considered as the embodiment of man's aspirations, loyalties, traditions, of his illustrious successes and his tragic failures. The second is perfection of the individual soul. All the best work of Henry James is reducible by analysis to a case of saturation with these two human idealities. He is the historian of man's objects of art, his buildings, streets, cities, the outer shell and the inner decorations of his culture; and he is "the historian of fine consciences."

If we state the two together, it is because of their interpenetration and essential oneness. It is in fact in Henry James's treatment of backgrounds that one begins to detect the infusion of his social sense. Not only does he catch the exact shade or tonal nuance of his scene, his Rome, London, Paris, or New York; he unravels its cluster of inwrought relations and connections with society, he makes it ramify spatially in every direction and temporally into the known past or the implied future. Geographically, the Paris of *The Ambassadors* is France crystallized, an affirmation of scores of towns and countrysides. Still more, it is a marginal commentary on England across the Channel, a critical analysis of America across the Atlantic—always with accentuated reference to Woollett, Massachusetts. The metropolis is presented, through Strether's observing and contrasting mind, in terms of everything that it isn't. And temporally one feels Paris as the child of Empire, the grandchild of Revolution. By innuendo, the yesterday is shown as penumbrally lurking behind and round the to-day. In the salon of Madame de Vionnet "the ghost of the Empire walked." And—"The light in her beautiful, formal room was dim . . . there was a pair of clusters of candles that glimmered over the chimney-piece. . . . He heard . . . from the empty court, the small plash of the fountain. From beyond this, and as from a great distance . . . came, as if excited and exciting, the vague voice of Paris. . . . Thus and so, on the eve of the great recorded dates, the days and nights of revolution, the sounds had come in, the omens, the beginnings broken out. They were the smell of revolution, the smell of the public temper—or perhaps simply the smell of blood." This is the process of saturation, the saturation of the subject with all manner of discovered contacts and values. Its effect is indescribably to thicken and augment the social significance of places and of things, which, at their best and under such auspices, amount in themselves to criticism of life.

The second and far more important kind of saturation is that of personality, of the fine individual conscience. In more and more fully achieving it, Henry James arrived, by the middle of his career as a novelist, at the practice of tincturing the material of each story as vividly as possible with the finest consciousness present in it. He views the action of the given story, not as the omniscient reporter whose only limitation is that of plausibility, and who can observe actions in different spots simultaneously, nor yet as the narrator who hands over his material to a first-person-singular, a convenient eye-witness or participant delegated to talk the story for him, but in a somewhat different, a very special and characteristic way. He creates for the subject, and puts into it as observer and actor, the one personality or point of view in and through which the operation of the subject becomes most significant and most rewarding: then he studies the action from that point of view supplemented by his own. By this we mean that his chosen observer views the action objectively, while the author views the observer objectively. The story that he tells is not of the facts only: it is, especially and primarily, of some one's enlightened perception of the facts. Thus our realization of the facts is suffused with the sense of another's realization of them; we know the facts through seeing what shape and color they assume for a consciousness felt by us as vividly present throughout, and known to us as that of the invisible author can never be. The task becomes then to behold the subject through the mind in which it can take on the finest shapes and shades, the rarest values. On these terms every one of Henry James's best pieces tends to become a story *about* a story, a recital of some one's perception of events, that perception being sifted and weighed and in general selectively reëdited by the author as he passes it on to us.

In certain important ways too devious for our space, this trick of method determines and explains the incomparably finished technique of Henry James, every one of whose artistic manipulations exists solely for service of the will to know, to understand, to unriddle the central mystery of character. It is this incessant and indomitable will to know that leads him to his studies of the finest, rarest, most specialized of human relationships: that of the painter to his still unpainted "Madonna of the Future," that of the "Passionate Pilgrim" to his ancestral home, that of poor little Maisie to her scandalously divorced and squabbling parents, that most frequent relation of the lover who renounces his hopes because only so can his conscience define itself in action, that of the artist's wife who has an unquenchable distaste for her husband's work—these and a host of others still more complex or richly ramifying, all of them proposed first, and presently brought to dramatic focus, as struggles of the individual soul rendered transparent to the reader.

IV

If we turn back a moment to qualify this insistence on the rewarding richness of the minds through which Henry James did his reproducing, it is only for defiance of an exaggerated public impression that most of his protagonists are formidably intellectual persons. He does of course exert some of his best gifts in the portrayal of intellectual types; and it is true that he has never found his interest shift its center of gravity very far toward the street, the shop, or the factory. But to let the mind course at random over the list of his most arresting and communicative personæ is to experience a difficulty in recalling a great number who are intellectuals primarily, whereas the others, the ones who think with their nerves, positively throng. The values that recur and persist are passion and quickness of intuition, rather than profundity of thought. Even when the case proposed is that of the artist incarnate, we see him primarily outside the studio, in trouble, in love, in some light romantic escapade, or perhaps in debt; and our awareness of the creative talent in him is only our tribute to the general adequacy of Henry James's characters—their adequacy, that is, for plausibly living up to any high requirement he makes of them. The task is to invent for each case as it comes up the one personality in presence of which it yields the most of its distilled essence, not by any means always the greatest personage. "A subject residing in somebody's excited and concentrated feeling about something—both the something and the somebody being of course as important as possible—has more beauty to give out than under any other style of pressure." That is one declaration of moment. But it needs this supplement: "The thing is to lodge somewhere at the heart of one's complexity an irrepressible *appreciation,* but where a light lamp will carry all the flame I incline to look askance at a heavy."

If there is any one type of appreciation in the analysis of which this author definitely excels himself, it is that of the very young girl in a difficult social situation, carrying it through with "acuteness and intensity, reflexion and passion," "a high lucidity," taking above all "a contributive and participant view of her situation." Of the lesser known of this type there are Maggie Verver in *The Golden Bowl,* Nanda Brookenham in *The Awkward Age,* Rose Tramore in

The Chaperon, Laura Wing in *A London Life*—to all of whom the best known Daisy Miller becomes, through her one last half-delirious flash of insight, the worthy elder cousin. Their altogether charming and lovable junior is of course little Maisie in *What Maisie Knew*—a mere wisp of childhood, bundled back and forth between parents divorced after an unsavory scandal, flung about as though she were a recurring taunt in some spiteful and monotonous argument, yet sweetly saved from the unlovely total of what she "knew" by just her appreciation, her adjustment to the homely oddness of her standing—the answer of the responsible child in her to the irresponsible child in each of her parents and their various connections.

Of the others, the variegated types that make up the world of Henry James's characters, there is no room to speak in detail. They are the select motley of all Cosmopolis. Let us content ourselves for the moment with noting that the best of the men, men such as Christopher Newman and Strether and Nick Dormer and Prince Amerigo, shine in the panoply of such virtues as we see in the best of the women: intuition, a grave and kindly solicitude, impressibility, readiness for the give-and-take of friendly intercourse—and in addition something which Europe mainly teaches them, a finished gentility, gentleness refined upon by breeding, the ideal consummation of chivalry. All of Henry James's best—and his aristocracy is genuinely of bestness—are agents of the same social law, in the light of which his less than best are judged: the law of understanding of one's fellows and of perfect charity for them—"never rashly to forget and never consciously to wound."

This formula, the formula of Henry James's large general definition of breeding, is the most important element in his work on the non-technical side. To see life steadily and see it whole has denoted in his practice the attempt to see it through the greatest faculty or motive applicable to it—the insatiable will to know, to understand. That will, a necessity to him and to his most representative men and women, rules and includes every lesser motive. It is simply the generalized version of his prized qualities of passion, intuition, reflexion, intensity—the "contributive and participant view" of life. He finds no need to write grim tragedies, which at their artistic best are the product of crucial misunderstandings, because he is always writing about the thing that makes the crucial misunderstanding impossible—the faculty of sympathetic insight working among difficulties, picking its way through them, achieving in the end, if it be worthy, the contact of understanding spirit with spirit understood. He confronts his personæ at the outset with a social situation that is like a very complicated lock, to which there is, there must be, they feel, somewhere a key. It is possible to break the lock; and oftentimes there is plenty of good sound raw common sense to be alleged for that course, on the usual blundering human theory that life is too short for anything but bold and violent action, the swiftest means of "getting there." But that is not the philosophy of our personæ in the given *impasse:* their one highest duty is to find the key. That it happens to be also their one highest privilege is the reason why their striving is seen as going on before us in the flush and glow of a warm human appeal. If they were seeking their ideal, a beautiful rightness of conduct, in the cold white light of some bloodless and sterile theory of obligation, the whole affair would strike us as intellectualized, flat, arid, and unrewarding. But all their waiting and wondering and subtle devising is in behalf of something they profoundly want, something profoundly worth wanting. By exhibiting the patience of self-knowledge, of slow self-mastery, they bring the issue out of their conflicts without the stress of a fiery or tragic dénouement. Their escape from that danger is the success of their understanding. The reasoned conduct that provides the way of escape is an expression of the social conscience, the inveterate human instinct of solidarity—Henry James's greatest thing in the world.

V

As we pass on to the description of Henry James's "art," using that sometimes despised and rejected word in its broad structural sense, we shall find a unique distinction in his procedure with a subject from the point of his first contact with its primary "germ." The accepted procedure of the realist is of course the collecting, note-taking, "documenting," or at any rate some form of the additive, whereby the germ is induced to multiply itself to the desired size. Henry James's first thought, on the other hand, was to secrete his first tiny "wind-blown particle" of suggestion, to shield it from the touch of any actuality outside his own imagination. We know the realist who conceives a story in his own mind and relies on life for the rest. Henry James, by his own repeated account, drew his initial conceptions from life and relied on his own mind for the rest. It is clear, again by his own account, that he distrusted life as an artistic selective principle, considered it in fact an artistic bungler and wastrel. Its way was to furnish the nucleus of a story, and then wantonly to wreck the story. By this we mean, not that he parted company with life or shirked important truths, but that he was far too interested in the *law* of life to dally among accidents or to prize odds and ends of reality just because they existed. A comment of his own illumines this point:—

> . . . the very source of interest for the artist . . . resides in the strong consciousness of his seeing all for himself. He has to borrow his motive, which is certainly half the battle; and this motive is his ground, his site and his foundation. But after that he only lends and gives, only builds and piles high, lays together the blocks quarried in the deeps of his imagination and on his personal premises. He thus remains all the while in intimate commerce with his motive, and can say to himself—what really more than anything else inflames and sustains him—that he alone has the *secret* of the particular case, he alone can measure the truth of the direction to be taken by his developed data. There can be for him, evidently, only one logic for these things; there can be for him only one truth and one direction—the quarter in which his subject most completely expresses itself. The careful ascertainment of how it shall do so, and the art of finding it with consequent authority—since this sense of " authority " is for the master-builder the treasure

of treasures, or at least the joy of joys—renews in the modern alchemist something like the old dream of the secret of life.

This dream and this secret are the explanation of Henry James's unvarying scorn for "the story that can be told" and of his life-long endeavor to tell "the story that cannot be told."

> "Heard melodies are sweet, but those unheard
> Are sweeter . . ."

Henry James found his interest at the central truth of things, and let who would be interested in the surface facts.

Of the swarming consequences of this interest as his art worked them out in one case after another, we have space to name only the most significant. It explains, first, the progressive simplification of his art through the forty years and more of his productivity. He withdraws from himself every factitious external aid, leaves himself more and more with a free hand. Austerely alone with his theme, taking it on its own terms, making the most of its peculiar intensity, he finds actually a notation for cadences of the unheard melody, "the story that cannot be told." A second momentous result is the breaking-down of the canonical distinctions between novel and short story—this latter, with its specialized and arbitrary "technique," a greatly overrated form at best. Obviously a theme developed on the conditions just described admits of no academical control from without it; and it is consequently impossible to locate the point where the "anecdotic" short story becomes the "developmental," or where the "developmental" short story becomes the novel-according-to-Henry James.

Again and, in the present connection, finally, this same austere use of the imagination accounts for the sense we all have of the profound *originality* of Henry James. Realism on the lower plane never gives us that sense: its whole force is of the opposite appeal, that to memory or recognition leaping out to embrace undoubted actuality. No critic has ever questioned Henry James's possession of the more fundamental and creative originality; but, most oddly from the present point of view, he has been praised above all for the novelty of his plots, which, as we have seen, are the one element of his art which he derived straight from brute material or factual reality, and which therefore can hardly justify our sense of his being so overwhelmingly individual. His true originality is first and always that of treatment. It is the outcome of his living at the center of his subject. His process, like that of Meredith's Comedy, "rejects all accessories." The realist lives, of course, all round the circumference of his subject and clutters his scene with accessories, and he is lucky if, in the end, he has made us aware that the subject *has* any center at all. In reading Henry James we are aware of hardly anything else; everything in him has the magic of supreme relevance. His best performances have the self-evident and self-sufficient beauty of a solitary cloud hung in a still sky, or, in his better phrase, "the hard beauty of the diamond." It is that splendid isolation and separate completeness of his themes, rather than their novelty as ideas, that surrounds us as we read with an eerie sensation never yet evoked by the novel which is a mere "slice" of life: the conviction that here is something that was never in the world before, something that is indestructibly and perfectly itself.

VI

The body of Henry James's work is, then, its studied formal exquisiteness. But it has a soul as well as a body; and its soul is a faith, a philosophy of the social conscience. Stated in one word that has all the air of being as old as Latin, that philosophy is Renunciation; but in a very special sense, quite remote from that of Christian dogma and on a different moral foundation. The Christian consciousness of guilt is replaced by the consciousness of worth; the soul renounces, not that it may be tempered and sensitized in suffering, but simply that it may live up to itself. It suffers, not blindly, but with eyes open and intent, after all the questions have been asked and suffering has been proved the one thinkable answer. Renunciation in this view is obedience to an inner law of necessity, the immediate exercise of a highest privilege.

The social sense of this view becomes intelligible if we remember that the highest privilege in the world of Henry James's characters is expressible only in terms of their relations to their fellows. There is nothing in their world except attitudes; a personality is the sum of its relations. One is happy just in proportion to the gift for surrounding one's self with intimate and flawless relationships; one must learn to think out of one's own point of view, think the thoughts of others, and in so doing partly cease to think of one's self. A social situation is a network of gossamer threads floating invisible, binding life to life in bonds fragile and perfect. A blunderer may tear all those threads from their contacts and leave half a dozen lives detached, shorn of half their meaning. The indispensable social grace is, then, to walk softly enough to feel the faintest brush of those intangible relations and to retreat, if need be, in time. The retreat is one's personal loss. But one must have seen far enough into the situation to apprehend the still greater loss of having one's way at the expense of muddling situations and spoiling lives and generally proving one's self an impenetrable brute. Self-esteem of this sort is practically a synonym for consideration of others.

If we have understood that renunciation of something immensely valuable for the sake of something quite without price is the crux of Henry James's greatest stories and his all-inclusive test of character, we see in the same glimpse why his most fruitful theme is international in scope. As the spokesman (and he is almost never the satirist) of the American abroad, he has an opportunity to present in a large way the contact of international ideals, influences, civilizations —the contrasted values of different traditions of breeding, each with merits, splendors even, that only the touch of the other can fully reveal. And through that juxtaposition of excellences the individual may find himself in a tragic dilemma, involving, by whatever way he escapes, the loss of important things relinquished. The measure of his worth is simply what he chooses to spare and what to cling to. *The Wings of the Dove* shows him, for example, choosing to renounce a living love for a memory that exerts a peculiar claim. The problem of the international novel as Henry James practised it was to bring out of a concrete social contingency so many conflicting ideals, all in their several ways desirable, that the individual soul must prove its fineness through choice and consequent sacrifice. The philosophy that comes out of this favorite theme is all in Strether's words as he effaces himself from the tangled situation of *The Ambassadors:* "That, you see, is my only logic. Not, out of the whole affair, to have got anything for myself." Materially, he has got nothing; spiritually, he has lost much but gained more.

That renunciation of this order is anything but the casual affair of one story or one period, we may prove by the case of *The American,* a story of twenty five years earlier. The "American" is Christopher Newman, a youngish retired business man taking his first long Continental holiday. He becomes engaged to Madame de Cintré, the widowed daughter of an ancient and distinguished house; but his fiancée's mother, a personage of sinister and, as it proves, lethal potentialities, cruelly contrives the breaking-off of the engagement. Then Newman finds his revenge prepared and waiting in the shape of a grim secret out of the past, involving unbearable disgrace for the family that has but just disgraced him. He has only to open his lips to destroy them. But somehow the fancied taste of revenge stales in his mouth—perhaps because he has savored it too long. He stands before the house of the Carmelites where Madame de Cintré has walled herself away from the world, and realizes how dead and meaningless is the whole story, how "the days and years of the future would pile themselves above her like the huge immovable slab of a tomb." Then he wanders into Notre Dame and sits down absently in the "splendid dimness."

The most unpleasant thing that had ever happened to him had reached its formal conclusion; he had learnt his lesson—not indeed that he the least understood it—and could put away the book. He leaned his head for a long time on the chair in front of him; when he took it up he felt he was himself again. Somewhere in his soul a tight constriction had loosened. He thought of the Bellegardes; he had almost forgotten them. He remembered them as people he had meant to do something to. He gave a groan as he remembered what he had meant to do; he was annoyed, and yet partly incredulous, at his having meant to do it; the bottom suddenly had fallen out of his revenge. Whether it was Christian charity or mere human weakness of will—what it was, in the background of his spirit—I don't pretend to say; but Newman's last thought was that of course he would let the Bellegardes go. If he had spoken it aloud he would have said he didn't want to hurt them. He quite failed, of a sudden, to recognize the fact of his having cultivated any such link with them. It was a link for themselves perhaps, their having so hurt *him;* but that side of it was now not his affair. At last he got up and came out of the darkening church; not with the elastic step of a man who has won a victory or taken a resolve—rather to the quiet measure of a discreet escape, of a retreat with appearances preserved.

Thus one of the earliest, assuredly one of the finest, versions of the reiterated lesson, the lesson of the sensitive conscience expressing itself in social terms. It is the moral foundation of every piece of ideally right conduct in the thirty volumes of Henry James. It is the sense too of the one grand public gesture of Henry James's life, his thrilling personal renunciation. We are *glad*, those of us who think we humbly understand him, that in the second summer of the war he saw the way to bring himself so immeasurably nearer to us. We knew he would do it; how, being himself, could he not do it? And when he stepped from under our flag—our poor dimmed blurred stars he must have thought them—he stepped straight into our hearts. We are not told that his thought was to reprove us. At least we know that, if it was, he had earned the right by first immensely loving us; and how should we not be able to bear "the gentle reproof of exquisite solicitude," as Professor Wendell has called it? But the emphasis was not on that, on the reproof or the loss: with Henry James it never was on either. Still less could it have been on himself. He was committing himself, we know well, to something vaster even than England, vaster than empires and the Empire, and more enduring than they—the future of human solidarity in the world. He was living a chapter, the last for him, of the story that cannot be told.

IV

WILLIAM DEAN HOWELLS

(January 1, 1917, for Mr. Howells's eightieth birthday)

I

It is thirty years since Mr. George Moore set down his version of a comparison which had already promised to become as stereotyped in criticism as that of Thackeray with Dickens. "Henry James," said Mr. Moore in one of the books which are still the Nemesis of their author, since they have never managed to bring him fame quite unmixed with infamy, "went to France and read Tourgenev. W. D. Howells stayed at home and read Henry James. I have no doubt at one time of his life Henry James said, I will write the moral history of America, as Tourgenev wrote the moral history of Russia—he borrowed at first hand, understanding what he was borrowing. W. D. Howells borrowed at second hand, without understanding what he was borrowing."

Now, some things have become obvious that were not even visible in 1887; some other things that are forever meaningless to a sterile æsthetic cosmopolitanism such as George Moore's of thirty years ago were as obvious then as now, if one but had eyes to see. Mr. Howells has had his share in both kinds of verity. He taught us some new lessons the worth of which was all in their timeliness; he reminded us of many a truth that had always been true, whether or not any one had taken the trouble to appreciate it. And of these latter, no other is half so important as that which Gallicizing æsthetes of the '80's most despised: the supreme value of having a home, a definitely local habitation, not to tear one's self away from, to sigh for, to idealize through a mist of melancholy and *Weltschmerz,* but simply and solely to live in, to live for. And so, while George Moore has said his worst in saying that Mr. Howells stayed at home, we dare urge the same fact as the very best that can be said—the special crown of Mr. Howells, and the open secret of his democratic grandeur. Nearly all of what one can profitably say of him distributes itself about this central and magnetizing fact, his unshakable foundation in a provincialism which is as remote from provinciality on one hand as from cosmopolitanism on the other—the "wise provincialism" of Royce's *Philosophy of Loyalty.*

Mr. Howells is quite the most American thing we have produced; that is, the most broadly and soundly representative. And his work falls in the era of the great transitions of our national life, the confusion of shifting ideals and mislaid ideas which led to the most American thing we have ever done—our specialization of everything. The war is over, and Howells comes back from his Venetian consulship to watch the phenomena of reconstruction, the emergence of a more centralized political system, and the dawn of a new unity. Agriculture grows relatively less important, manufacturing relatively more so; and thereupon begins the flux of young men and women from village to city, from farm to factory and office, and the consequent specialization of multitudes of lives. In industry, the epoch of individual enterprise merges into that of great combinations and corporate monopolies; business too becomes specialized. As commerce gains respectability, idleness becomes dubious and finally odious; and the result is a cleavage between generations in many a patrician family, the parents clinging to an old ideal of the leisured ornamental life, the sons drawn by a new ideal of useful prestige. When the new arisotcracy of vigor has supplanted the old aristocracy of cultivation, there arises the new cultivation, through efficiency. The laboring class, disproportionately augmented by immigration, develops a self-consciousness; its problems become insistent and terrible. In the professions, the general practitioner of an elder time turns into the specialist. Journalism and advertising, the quintessentially modern professions, begin to have their day. Among women too a ferment is at work; they swarm through doors once closed, they begin to know something, subtle changes take place in the home, marriage itself hears questions asked of it and knows that sooner or later it must answer them. Dogmatic theology is sharply challenged when the physical sciences reconceive the world, and the social sciences the people in it. The sense of an organic unity replaces that of an organized unity—and the world begins to wonder what purpose it serves, what it can possibly *mean.* Casting about, it begins to think it sees a purpose in unity itself. And through the confusion there crystallizes slowly the dream of a real society in which the common interests shall overthrow the conflicting ones. In a score of ways, the America of 1875 was at the crossroads. And William Dean Howells was the man who was there with her to see everything. He saw—and he understood.

All these tendencies and forces—the recital of them may be tedious, but it is certainly indispensable—are charted in the fiction of Mr. Howells, with an amplitude and a fidelity applied elsewhere, as in the novels of Trollope, to much narrower sectors of life, but never before in English to all the important phases in the life of a whole nation. It is as lavish as anything since Balzac, and it is focal. Howells is master of village and town, farm and city, New England and the Middle West; he is at home in factory and lumber-camp; he knows artisan and idler, preacher and teacher, the scientist, the journalist, the commercial traveler, the nouveaux-riches and their débutante daughter, the country squire, the oldest inhabitant, the village scapegrace and the village fool, the doctor and the lawyer; he misses nothing, as a review written by his greatest American contemporary once phrased it, of "the real, the natural, the colloquial, the moderate, the optimistic, the domestic, and the democratic."

And he has through all this, in addition to the notion

of where we are, the vision of where we are going. His novels convey the impression of greater lapses of time than any one of them actually records, because each one of them is an inquiry into something that is about to become something else. *The Rise of Silas Lapham,* our first and greatest analysis of the self-made man and of the social implications of his money, is a tragedy whose significance reaches nearly the whole of self-made America. Written at the nexus of so many tendencies and interests, it remains to-day as poignantly contemporary as ever, a drama of transitions not yet more than half accomplished. We clamor still for "the great American novel"? Why, we have been reading it these thirty years and more.

II

The remarks quoted above from *Confessions of a Young Man,* for the sake of finding in them something incomparably more important than their author intended to put there, seem to us to break down hopelessly as accounts of literal fact. One is justly reminded of the old lady who testified, first that the pot was broken when she borrowed it, secondly that it was whole when she returned it, and finally that she had never borrowed the pot anyhow. Mr. Moore was similarly pampering his intuitions at the expense of his facts.

It should have been evident, for example, even in 1887, that it was Mr. Howells, more than Henry James, who had set out to write the moral history of America. Also, Mr. Howells knew at first hand, not only his Tourgenev and his James, but Gladós and Valdés as well. If his critical interest was never quite so intensive in its workings as Henry James's, it was certainly much more eclectic. Its boundaries in 1887 did in fact touch everything that we now recognize as having been at that time important in Continental fiction and drama, with the single exception of Meredith, who seems, lamentably, to have meant nothing to Howells. Many readers and some critics could still learn a good deal about Balzac and Zola, about Dostoievsky and Tolstoï, from what Mr. Howells wrote about them more than a quarter of a century ago.

But one of the principal effects of his excursions among Italian, Spanish, Russian, and French realists was greatly to intensify his appreciation of Miss Wilkins, Miss Jewett, Mrs. Cooke, Miss Murfree, and Mr. Cable—American realists whose worth, like his own, is all in their provincialism; whose breadth is, as he says, "vertical instead of lateral." If his fiction withholds the cheap tribute of imitation, it is doubly rich in its recognition of the inimitable. His way of learning from Tourgenev was not to copy Tourgenev, but to be as American as Tourgenev was Russian. In the profoundest spiritual and moral sense, he did stay at home; but neither physically nor intellectually can he be said to have done so. He not only understood just what he might have borrowed, whether from Continental fiction or British; he understood it too well to borrow it at all.

Even the resemblance between Howells and Henry James is a subject easily overelaborated by criticism, as indeed it has often been. What resemblance there is is so superficial, and leaves room for differences so fundamental, that it becomes a point for criticism of Mr. Howells's critics rather than of Mr. Howells himself. So many have conspired, both before and since George Moore, to make sure that neither great man shall be named without the other, that it is actually more invidious to ignore the point than to treat it.

To summarize, one may say that the similarities are more marked in the later work of Mr. Howells than in the earlier, and at the same time much less important, and that they appear most in his least important work. One of the two social strata in *The Rise of Silas Lapham* is, pretty exactly, the social stratum of *The Bostonians;* and here, where the "body of reference" in part of one book resembles that in the whole of the other, the similarity is most important. Later, it becomes almost purely verbal. However strange it may seem, it is true that Mr. Howells, whose style has for fifty years remained limpid and lacustrine, shows after 1895 a slight, perhaps an unconscious, infiltration of the much abused "third manner" of Henry James. For example, *Miss Bellard's Inspiration,* a tenuously delicate bit of high comedy, is wrought up to this parting comment by Mr. Crombie: "'Well, I suppose she didn't want a reason, if she had an inspiration'"—which, like many another such pretty sophisticated trifle in the book, is persiflage of exactly the Henry James idiom.

But this sort of thing is of very slight avail when one is dealing broadly with the question of "influences."

The earlier likenesses are so general as quite to lack any hint of a debt, however honorable to the debtor; later, when the likenesses become more specific, the all-important differences become proportionately more accentuated. Henry James withdraws farther and farther from the America we know, and penetrates more and more deeply into the queer world of his own intensely self-conscious art. Howells remains about as objective, as regional, and as little self-conscious as a modern artist can be. If it is as true as we have said that Howells stayed at home, the compliment is to America, not to a brother author.

There is nothing in all this to disturb our account of that provincialism which is the nourishing root of his greatness. Morally, it is the whole story. If we speak, as here we have had to for a moment, of lighter and lesser things,—æsthetics, comparative literature, the transmission of influences,—we have to revise the account only so far as to say that Mr. Howells, if he did not stay at home, *went* home. We find him going everywhere but to go back again; enjoying one after another his Continental journeys, of the mind and of the body, as turnings of the road; never forgetting that great sprawled-out provincial modern Rome to which, he knew, whatever road he was on must at length lead back; finding beauty, the beauty of self-fulfilment, in each successive reunion between the America he had left and the American he was. Concretely, his books of travel, his various *Italian Journeys* and *London Films*, are better and truer records because there is no affectation in them of being anywhere except "abroad." Provincialism, like religion, is a surrender of something for the sake of something else that means more. If you are at home everywhere, you have lost the meaning of home. Mr. Howells prefers to give up being at home everywhere, in order to see Europe through naïve yet shrewd "Yankee" eyes, very much in the mood of

> "You have curious things to eat,
> I am fed on proper meat;
> You must dwell beyond the foam,
> But I am safe and live at home."

The result is that his most casual sketches of Italy, Spain, and England are not less American than *A Boy's Town* and *The Lady of the Aroostook*—which are as American as Abraham Lincoln.

III

In speaking of the sacrifices with which Mr. Howells, like any one, must pay for a sound and wise provincialism, we have in mind first of all the penalty inherent in any choice, the mutual exclusion of opposites. It is in the nature of things that you cannot be at the same time cosmopolitan and provincial: you can have everything, or you can have something which shall mean everything to you, but not both. This is the inevitable penalty. And it is well for the artist who has the courage or the sublime innocence to pay it, as we see proved in the unpretentious successes of such authors as Trollope and Jane Austen. If we require proof that it is *not* well for the artist who lacks the courage or the innocence, we need seek it no farther back than the pretentious failures of the Celtic Renaissance—a movement which had its headquarters in France and its impulse from a cosmopolitan æstheticism, and which was everything else before it was Celtic. We are safe, then, while we laud Mr. Howells for giving up everything, and acquiring nothing, which could have made him less definitively cisatlantic.

But there is another kind of penalty, not in the nature of things but incidental and secondary, which Mr. Howells also elected to pay—with some slight danger, as it seems, to his permanent importance. And even though no serious doubt of that permanent importance may ever have occurred to one, still one must try honestly to consider whether the author himself has not subjected it to the handicap of some unnecessary sacrifices here and there. We do find that Mr. Howells, seemingly in sheer national self-assertion and a kind of fiercely proud joy in heaping up the measure of his self-denials, has refused some fairly important things that he might as well have had. These minor refusals, made in all conscience and with the finest recklessness, do faintly blemish his work as that of a rounded artist, while adding nothing to its value as a national institution.

One is happy to note, first, that he was constantly threatening some sacrifices which he never made, and that his work as critic abounds in precepts the consequences of which he refused to incur in his own practice. He despises care for style, and says that style becomes less and less important to fiction: yet he writes a style finer on the whole than Hardy's, since it is just as objective, just as clear, much more full of highlights and undertones, and less metallically cold. He condemns with faintest praise the necessary technical means of art; he seems to imply that the artist can draw the pattern of his facts, as well as the facts themselves, from life; his account of Jane Austen would lead one to suppose that the sum of her process was to look about and jot down what she saw; in short, he develops a theory of the relation between literature and life that would result, if any one literally practised it, in novels with masses of subject matter but no subject at all. "Out of this way of thinking and feeling about these two great things, about Literature and Life," there has indeed "arisen a confusion as to which is which"—a confusion which has become in the last decade one of the least promising symptoms of the novel. And Mr. Howells seems to welcome the confusion when he says: ". . . it is quite imaginable that when the great mass of readers, now sunk in the foolish joys of mere fable, shall be lifted to an interest in the meaning of things through the faithful portrayal of life in fiction, then fiction the most faithful may be superseded by a still more faithful form of contemporaneous history." Yet here again Mr. Howells follows infirm doctrine with sound practice: his own novels enjoy all the advantages of the definite issue carefully extracted from life and then displayed before the reader as having relevance to some unified critical purpose. To young authors he says: "Do not trouble yourselves about standards and ideals." Himself, he follows a better precept: "Neither arts, nor letters, nor sciences, except as they somehow, clearly or obscurely, tend to make the race better and kinder, are to be regarded as serious interests"—a dictum which is unintelligible unless it provides art with a *rationale.* The creative artist is made as much by what he *wants* as by what he knows; and what he wants involves, of course, the whole question of how he is to get it. It is strange that Mr. Howells, who never desired fiction to be less than a criticism of life, should so often have ignored this truism in his critical writings and so unfailingly have used it in his fiction.

Neither in the style nor in the architecture of his novels, then, does he suffer the logical consequences of what is narrowly provincial in his theory. But in one deficiency of treatment, the enormous excess of conversation over everything else, his stories do suffer from his contempt of design. He appears, as Henry James wrote long ago, "increasingly to hold composition too cheap"; he neglects "the effect that comes from alternation, distribution, relief." The dialogue especially needs to be "distributed, interspaced with narrative and pictorial matter." It is not that there is too much of the dialogue, which is uniformly of the first excellence, but that there is too little else. Mr. Howells is at his very best when he is giving his subject wrapped in interpretation of character and manners. He makes a woman speak "with that awe of her daughter and her judgments which is one of the pathetic idiosyncracies of a certain class of American mothers." He speaks of the deplored "infidelity" of a New Hampshire village squire as a time-honored local institution, "something that would hardly have been changed, if possible, by a popular vote." He is subtle in his notation of such realities as "the two sorts of deference respectively due to the law and the church" and "the country habit of making no comment in response to what was not a question." These touches are treatment, presentation at its finest, "the golden blocks themselves of the structure"; and when Mr. Howells dispossesses them in favor of talk and still more talk, he deprives us of that which he can more abundantly afford to give than we can afford to be without it.

IV

Unless one is in the heroic mood to require that the writer of fiction supply a full measure of everything one happens to like, one need not be greatly disturbed by the several details about Mr. Howells that one simply cannot understand. Why does it happen that, with all his coldness to technique, he instinctively warms to the most careful technicians, from Jane Austen to Hardy and Henry James? Why, against that same coldness, should he reject Thackeray because Thackeray pleased to "stand about in his scene, talking it over with his hands in his pockets, interrupting the action, and spoiling the illusion in which alone the truth of art resides"—a minor technical quiblet if ever there was one? Why should he denounce Scott for "acquiescence in the division of men into noble and ignoble, patrician and plebeian, sovereign and subject, as if it were the law of God," without allowance for the fact that Scott often makes his plebeians nobler than his patricians, the subject more of a man than the sovereign? Why, above all, should he belittle Dickens because of the occasional caricature of people and the romantic distortion of facts, and not see that Dickens was *on the whole* a valiant fighter in the cause of realism against an effete romanticism, precisely as Mr. Howells himself was?

The only explanation of these sophisms is that Mr. Howells loves truth—by which he nearly always means factuality—so much that the most trivial violation of it affronts all his sensibilities. Let an author, especially a British author, tell more truth than anything else, let him further truth in intercourse and sternly rebuke whatever tends to defeat it: all this goes for naught if, in a moment of deference to some innocent romantic fashion now discredited, he is caught dodging realities. Why, the fellow cherishes "shadows and illusions," he is "very drolly sentimental and feeble"; Mr. Howells will have none of him. We can think of hardly any other critic of equal repute who has allowed so little that he disliked to overrule so much that he would have liked if he could have taken trouble to see it. This is an explanation, of a limping sort; but it does not materially reduce the deficit chargeable to Mr. Howells as critic.

What does materially reduce it is, of course, his historical position and influence. Preaching realism and democracy at a time when the novel, under the sanction of Stevenson and Anthony Hope Hawkins, was trying as hard as it could to get back to Scott and Dumas, he was in the position of a man who must shout if he is to make the unwilling crowd listen, and even so can make them hear but one thing. Most of Mr. Howells's criticism, despite its urbane moderateness of tone, is essentially controversial. He was decrying a fashion which he hated as spurious and silly; his one message was the ugliness of whatever denies or shirks reality, and his exaggeration of that ugliness was simply the raising of his voice to overcome inattention. We do not think that he said what he did not mean, in order to be heard; but unconsciously he was carried away by his enthusiasm, as any small minority tends to be. The measure of his usefulness was the universal need of just that message, and his justification is its later universal acceptance. He fought the costume romance, and it is dead; he predicted the "sociologic" novel, and it has come, to the exclusion of pretty nearly everything else.

In short, the author of *Criticism and Fiction* (1891) was one of the very few great modern men who have been deeply enough immersed in the stream of historical tendencies, and sensible enough of main currents in the life about them, really to understand and work for the future. He decried the romantic novel when it had most applause, in terms which show that he thought of it as already discredited. More characteristically, he decried a certain mawkish and very fashionable kind of sentimentalism: the sentimentalism of useless self-sacrifice in a bad cause, on the theory that self-sacrifice is in itself a great enough good to be sought at the expense of everything else. Many readers will recall the instance in *Silas Lapham*: a girl's refusal to marry a man because her sister is madly in love with him, and the author's admonition (expressed, it happens, through a minister of the gospel) that it is better for two people to be happy and a third unhappy for a time than for all three to be permanently wretched. In both these particulars Howells is of the twentieth century more than of the nineteenth.

But even these are as nothing to his vision of what the future was to do for brotherhood among men, the increase of economic and social community, and the sense of "living in the whole." That sense, he saw, was what fiction must acquire unless it were altogether to lose step with the world; and in precept and practice he helped fiction acquire it. "Men are more like than unlike one another," he said: "let us make them know one another better, that they may be all humbled and strengthened with a sense of their fraternity." "The work done in the past to the glorification of mere passion and power, to the deification of self, appears monstrous and hideous. . . . Art, indeed, is beginning to find out that if it does not make friends with Need it must perish." And to Matthew Arnold's complaint that there was no "distinction" in our national life, he justly and eloquently retorted:

"Such beauty and such grandeur as we have is common beauty, common grandeur, or the beauty and grandeur in which the quality of solidarity so prevails that neither distinguishes itself to the disadvantage of anything else. It seems to me that these conditions invite the artist to the study and the appreciation of the common, and to the portrayal in every art of those finer and higher aspects which unite rather than sever humanity, if he would thrive in our new order of things. The talent that is robust enough to front the every-day world and catch the charm of its work-worn, care-worn, brave, kindly face, need not fear the encounter, though it seems terrible to the sort nurtured in the superstition of the romantic, the bizarre, the heroic, the distinguished, as the things alone worthy of painting or carving or writing. The arts must become democratic, and then we shall have the expression of America in art; and the reproach which Mr. Arnold was half right in making us shall have no justice in it any longer; we shall be 'distinguished.'"

V

Because Mr. Howells's love of reality is more intense and consistent than that of any other important novelist we can think of,—and we have thumbed the list of others with some pains for the possible exception,—his realism is inexpressibly more vital than most realism. Of writers who explored the actualities because they distrusted or feared them, despised or did not know what to make of them, we have seen many, perhaps too many, since the turn of the century; but Mr. Howells is not of this company. No one has done him justice who has not seen that his love of life is his belief in life, and that it is to him quite literally a *faith*. By this we do not mean that he accepts everything as it is, proposing no improvements,—we have already seen how much courage he derives from the facts of social evolution,—but we do mean that he sees in life itself, ever struggling to articulate consciousness and beginning to operate, all the forces that are necessary to a great society and a great art. For him, there is no need of a fiat to legislate order into society from without; nor does he go to the opposite extreme of giving up the hope of order. All things work together for good, because that is the nature of them—even of things not in themselves good.

Thus, for him, intimacy with the real stands in the room of more prerequisites to art, and is altogether more sufficient, than we commonly know it capable of. He is a generation farther along in the chronology of art than such a realist as Gissing, with whom reality was a distressing makeshift for lost faith. Mr. Howells appears never to have cherished illusions. Partly because he brought over from his early work as journalist and editor a vivid sense that life was in itself enough, and more because he was born with the probing mind that will not believe without sight where it is possible to see, he picked his way serenely through the religious disturbances of the decades when even Huxley and Arnold were spending themselves in theological controversy. He reports the disturbances indeed, but tolerantly, indulgently, as things milder than they seemed, more ephemeral, less real. Here again his faith took him forward beyond the stresses of his time; he looks back on struggles little more than begun.

This faith in the reality which is our daily life is

strikingly exemplified in everything Mr. Howells has written about the phenomena of mysticism. It was only the other day that he gave us, after a long incubation, *The Leatherwood God*, his record of religious imposture in a small Ohio community of the early nineteenth century. It shall not be said here that he intended this story as a sly and subtle *exposé* of all religion through direct physical revelation; all that the evidence warrants is the assertion that he *may* so have intended it, and that if so he could not have done much more to sharpen its point. Clearly it expresses his contempt of the faith that demands a sign. And in Squire Matthew Braile, the shrewd and humorous "infidel" of Leatherwood, we have not only a striking individual of one of Mr. Howells's most sympathetic types, but also the intellectual point of view of the book. "Why," says Braile, "I don't see what you want of a miracle more than you've had already. The fact that your cow didn't come up last night, and Abel couldn't find her in the woods-pasture this morning, is miracle enough to prove that Dylks is God. Besides, didn't he say it himself, and didn't Enraghty say it? . . . When a man stood up and snorted like a horse and said he was God, why didn't they believe him?" In all this quizzical irony did Mr. Howells mean to say, for hearing ears only, that Christianity is to him, not the water and the wine, the loaves and fishes, the empty tomb, the harps and crowns, but a rule of life which can neither be given nor taken away by any of these, and which is real whatever becomes of them?

We ask, not answer, the question. But it is worth while to note that the conjecture interlocks most adroitly with something Mr. Howells had written more than thirty-five years earlier, his analysis of spiritualism and its materializations in *The Undiscovered Country*. "All other systems of belief, all other revelations of the unseen world, have supplied a rule of life, have been given for our *use* here. But this offers nothing but the barren fact that we live again. . . . It is as thoroughly godless as atheism itself, and no man can accept it upon any other man's word, because it has not yet shown its truth in the ameliorated life of men. . . . As long as it is used merely to establish the fact of a future life it will remain sterile. It will continue to be doubted, like a conjuror's trick, by all who have not seen it; and those who see it will afterwards come to discredit their own senses. The world has been mocked with something of the kind from the beginning; it's no new thing." The quoted words are Dr. Boynton's: who can doubt that the meaning is the meaning of Howells? He will have nothing to do with the mysticism which is only "a materialism that asserts and affirms, and appeals for proof to purely physical phenomena." Its sole effect is to drive him homeward to the plain every-day faithful and courageous actual. His philosophy is all in the cry of a foolish woman who has given a bolt of linsey-woolsey that the Leatherwood God may turn it into "seamless raiment": "'Oh, I don't care for the miracle,' she kept lamenting, 'but what are my children going to wear this winter? Oh, what will *he* say to me!' It was her husband she meant."

VI

The corollary of faith is peace. And the faith of Mr. Howells in the realities of life brings to him, throughout the inordinate busyness of his career, a peace, a large serenity, that one instinctively thinks of in Scriptural phrases—"the peace that passeth understanding," "He that believeth shall not make haste." We have seen how little friction and loss he suffered during years when the fading of supernaturalism brought a tragic unrest into nearly the whole Western world. Through those years while others fought, he enjoyed; and even when he fought, as sometimes one must for opinions worth holding, it was in the jolliest fighting mood, and with a good-nature as uncompromising as the opinions. If he had enemies to tackle, at least he was on the best of terms with himself. If it were not so, how should one account for the preponderance in him of humor, a tranquil attribute, over wit, a restive?

We would be at some pains to distinguish this deep composure of Mr. Howells from the merely vegetative contentment of which he is rather irresponsibly accused in several quarters. To words already quoted Mr. George Moore adds, in the mood of patronizing impishness which had then become his fixed mental posture: "I see him [Mr. Howells] the happy father of a numerous family; the sun is shining, the girls and boys are playing on the lawn, they come trooping in to a high tea, and there is dancing in the evening. . . .

He is . . . domestic; girls with white dresses and virginal looks, languid mammas, mild witticisms, here, there, and everywhere; a couple of young men, one a little cynical, the other a little overshadowed by his love; a strong, bearded man of fifty in the background; in a word, a Tom Robertson comedy faintly spiced with American." These are indeed the ingredients, this is a large part of the formula—and it is a large part of America too.

What George Moore really meant was that Mr. Howells had not chosen to be turgidly frank about sex. To which the answer is that Mr. Howells had chosen *not* to be, for the good reason that America does not share the Continental obsession, and provides singularly little in sex to be turgidly frank about. Mr. Howells explains himself on this point in two chapters of *Criticism and Fiction;* and in *A Modern Instance*, which contains some of his most inimitably faithful tragi-comedy of New England village life, he makes these observations upon the girl entertaining her suitor at midnight in a sleeping household: "The situation, scarcely conceivable to another civilization, is so common in ours, where youth commands its fate and trusts solely to itself, that it may be said to be characteristic of the New England civilization wherever it keeps its simplicity. It was not stolen or clandestine; it would have interested every one, but would have shocked no one in the whole village if the whole village had known it; all that a girl's parents ordinarily exacted was that they should not be waked up." This is not the ignorant bliss: it is the *pax Americana* that leaves youth blessedly and uniquely free from the experience of guilty love,

> ". . . a heart high-sorrowful and cloy'd,
> A burning forehead, and a parching tongue."

No: the equableness of Mr. Howells is something other than the languor that aspires "to sit in a corner tippling tea." It consists of elements dynamic but under the control of knowledge and faith. Set a taut wire vibrating and touch it with the thumb-nail: it gives forth a jangling buzz. Mr. Howells's criticism of life is the wire left to vibrate harmoniously; there is nothing to disturb its free play in the vast quiet space of his charity, his faith, and his self-command. The Celtic rebelliousness which he inherited gives it *timbre* and poignancy but not discordance; and again and again the rarely beautiful overtones, such as that poor defrauded woman's cry for her lost labor, prove that it is taut, not slack.

And, finally, Mr. Howells proves his profound calm in his most American appreciation and retention of the ardors of youth. We cannot see that he wrote better about youth when he had it than latterly, with all his weight of years and honor; or that he knows the meaning of age better in his eightieth year than in his fortieth. In his philosophy, things must always be renewed if they are to live; the present must re-create itself out of the dead past, and be perpetually attaining perpetual youth. Language renews itself: "no language is ever old on the lips of those who speak it." Literature renews itself: "most classics are dead."

And life renews itself. When, in *The Son of Royal Langbrith,* Mr. Howells treats the problem of wealth got through the chicane of the father, and the serious question of the children's attitude toward it, he makes an end of the whole matter by letting the sleeping dog lie. "It came to Anther again, as it had come before, that each generation exists to itself, and is so full of its own events that those of the past cannot be livingly transmitted to it; that it divinely refuses the burden which elder sins or sorrows would lay upon it, and that it must do this perhaps as a condition of bearing its own." There is more than a touch of this indomitable youth in the characters, the best of whom live on, no older now than when we last saw them. Rarely, they step, like Trollope's characters, from one book into another—and then they are doubly welcome, doubly alive.

This year of Howells's eightieth birthday is also the centenary of Jane Austen's death—fitly, because he has honored himself in honoring her, and because she too loved reality and made successful war, from her provincial citadel, on superstition, on mawkish sensibility, and on the tinsel romanticism of the fashion then current. The years in which she was quietly fulfilling her allotted task were, like this year, made terrible by war and the pouring out of blood; yet she pursued her way and kept her faith, in a quietude untroubled by the great stirrings of empire abroad.

It is to be feared that Mr. Howells has not known how to keep himself similarly untroubled—for the world is smaller now, and crowded, and what hurts one hurts all. Our wish for him on New Year's Day, when these words are written, is that he may wring from this very fact, the community of pain, a confirmation of solidarity in the world, and a hope for its eventual triumph. If we could venture to wish him anything else, it would be that he might find somehow the way to keep on believing in America—his America of the soiled hands and the good heart.

The Specialist in Place and the Specialist in Time

THOMAS HARDY
WILLIAM DE MORGAN

The [illegible] and the [illegible] of the Time

THOMAS HARDY
WILLIAM DE MORGAN

In it perhaps [illegible]
and still more [illegible]
erel discussion of the [illegible]
self introduction [illegible]
we are not [illegible]
Mr. Hardy's [illegible]
last, the [illegible]
ments. And [illegible]
expressed [illegible]
forbidding [illegible]
questions [illegible]
with that [illegible]
much because [illegible]
as because [illegible]
after light [illegible]
for such [illegible]
case of Mr. Hardy [illegible]
pessimism of [illegible]
expression, or [illegible]
of character. [illegible]
that there [illegible]
with Mr. [illegible]

V

THOMAS HARDY

I

It is perhaps unfortunate for Mr. Thomas Hardy, and still more unfortunate for criticism, that all general discussion of the Wessex Novels tends to resolve itself into discussion of *Jude the Obscure*. *Jude* achieves, we are not forgetting, a singular emphasis among Mr. Hardy's works of fiction, both because it is the last, the terrible outcome of a long series of experiments, and because it has the sanction of its author's expressed approval. Hardy did indeed arrive at a forbidding unity of purpose, a misanthropy at once querulous and brutal. But he is often identified with that extremity of his thought and feeling, not so much because it is traceable in him from the beginning as because its intensity is so great that it casts a sinister light backward over all that precedes it. If only for such factitious reasons, any fundamental criticism of Mr. Hardy has to begin with the celebrated pessimism of which *Jude the Obscure* is an ultimate expression, or, in the least favorable view, a *reductio ad absurdum*. But it is very important to remember that there is only one *Jude*. A critic who undertakes, with Mr. Chesterton, to classify Thomas Hardy as "the village atheist . . . blaspheming over the village idiot" makes the mistake of rewriting *A Pair of Blue Eyes* and *Far From the Madding Crowd* in order to prove that a great novelist was always the same person, and that he has always read the universe in the same dark light. Whereas it is our point, by all odds the most important producible, that Mr. Hardy has been several persons in succession, so that to reject *Jude the Obscure* is by no means to reject the whole of Hardy. When we look for the element of consistency or continuity in Hardy, we find it in his art, not in his philosophy. The development of his art is a growth; that of his philosophy is a change.

The truthful critic must describe the pessimism of Hardy as simply the extension of his earlier temperamental bias toward appreciation of incongruity. Probably no novelist has ever had a keener appreciation of the incongruous for its own sake. The quaint home-made song-books of his Mellstock Choir, made up of sheets hand-ruled by the horny fingers of country artisans, wheelwrights, plowmen, cobblers, and containing between the same covers the most bizarre extremes of pious and unprintably profane, can stand as an image of character, of life, and of the world as Hardy tended from the beginning to see them. The incongruous mixture of elements in the same character; the incongruous domination of the strong or unified character by impersonal forces, nature, heredity, or simply chance; pranks played on the helpless human soul by the mocking irresponsibility of the whole world-scheme—these are the familiar and characteristic appeals of Hardy after a certain point; and even from the first they are a vaguely implied destination.

The subtly pessimistic bent of Hardy's mind is shown in the group of novels which may be called, for want of a really apt name, his idylls—such novels as *Under the Greenwood Tree, Far From the Madding Crowd, A Pair of Blue Eyes*, and *The Woodlanders;* a group not compressed into a few years, a recognizable "period," but scattered from 1872 to 1887, and interspersed with others less great, such as *The Hand of Ethelberta*, and far greater, such as *The Return of the Native.*

The figure of a cadence marred by a half-inaudible discord will serve to describe life as Hardy sees it in these tragi-comic idylls, especially since it is in the endings of such books that he comes nearest to his later pessimism. *Under the Greenwood Tree* closes with the conversation of two just-married lovers, the husband exclaiming fondly over the perfect confidence they share and the impossibility of either's having a secret from the other, the woman coolly assenting even while she thinks, in the last phrase of the book, "of a secret she should never tell"—a secret which, told, would discolor the entire future of their relation. *A Pair of Blue Eyes* and *The Woodlanders* both end with grave-scenes which show how Time has made, as is his wont, a laughing-stock of love. Still more characteristic, because in the tone of humor rather than of pathos, is the close of *Far From the Madding Crowd.* Farmer Oak has at last, after many vicissitudes, married Bathsheba, who resorts to him after all else has failed her. When the neighbors come to chorus their good wishes, the dominant strain is somehow not the serene contentment it seems to be. No one means to touch a discordant string: yet—"Why, it might have been worse, and I feel my thanks accordingly," is all Joseph Poorgrass can say. And somehow the reader can say no more; for Bathsheba's gift is that of a spent, an all but wasted self, worn out by the stresses brought into her life by caprices and petty vanities.

All the novels of this group mingle light and shadow in somewhat the proportion of life. Their resultant taste is bitter-sweet, like that of life. If any one trait in them more irritates than pleases, it is the conscious effort to disentangle and accent the note of irony above its natural vibration. The reader experiences a lurking wonder whether after all the artist has given the goodness of life a quite fair chance. This wonder recurs most often in connection with the women characters, in the treatment of whom Hardy's insistence is always upon the lighter qualities. His judgments of women are censorious in the extreme; indeed, his favorite motif is the situation which might be of ideal felicity but for a woman's failure in constancy or candor. Fancy, Elfride, and Viviette spoil the future by white lies, deceits petty intrinsically but overwhelming in their consequences; Bathsheba fails through vanity or self-regard; Grace through inconstancy.

To these qualities of his unsparing analysis, Hardy adds an almost lyrical sense of the cruelty of Time, which makes beauty fade and love grow cold. No artist has ever had a more plaintive sense of the pathos in shriveled cheeks and whitened hair, or a less adequate sense of their dignity. We can think of no character in Hardy who promises an old age of ripened wisdom and contentment, fire-lighted ease and musing placid retrospect. Most of them are victims of the irony that waits on the vows of lovers, who pledge themselves to eternity and, like Wilfrid Pole, forget before eleven o'clock of the morrow morning.

The mournful beauty of these idyllic books is so haunting largely because throughout them the possibility of happiness, though unfulfilled, is so vividly present and near. They are marked by a sense of the insubstantial character of the wall that shuts men and women out of their beatitude. Spare one trifling element of the ironic, let so much as a pin-point of light through the wall, and the characters can find their way to happiness; not otherwise. This is the latent cruelty of even these earlier and purer interpretations of life—a cruelty foreshadowed in such title-phrases as *Far From the Madding Crowd* and *Under the Greenwood Tree,* wrenched from idyllic poems about the beneficence of nature to man, to be applied to idyllic novels about Mr. Hardy's favorite idea, the ironic contrast between nature and man.

II

Hardy always perceived, then, the ironies that make for humor or for the bearable degrees of pathos—"Life's Little Ironies," as he calls them in a familiar title. But it is not until nearly the end of his career in the novel that he begins to add these up into the great fundamental ironies that make for despair. We see his drift as a thing self-propulsive. The tendency grows by what it feeds on, progressing, not evenly but on the whole decisively, toward its own logical fulfilment. In the seventies Hardy found humanity in many ways a sorry spectacle, but still rather a lark; in the eighties, a forlorn hope; in the nineties, a desperate failure. When he wrote *Two on a Tower* his purpose was "to set the emotional history of two infinitesimal lives against the stupendous background of the stellar universe, and to impart to readers the sentiment that of these two contrasting magnitudes the smaller might be the greater to them as men." Ten years later his purpose would have been to engulf and extinguish the lesser magnitude. After 1885 he might have written a book called *Desperate Expedients*, but hardly one called *Desperate Remedies*. By 1890 he is almost exclusively concerned with Man the Ridiculous—"Time's Laughing-Stock."

It is only at this last stage where his somber temperament vents itself in a black philosophy that he becomes the exact antithesis of Meredith. Meredith's parting word of "There is no irony in nature" he would have turned at length into "There is nothing but irony in nature"; he would have taken the "Fifty years for one brave minute!" of Kirby the Old Buccaneer and given it the ironical inflection to make it mean all the accumulated good of fifty years existing for no better end than annihilation in one tragic instant. But not even Mr. Hardy can give us the right to identify him throughout with this eventual grim fixity of despair. An artist's meaning, after all, is less what he says than what he makes you feel; the malignant words in *Jude the Obscure* may deny, but they cannot destroy, the compassion evoked by such a tragedy as *The Return of the Native*.

We mean of course to face, not to obscure or belittle, the significance of *Jude the Obscure*. Incomprehensible as one may find a world in which men and women are destroyed, not through their weaknesses, but actually, like Tess and Jude, through their virtues; Hardy did create that world of evil principle, in which man is only a "disease of the dust"; and one may not merely cover one's eyes with horrified protesting hands. Because that one book contains a great artist's final summary of man's tragic life, the consideration of it is on no account to be shirked.

The central fact of the nightmare seems to be that man's very powers of hope, of faith, of resistance have become agents of tragedy. The sad thing is no longer that the little evil in life can sometimes triumph over the great good: it is that the little spark of good must linger unquenched by the flood of evil. The heart must keep on longing for fulfilments which exist only as illusions. Strength is more tragic than weakness, for strength means resistance, and resistance means only the prolonging of futile pain. There is no bitterness in the Wessex Novels to be compared with the bitterness of this final paradox, that the one greatest evil in the cosmos is the goodness in man's soul. But for that goodness, the argument seems to run, we should not know evil as evil, or suffering as suffering. Jude, a man at the last gasp, is not even allowed to curse God and die with a shred of human dignity. Arabella, the most heartless of Hardy's women, conceals the fact of his death for several hours in order that she may finish a tawdry frolic with tawdry companions. Of Jude's faithless love of earlier days, it is said by Mrs. Edlin, a motherly soul: "'Well—poor little thing, 'tis to be believed she's found forgiveness somewhere! She said she had found peace!'"—on which note the drama might almost bearably have ended. But there comes Arabella's harsh retort, literally Hardy's last word in the field of the novel: "'She may swear that on her knees to the holy cross upon her necklace till she's hoarse, but it won't be true! . . . She's never found peace since she left his arms, and never will again till she's as he is now!'" By this last word we are ushered into a cosmos where goodness is foredoomed, denied even a fighting chance, and made at length to crave oblivion as the sole thing left to believe in.

It is one thing to let the imagination enter that cosmos, and another to accept its conditions. The answer to such a last word as Hardy's depends on considerations somewhat abstract but, surely, not obscure. First of all, *Jude* is one illustrious example of a familiar artistic fallacy: the attempt to prove a general truth about life by imagined facts. It is useless for Mr. Hardy to protest that life stacked the cards against Jude, when it is so very obvious that Mr. Hardy stacked them. "By ten o'clock that night Jude was lying on the bedstead at his lodging covered with a sheet, and straight as an arrow. Through the partly opened window the joyous throb of a waltz entered from the ball-room at Cardinal." By such gestures—*Jude* is full of that machine-made irony—the case is tricked out in gloom. That particular gesture is Mr. Hardy's way of saying that life does not care what it does to the deserving unfortunate. But his proof is purely arbitrary—as arbitrary as though, at the opposite extreme, he had suddenly filled the lodging with Good Samaritans come in from the street to ask how they could help. The trouble is that his theory has become so important to him that he lets it first select and then discolor the facts. He overlooks the facts that do not fit the theory and distorts the ones that half fit it, instead of choosing the facts broadly for their human interest and letting them prove what they will.

Was it the late Samuel Butler who remarked that extremes alone are logical, but that extremes are always absurd? That Hardy should once have overlooked this truism is the more remarkable since he had formerly given an ingenious illustration of it. In recounting the summary execution of a young sheep-dog who had chased the sheep to their death, and was considered "too good a workman to live," Hardy calls the transaction "another instance of the untoward fate which so often attends dogs and other philosophers who follow out a train of reasoning to its logical conclusion, and attempt perfectly consistent conduct in a world made up so largely of compromise." The logic of an inexorable pessimism appears to be one of the absurdities denied to literature, not by the nature of pessimism as a philosophy, but by that of literature as an art. If it be asked whether optimism is not in its way as arbitrary as pessimism, the answer is: Philosophically, yes, but not artistically. For there exists in practical application of the two this gigantic difference: The optimist in literature leaves the powers of darkness really powerful, because the triumphant strength of goodness is exalted just in proportion to the forces it has to contend against, and his result is a balanced picture of life as a struggle; whereas the pessimist is restricted from telling the whole truth about the goodness of life, because at any cost he must make evil triumph over it. Consequently we view the singular spectacle of the pessimist leagued with the powers of darkness against the human hero, that their victory over him may be assured; and the struggle is not equal enough to produce tragedy in the true sense. This is why all the greatest tragedies have been written by optimists—men who have enough faith in life to understand that it is good even when it does not seem so. The pessimist has not enough faith in life to understand that it is good even when it does seem so; and therefore he falsifies the immediate seemings of things in deference to his ultimate principle. But the proper concern of fiction is with the immediate seemings; and if it miss the truth about them, it has failed at the all-important point, the point of access to the reader. However adequate it may be as self-expression, it stops short of self-communication, without which the work of art dies at its source.

III

These matters go to the root of the tragic emotion. "We can give good critical reasons," says Professor Winchester, "for our natural demand that a novel should, in some sense, turn out well. It may not end in sugared marital felicity, with 'God bless you, my children,' and ten thousand a year; but its total effect upon the emotions should be healthy and strengthening. Shakspere's most terrible tragedies brace and hearten our spirits. They never leave us with a sense of mere horror, or with a discouraged or nerveless feeling. Their close is often pitiful, sometimes supremely and solemnly tragic; yet we shut the book with a feeling of the beauty and value of the great virtues. Such art solemnizes and fortifies our souls. It meets Aristotle's requirement for tragedy; 'it purifies the passions by pity and fear.'"

We have, when all is said, our lives to live; and art is very properly concerned with the terms of our living them. It is irrelevant, as well as paralyzing, to say that we are fools to live them at all, for we cannot think of ourselves as having a choice in the matter. Great tragedy is not moral justice, because it is essentially disaster to the good; but its appeal is to our sense of moral justice, since it makes us feel the abnormality of the destruction of good by evil. Let such disaster be presented to us as normal, a fulfilment of the world-purpose, and hope atrophies in the heart, the will is benumbed—the tragic emotion is gone. If *Othello* proves that jealousy is a terrible thing, it certainly does not prove that life is a terrible thing.

If it did, it would entirely miss its point about jealousy; the smaller evil would be lost in the greater. So *Jude* misses its point about man's inhumanity to man by covering all human nature with mud.

If, at the last, we find Hardy thus offering us spurious tragedy without the compensations of tragedy, we have only to follow him backward and upward to where the compensations are richest. To get from an abyss of impotent despair to a great height of moral indignation, we need go no farther than to *Tess of the D'Urbevilles*. Jude is weakly good; but Tess is so strong that it takes the whole world to conquer and destroy her. She is an inspiring picture of the fortitude of the human soul expressing itself in the virtues of steadfastness, obstinate devotion, and self-effacement. Elsewhere the insistence is on the capacity of the world to inflict sorrows: here it is on the capacity of the soul to endure sorrows without being broken. Tess is the one resplendent example of her sex in the Wessex Novels, a figure of solitary greatness. She has almost nothing of vanity, itching curiosity, or deceitfulness—the three Fates, almost the three Furies, of Hardy's women. She is "a pure woman faithfully presented" in her struggle against all the impurities in the world. Her greatness of heart, her indomitable courage, her stubborn persistence in hope on the very borderland of despair—these give the approach to equality between the contending powers; and it is that approach to equality that makes the splendor of authentic tragedy.

The compensations of tragedy are likeliest to take, as here, the form of the moral or social emotions.

"Poor wounded name! my bosom, as a bed,
Shall lodge thee, till thy wound be thoroughly heal'd"—

in that mood of compassion Tess is imagined, and at that altitude the treatment is sustained—a far remove from, say, the superciliousness with which Bathsheba Everdene is drawn. Hardy performs his task here under an instinctive sense that there may be, that there indeed must be, something in compassionate understanding alone that can all but redeem the lost world. By such appeals the heart is wrung, and its springs of pity are not dried. It is true, as Mr. Copeland once put it, that "the historian of Wessex celebrated the three Fates until people shuddered to see the thread both spun and cut." But it is further true that in this one instance the historian himself shuddered, and thereby humanized his message.

The critic owes it to Mr. Hardy to see that what brings him eventually to the mood of frozen despair is precisely his susceptibility to the moral emotions, the warmest, most expansive possible. The sense of sympathy cries out against the tragic in life; or, more philosophically, the sense of order protests against the waste in the world. The sense of order has only to be tender enough, to find itself lacerated at every contact with reality. If Hardy once gnashed his teeth at life, it was for no other reason than that life was hurting fellow-creatures whom he loved. The trouble is not that the feeling is misguided, but that it has overleaped the human power of expression.

It is this baffled humanitarian rage of the altruist that leads Hardy to the uttermost resort of his style, the personification of evil chance, or the massed injustice of the universe, as God. Hardy's smoldering indignation flames out, as in *Tess*, against man's inhumanity to woman, and its characteristic subterfuge the "double code"; but, more important, it flames out against the empty heavens, the inveterate mercilessness of the whole cosmic organization. The defiance sounds with a more austere dignity than in *Jude*, where the persistent note is querulousness. And the dignity comes through a characteristic resort of modern pessimism in literature—a species of pure symbolism, almost of pure poetry. Hardy knows that God does not exist as the object of either prayers or curses; his world is that of naturalism, the rationalistic world of George Eliot. But he adopts the imagery of despair, personifying the new meanings under the old names. He takes the personal God in whom he has ceased to believe, and turns him into a personal devil in whom he never believed. And at the end of the tragedy, as the black flag mounts the staff, we read: "The President of the Immortals had ended his sport with Tess." This reversion to the old terminology is partly a habit of speech, like the profanity of some atheists; partly it is a baffled attempt to get beyond the point where language can go; most of all, it is simply a conscious poetic symbolism, a figure of speech perverse and sublime.

It is easy enough, on logical grounds, to ridicule this inverted theology, in which the best in human nature becomes the scornful judge of evil chance personified as God. Indeed, Mr. Chesterton has ridiculed it in these words: "It has been said that if God had not existed it would have been necessary to invent Him. But it is not often, as in Mr. Hardy's case, that it is necessary to invent Him in order to prove how unnecessary (and undesirable) He is." To which, long before it was written, Mr. Hardy neatly retorted by a precedent from King Lear:

> "As flies to wanton boys are we to the gods;
> They kill us for their sport."

But the one really decisive retort is that to brandish one's fists at a heaven under which things chance as they did with Tess is essentially an ennobling gesture—whether by that heaven one understands a personally malignant God, the injustices of man, or simply the collective insensibility of things.

IV

However long we find it necessary to dwell on the elements of tragedy in Hardy's genius, we are in small danger of forgetting that after all its most irresistible qualities are of the comic order. We turn to the realism of Hardy, and find the doleful philosopher an inimitably comic artist. His realism is exhibited most, of course, in his command of folk-lore and of the folk-spirit, his extension and specialization of George Eliot's early treatment of rustic life and character.

The first to specialize rigidly in a provincial district marked principally by quaintness, naïve archaic oddity of speech and tradition, of custom and dress, he disinters a thousand charming odds and ends of the past. These range from whole institutions re-created bodily, such as the Mellstock Choir, down to such curiosities as the "two-handled tall mug" from which Gabriel Oak drank on his first evening at Warren's Malthouse —an ancient vessel, warm and crusted with ashes from the hearth, and called a "God-forgive-me," "probably because its size makes any given toper feel ashamed of himself when he sees its bottom in drinking it empty."

Much more important are the minor characters, the Greek-chorus bystanders in alehouse kitchens, at rehearsals, weddings, dances, sheep-shearings, christenings—such women as Bathsheba's attendant Liddy and the three dairy-maids in *Tess*, such men as Granfer Cantle and Christian, Joseph Poorgrass, the timid William Worm, and a dozen others. All of these are delightful, most of them superlative; all have the undeniable stamp of authenticity. And they are intrinsically funny, as the clowns of Shakspere are funny.

But we would speak primarily of the uses to which they are put; of what may be called the structurally comic element in the art of Hardy. He weaves together the lives of these rustic folk and the lives of his protagonists, who are likely to be from more cultivated, even from exceedingly sophisticated classes. His heroes are often of the artistic and scientific professions. He is master of the astronomer, the architect, the writer or student of affairs, the teacher or preacher, the archæologist or historian, placed in rural solitudes on his holidays or his professional errands, and sharply characterized through his chance contacts with simple, naïve folk. These are used in turn for two purposes: for expository comment on the principal action, and effects of broad relief or comic contrast.

It is in this second, somewhat technical respect—where once more, by the way, we find an innate love of the incongruous explaining much—that Hardy may accurately be said to have drawn his structure from the Elizabethan play. In an age like the Late Victorian, of smooth-textured art more and more highly polished, this rough chiaroscuro of Hardy, an affair of broad belts of light and shade, especially denotes artistic virility. In the boldest of these contrasts there is a primitive hacked-out quality that recalls, of English comedists in prose, Fielding, Smollett, and Dickens.

One of the best illustrations of this matter is the series of five chapters culminating in the major crisis of *Far From the Madding Crowd.* Fanny Robin is an obscure girl whom Sergeant Troy has wooed and dashingly won; then his fancy for Bathsheba has diverted him, and his marriage to her has made him lose track of Fanny's plight. Troy and Bathsheba, driving, encounter her on the road, miserable and exhausted. We follow her painful and labored progress toward Casterbridge. Night comes on; she falls, but helps herself up and on with crutches improvised of sticks. With the aid of a stray dog, a powerful and kindly friend, she drags herself the remaining half-mile to "the Union." A man and a woman lift her up and help her in. The next day Troy borrows money of Bathsheba. The next morning after that, just after Troy has started off, the news comes that Fanny has died in the work-house. Bathsheba sends Joseph Poorgrass with a wagon for the body; for Fanny had once been the servant of her uncle. Meanwhile Bathsheba, who has been putting two and two together into an uncertain and complicated four, begins to suspect her husband's perfidy.

All this is of a prolonged tenseness, with the tension still to be increased; and it is at this point that Hardy interposes his emotional relief. The expedient is simple; but it suffices, and it is contrived so as to help the plot as well as the mood. Poorgrass, conveying the body through solitary woods at nightfall, finds his nerves in a tremor. The tapping of heavy raindrops on poor Fanny's coffin becomes at length too much for him, and it is with enormous relief that he approaches the Buck's Head. Mark Clark and Jan Coggan are there. Malt flows, tongues loosen; time glides. When Gabriel Oak comes looking for Poorgrass, he finds the party fuddled with drink. "Coggan looked up indefinitely at Oak, one or other of his eyes occasionally opening and closing of its own accord, as if it were not a member, but a dozy individual with a distinct personality." Gabriel drives on with the body. But he has forgotten to take the death certificate from Poorgrass, and the coffin is left, by Bathsheba's direction, in her house, instead of being buried at once. Gabriel lingers by the coffin long enough to erase the last two words of the chalk inscription on the lid—"Fanny

Robin *and child*"—in order to shield Bathsheba from the full knowledge.

This comic interlude of the tavern scene both serves the plot, by insuring yet postponing the revelation, and slackens the emotional tautness of the reader, in order that the next effect may exert its full tug of contrast. The final thrust comes when Bathsheba, left alone late at night and obsessed by suspicions, makes up her mind at last to *know*. She opens the coffin. While she kneels by the bodies of mother and still-born child, her husband comes back from his unexplained errand. No need to explain now: the situation is beyond pretense, and, for the reader, almost beyond the pale of the endurable.

Tess of the D'Urbevilles may be, as a whole, the greatest of the novels; but Hardy never surpassed this sequence of five chapters, with its comic impediment so placed as to double the impact of the culminating scene. As in the best drama, each inexorable stroke tells for more than its intrinsic worth. The result shows all of Mr. Hardy's distinguished powers working as one toward a predetermined artistic effect—his irony, his humor, his extraordinary narrative power, his sense of atmosphere, his compassion; and, one must add, that unsparing and unyielding love of truth as he sees it that does more than anything to give him his place of intellectual honor among the great modern practitioners of fiction. But even that moral inexorableness would appear as so much diffusion and waste were it not for the use that, through the most rigorous artistic self-command, is made of it.

All the elements *must* work as one, or none of them will work at all. The tremendous crisis, "Fanny's Revenge," could never have been swung in complete equilibrium to its tragic fulfilment except on some such precarious and delicate pivot of the comic.

V

Those readers who find Mr. Hardy everywhere, as in *Jude the Obscure*, a victim of his own ironic temperament, seem to us to have overlooked several important aspects of his art, not least among them this impersonal economy which rules and explains his boldest contrasts. But we shall not have made a proportioned sketch, even within the present narrow limits, until we have reverted to an equally impersonal trait of his philosophy itself, as distinguished from his art—a trait which, more than any other, modernizes and vitalizes both philosophy and art, making them harmoniously one. We find in him from the beginning a certain scientific detachment of spirit which he was the first to bring conspicuously into the regional novel, and which is fully as important as either his structural genius or his irony.

For an expression of it in its earliest intensity, we have to go back as far as *The Return of the Native*, where for the first time he deserts the local color that is merely quaintness for the local color that is interpretation on the grandest scale. We do not understand *The Return of the Native* until we understand that its real hero is the *genius loci*. If we analyze the plot alone, we shall find it a tissue of improbable coincidences, a prolonged strain on the credulity. Like *The Mayor of Casterbridge* it is a drama of retribution brought home to the sinner, and involving disaster to the innocent; and as in *The Mayor of Casterbridge* the expiation is wrought out in a very elaborate and ingenious machinery of events. But there is this all-important difference: that the events in *The Mayor of Casterbridge* take place in the clear light of normal day, a compromising glare in which the plot seems as artificial as a mechanical toy; whereas in the earlier and greater spectacle the human figures move through a sinister gloom which discolors ordinary probability, and in which anything can happen. The personæ are puppets of the spirit or atmosphere of place, creatures of the gloomy twilight that broods over the Heath to work out with human pawns the moves of its inscrutable game. The first chapter, "A Face on which Time Makes but Little Impression," raises a curtain on some mighty drama presently to be enacted in shadow. The opening is one of those stupendous effects of mood which can only be compared to such things as the first scene of *Hamlet* or the Prelude to *Tristan und Isolde.* Night and day struggle together in a sort of endless twilight.

And the heroine, Eustacia Vye, is a translation into flesh and blood of the dark spirit that presides over the waste where she lives. Night and day, light and shadow, mingle and struggle in her soul too. This parallel is not a fanciful one for criticism to draw: indeed Hardy draws it at some length himself, in the chapter named "Queen of Night," and even extends it to his heroine's appearance. She is "without ruddiness, as without pallor." "To see her hair was to fancy that a whole winter did not contain darkness enough to form its shadow." Not that Eustacia Vye is an inhuman symbol, an abstraction: decidedly she is one of Hardy's most real women, as Egdon Heath is one of his most real landscapes. But both the place and the woman are real with a faintly abnormal intensity; they are two pagans between whom exists a subtle accord. There is something more than a purely decorative harmony in Eustacia's love of darkness, her prowlings at night, her stolen meetings with Wildeve at the edge of the dismal pool into which he throws his signal-stone. There is a still stranger fitness in her death in Shadwater Weir on a night when the heath has unleashed all its furies of darkness and storm. Thus the microcosm of personality is made a stage for the interplay of almost cosmic forces.

There is one more important aspect of this impersonal power of Hardy: his essentially modern faculty of taking scientific fact and utilizing it on a vast scale for effects of poetic grandeur. The obvious instance is *Two on a Tower*, where the characters are shown against the whole stellar universe, for ironic commentary on the somewhat petty terms of their human drama. A briefer expression of a somewhat similar concept occurs in *Far From the Madding Crowd*, in description of a clear night when "the twinkling of all the stars seemed to be but throbs of one body, timed by a common pulse." The greatest example of all, perhaps, is one which utilizes a different kind of scientific fact, the geologic. In *A Pair of Blue Eyes* Henry Knight, scientist and scholar, loses his footing at the edge of the "Cliff Without a Name," and hangs for some minutes precariously clinging on the rounded edge by a tuft of sea-pink. Time closes up "like a fan" before him, and he sees himself "at one extremity of the years, face to face with the beginning and all the intermediate centuries simultaneously." Lost to all but the curving face of the cliff round and beneath him, and prompted by an imbedded fossil that stares at him from the rock, he relives the whole cycle of organic evolution on the earth. The Hardy who could make so much scenic and emotional impressiveness out of the facts of a special science does quite clearly represent a generation beyond that of the rationalist George Eliot.

Criticism has been on the whole rather generous in providing points of view for the study of Mr. Hardy. But they all—historical, technical, or philosophical—fail us if we ask much of them. And we are brought back to the necessity of partly rejecting them all, and of defining our author very largely in terms of himself. We do well, surely, to beware of the conventional tags and labels, the catch-words invented for dealing on the quickest, least costly terms with the Poes and Ainsworths and Oscar Wildes of literature, but proved to be least helpful here where there is more than we can see at any one glimpse or from any one angle.

There are some affairs which pay themselves the compliment of bursting any mold of formula into which one tries to pour them, whose distinction is, as we say, to "defy analysis." The great 18th century novelists have this variousness and elusiveness; Scott and the great Victorians have it; Hardy has it also, to a degree that gives him his impressive character of survival from an age of grander dimensions than ours, an age of more burning creative intensity and of genius magnificently rioting. Even if the future should strangely overlook the greatness of such a man, it could hardly overlook his largeness. Wherever he failed, he failed spaciously, grandly, and his very failures are more to be prized than the safe successes of lesser men; just as the desperately bad things in Thackeray are better literature, if worse art, than the unusually good things in Bulwer-Lytton. This general largeness or capaciousness, which we associate with tumultuous periods such as the Elizabethan, is especially marked in Hardy because his last fifteen years of creative activity in the novel fall in a period otherwise mostly given over, except for Meredith, to the excellence of little things. And, quite apart from particular small merits and defects, it demands for him a special consideration. He looms, however jaggedly or unsymmetrically, over our modern landscape, he is a mountain that towers. We may, if we will, turn from the ascent; but at least we cannot help being in his shadow.

VI

WILLIAM DE MORGAN

(January, 1917)

I

Only a little more than a decade ago, a young lad was lifted by the slack of his trousers into a distinction close to absolute fame—as close perhaps as any creature of mere books can come in this book-weary age. The scene of his elevation was unpretentious to the last degree: the dingy barroom of a London public-house. And the persons present might have seemed, to a nicely discriminating judgment, vulgar and not too clean. They were the father of the young lad, already "getting towards the quarrelsome stage of beer," "a Sweep with inflamed lids," a phlegmatic young barmaid "behind a fortress of brass and pewter" (the brass being, in this instance, not altogether literal), and a familiar barroom motley of artisans and loafers, all good-natured and hearty and spoiling for a fight, which they were willing to watch and, to the last man, rather more willing to participate in.

And presently, of course, the fight came. The father of the "young nipper" discovered a "hinseck" —genus and species never divulged—in the dregs of his ale, and shook the wriggling thing out on the metal counter. It was at this point that the young nipper asked to be lifted up—"For to see the hinseck." Thereupon ensued an altercation about the ownership of that unenviable speck; the Sweep being all for "crocking" it with his finger-nail, the father insisting that he had paid for it, and that it was not to be assaulted without his consent. "'Anyhow you put it,' said the Sweep, 'I'd crock him for a farden.' And without waiting for any security of payment, he did it straightway." There was a blow, too quick to be parried, from the irate father. Then came a scuffle of men who had already taken sides, and the belligerents were forced out of the barroom to finish their quarrel where there was less danger of officious interruption.

The young nipper slipped down from his perch on the bar and joined the stragglers headed for the fight. He was in time to see his father stretched on the ground, and the Sweep being led away between two policemen; in time, too, to pick up a heavy and jagged fragment of glass bottle "lying against a dead cat by the roadway," and hurl it at the triumphant Sweep, one of whose inflamed lids it pierced. And after this act of filial heroism, executed from behind a fence, our midget of seven scuttled off home, too terrified to wait for the outcome and convinced that his father was killed.

These events occur, of course, in the first chapter of the first novel of William De Morgan, till yesterday one of the oldest men actively engaged in producing fiction, and one of the very youngest authors. Nearly all of us know the subsequent history of Joseph Vance, the young nipper who sat on the bar. And nearly every one who reads English for pleasure has read that history as Joseph Vance tells it in the first person. We know that Joe Vance's father was to live for many years after all, to hear on his death-bed the story of that piece of glass and of who had thrown it; we know that Joe himself was not to end his story until he had risen far above his birth and first surroundings, taken a university degree, become a scientist and inventor, assumed the guilt of another's misdoing, allowed that other to appropriate his name in order to spare the woman he loved some sorrow, and received at last, though almost too late, his fitting reward.

There is a legend—we do not know how true—that Mr. De Morgan, ambitious young author of sixty-five, tried this first of his stories, when it was only an enormous bundle of manuscript, on one publisher after another before he succeeded even in getting it read; and that finally, when he discovered a firm with the hardihood to pay for having the story typewritten, it was accepted because the girls among whom it was parceled out were caught crying over it. The legend may not be true; but it is certainly true criticism. As well as the first chapter of *Joseph Vance* it introduces the celebrated Early Victorianism of De Morgan; it and the first chapter taken together all but summarize his Early Victorianism.

For, in spite of Mr. De Morgan's own frequent and impatient disclaimers, he did reunite us in a singularly powerful way with the Early Victorian past. We do not say that he belongs to that past. He belongs to us; and, unless we are wholly armored in our favorite modern kinds of self-sufficiency, we can find him nothing less than one of the most lovable of our literary possessions. He belongs to us no less, though, because the England of the forties and fifties, the England of Dickens and Thackeray, belongs to him. That fact was his special crown, and not merely, as criticism has sometimes assumed, his special shortcoming. It constituted a great part of his difference from any one else, his force and his originality.

A large part of the discussion of him is, then, necessarily the discussion of his comfortable ownership of a great deal that belongs, not to yesterday or to the day after to-morrow, but to the vanished decades that brought forth Pickwick and Pendennis, Cranford and Barchester, the potato famine and the repeal of the corn laws; the past of his own childhood, softened in retrospect but still vivid, seen not through the eyes of a note-taking novelist on the trail for "copy," but rather in the mellowing light of the studios and stained-glass windows among which Mr. De Morgan spent the most of his working life, and in which he got his training for the craft through which we are most likely to know him. It is necessary to admit that, although he was the most delightful and the most gladdening of anachronisms, he was still an anachronism.

II

The more material and obvious side of De Morgan's Victorian quality is suggested in that first chapter of

Joseph Vance, which shows the beginning of its author's mastery over the men and boys, the buildings and places, the manners and presiding spirit, of a time before mid-century. It was in 1906 that little Joe Vance climbed into fame under our eyes; but it was really, we never forget, in the late forties that he mounted the bar and dangled his diffident little legs in that loud company and threw the glass at Peter Gunn. The creator of Joe Vance knows the London of that period as Dickens knew the London of his own boyhood.

Mr. Chesterton has said of Dickens, in a finely applied phrase, that he had, beyond any other in English letters, " the key of the street." His possession of it is not the less remarkable because a thousand other men then living might have had the same key. But De Morgan's achievement is decidedly the more remarkable because he had the key of a street that no longer existed, except in the memory of a few and in such printed pages as he has given us. Dickens was at home in places which he alone found. De Morgan was at home in places which no man can ever find again, because they have been buried in progress, hidden under a covering of expansion and rebuilding as deeply as Pompeii under its ashes. Half the enchantment of that Court where Dave and Dolly Wardle scaled the dust-bin and draggled themselves in the mud is that no man can ever again turn under its archway. We shall never locate that " extensive basement with cellarage " where Alice saw the " lidy with the spots," or drink a mug of ale at The King's Arms where Uncle

Mose and Mr. Bob Alibone enjoyed their afternoon pipe and read the *Morning Star*. De Morgan's places had long been swept among the rubbish of London's yesterdays before it ever occurred to him to delve for them with a pen. He combines therefore something of the historical novelist's romantic remoteness with the vivid intimacy of the eye-witness.

But all this is only the mechanical and really the less important side of De Morgan's Victorianism. It is the less obvious side that some criticism has slighted: the side that concerns, not what he wrote about, but how he wrote about it. The whole basis and superstructure of his art was of the period before mid-century. He was Early Victorian in his entire contempt for the art of the novel, as the Continent has taught us to reconceive that art. His fiction sprang from no formula except that of pouring out in a turbid and generous flood the accumulated riches of a humane mind, the whole store of experience, memory, emotion, the whole man De Morgan. There was no other art in him. The contribution is essentially something to be measured by its amount, its stupefying abundance; and it was fitting and acceptable that the gift should offer itself in works approaching a third of a million words —the length of *Tom Jones* and of *Vanity Fair*. It is this directly human and naïve, this artless side of De Morgan's art, that one finds crystallized in the anecdote about the typists who wept over the copy of *Joseph Vance*.

Our anecdote presents too, naturally, the matter of De Morgan's pathos. For he dealt extensively in the pathetic emotion, and with range as well as mere quantity. It is not the least of his claims that he made us weep in an age when the novel had forgotten a good share of the virtue in womanly or, yes, manly tears, and when fiction, though it often made us think and sometimes shudder, cared little about making us cry. A great deal of De Morgan invites, among other tests, the test by tears.

Most often the pathos resides in a child's sweet unconsciousness of misery to which the child has grown accustomed or been born accustomed: in six-year-old Alice sent to the bar round the corner and afraid to return to her drunken mother because she has dropped and broken the beer-jug; in Lizarann's ignorance that her blind father is a beggar, as she goes each night to a certain corner to meet and guide him home, announcing herself with his old sea-call of "Pi-lot!"; in the waiting of Dave and Dolly for old "Mrs. Picture" (their version of "Prichard"), who was never to come though they made a daily ritual of setting out their toy tea-things.

But there are cases that concern men and women too: let us name only Joe Vance's all but hopeless love for Lossie Thorpe, and that last, most crushing instance of all, the reunion of Phœbe and Maisie Runciman, twin sisters of eighty years, each of whom has been made through a cruel stratagem to believe the other dead. Nowhere, probably, does the pathos become so maudlin as in some chapters of Dickens. Nor did Mr. De Morgan ever make so much of pathos as to come under the famous ban of Meredith: he kept his load of emotion for ballast, and did not let it be the chief part of the cargo. It is comedy, not pathos, that prevails even in *It Never Can Happen Again*, where occurs the most pathetic episode of all, the death of Blind Jim's daughter Lizarann.

The emotional quality of De Morgan's appeal rested, however, on more than pathos. It was not so much by excess of one emotion as by a bizarre mingling of all emotions that he triumphed over even the most stolid. No statement includes all of his method except the statement that it consisted in putting together the widest possible extremes, and the greatest possible number of them. His most touching pathos exists side by side with his most infectious humor; his human saints and his human devils inhabit the same chapters. He would take a plot like that of *Barnaby Rudge*, another plot like that of the Book of Ruth, a set of characters straight out of Dickens, another set straight out of Thackeray, a great county family, a family of the slums, a mystery, a murder, a buried skeleton or a lost manuscript, several people as farcical as Smollett's and several other people as subtle as Henry James's, and add even a would-be ghost—and mix all these ingredients into a tale of incredible complications, making the whole one only by the unbroken quality of his personal style, the clear and fluid medium in which all these elements are suspended in solution.

We who like realism and restraint, naturalism and the impersonal mode, may say that this is unity the most precarious. But the absence of unity means here, we do well to see, the presence of everything else —the general too-muchness, a glorified excess. There is no failure to " round out " the subject, no hint of what Miss Sherwood might call the timidity of our modern boldness. It is always a subject that craves rounding *in.* De Morgan knew all about this fine modern consummation of technique, as he proved in *An Affair of Dishonor,* the one novel in which he deliberately withheld a great part of himself. And with what result? Why, that the very voices which had clamored against him for trying to be Thackeray now clamored still more loudly against him for daring to be less than De Morgan. This failure of his fifth book was quite the oddest of all his perverse triumphs—the vindication, so far as he was concerned, of the nineteenth century against the twentieth, and a clinching argument for his earlier largesse.

III

In this love of mingled extremes, he belongs of course with the great Early Victorian novelists. It became usual to compare him with Dickens; and indeed he does resemble Dickens in many respects, including his passion for purely verbal pleasantries, the sort of verbal decoration which at its best is wit and at its worst " fine writing." But the list of possible comparisons does not stop here. De Morgan resembles Thackeray at least as much, especially in his possessing the key, not only to the street, but also to the country house and the town salon. In lesser ways he resembles Wilkie Collins, and Charles Reade, and Anthony Trollope. The Arkroyds of *It Never Can Happen Again* recall irresistibly some of the folk in the Barchester novels, and the Reverend Athelstan Taylor is Trollope's Francis Arabin in his habit as he lived.

The truth is that De Morgan cannot be summed up as an imitator of any one influence. What he mastered was the whole spirit and contribution of a period—a period of great individual geniuses who were like each other only in their abundance, their lavish and ungoverned invention, and their remoteness from any ideal that could make art of a visibly balanced or structural sort. We have all the new and symmetrical bottles; one is tempted, in moments of revulsion, to say that they had all the old wine. Mr. De Morgan was like them in caring nothing about the bottle except to make it hold as much as could be got in. Many people must remember thinking, at their first discovery of *Joseph Vance:* "Here is a man who has said to himself, 'Go to, I will play the game as Dickens played it.'" But within a few chapters they were adding— "'and as Thackeray played it.'" Long before the end of the book they must all have given up in despair. Mr. De Morgan synthesized an entirely new game. He tried to do in each of his five great novels pretty much everything that all the Victorians did in all of their novels put together—and then he added several things of his own. He was the pupil of no teacher except the age of the greatest personalities our fiction has yet known.

His mannerisms especially are of that age. Every one of his best stories is a personally conducted story, with an amiable and chatty relation between author and reader—the relation which Fielding learned from Congreve, and Thackeray from Fielding. Some of the characters are labeled forever by an omnipresent tag: Joe Vance's father always forgets proper names and extemporizes grotesque substitutes; Mr. Heath always catches up the last word of a remark and volleys absent-minded questions based thereon, to cover his inattention; Miss Dickenson always makes polite conversation of the encyclopædia ("Some people feel the effect of thunder much more than others. No doubt it is due to the electrical condition of the atmosphere. Before this was understood, it was ascribed to all sorts of causes"). Equally in the spirit of Dickens are the disjointed fragments of discourse caught up into the text in the phraseology of the original. When Dave cut his head falling off the post, Aunt M'riar's failure to rescue him is set forth in these terms: "If he'd only a had the sense to set still half a minute longer, she would have done them frills and could have run up the Court a'most as soon as look at you." De Morgan's style is a leisurely Victorian affair of quips and pleasantries, and it is full of the gaiety of deep and irrepressible self-enjoyment. The modern ideal is to give one's self strained through a fine mesh of philosophy or mood: De Morgan's way is to give himself whole, unmoderated and diffuse, with no other preparation than what he is. And, like Thackeray, he is fond of recurring to his ingenious conceits. When Challis begins to enjoy basking in the flattery of Judith Arkroyd and proportionately forgetting his "impossible" wife, his sensation is "like having the hair of his soul brushed by machinery." The simile recurs often; and *It Never Can Happen Again* without its soul-brush would miss one of its acutest pieces of analysis. In such points De Morgan's style was nearer to Thackeray's than to Dickens's, in which the popular and obvious string is the loudest plucked, and the most frequent. But it is nearer to both than to any since.

Nor, coming to more important matters, can one detect any new philosophy of the whole brought in to revitalize the old expedients. De Morgan expressed practically no philosophy at all, beyond the ardent Victorian will to believe that humanity is immensely enjoyable, and that the unpardonable sin is not to enjoy it—and even that faith he never expressed save through the medium of his characters and his own obvious enjoyment of them. He had no remedy for anything, no moral or social or political ax to grind. On matters of faith and dogma he was either strangely negative, or still more strangely non-committal. He gives a just portrait of a clergyman and another of a freethinker; he makes the two portraits satirize each other with arguments that one commonly hears—and the reader has no more idea than before where the author himself stands. Despite the intimacy which he took every means to cultivate with the reader, he seemed anything but a person with views. Aside from the cardinal virtues of manhood and womanhood, we cannot detect that De Morgan felt strongly on any subject. He had perhaps a mild contempt for faddishness and ineptitude. He threw good-natured ridicule upon the Grauboschian philosopher who proposed new and fearfully complicated names for all the old commonplaces; he had little use for the M. P. to whom things lay in nutshells and called for decisive handling, who would not presume to arraign the judgment of any fellow-mortal, but would venture to call our attention to a great variety of alternatives with which it was our bounden duty to grapple. But he had nothing against industrialism, or aristocracy, or marriage. He was not even a sentimental sociologic tinker, as Dickens had been. Aside from his impatience with the minor fads and futilities, he assumed a threatening posture toward nothing whatsoever except downright wickedness—and even that he pitied when he had punished it.

IV

The love of putting incongruous extremes together was in itself enough to account for whatever was most striking in the ornate architecture of De Morgan's stories. In him we saw the Victorian system by no means modernized, but specialized, extended; and to the end that he might find his amusement in great gaps of time annihilated, deep social chasms bridged. The central and essential De Morgan, the author of five prodigious novels and of the extravaganza called *A Likely Story*, is a man of two objects, two delights. First, he must fold a century of time upon itself until the ends touch and are superposed. Secondly, he must arrange the social order in an instrumentation to which patrician and plebeian, titled halls and the gutter, contribute harmonies queer and quaint, if not altogether new. In fiction where the effect of reality is so great a fraction of the whole effect, there is surely no other like instance of the desire and the ability to make both ends —both ends of anything—meet.

It is convenient to separate one of these matters from the other. De Morgan called his second novel, *Alice-for-Short*, a "Dichronism," because it has to do with a century-old mystery and with the only living mind that forms a direct linkage with that mystery. Now, with the single exception of *An Affair of Dishonor*, a strictly modern piece of realistic method, every one of the stories is a dichronism. Every one of them turns on some buried secret, disinterred from its moldy wrapping of circumstance in time to alter profoundly something in the present. In *Alice-for-Short* the past is divulged through old Mrs. Verrinder, a woman of ninety whose life had been broken off when she was thirty, by a fall and a blow on the head. A daring surgical operation reawakens her to a world that was waiting impatiently for the next novel of Mr. Scott, and leaves her a young bride with snowy hair and shrunken, trembling limbs, a bride whose husband and child have long been in the grave. Looking back from what is in effect her thirtieth year, she recalls childhood pictures and events that dovetail with other evidences to solve Alice's mystery.

In *Somehow Good*, an electric shock destroys a man's memory and blots out his early life. In that prolonged state of not being himself, he stumbles upon the wife from whom he had been separated years before, and who is now no more to him than a lovable stranger.

And in *It Never Can Happen Again*, a strictly modern social comedy which turns on the repeal of the Deceased Wife's Sister law, the central person, Alfred Challis the novelist, is almost trapped into a felony by a buried secret which is divulged just in time.

It is this type of plot, coursing over a stretch of time and involving endless tangles and coincidences, that De Morgan made peculiarly his own, by blending it with a modern species of realistic comedy. He recalls the Victorian novel once more in that his chief characters always end in bliss, as they always must in a story of complicated design. *Any* series of events, however simple, can yield a tragedy: it requires no ingenuity to manufacture despair. But what is the use of difficulties except to be overcome, of complications except to be wriggled out of? The more involved a story, the more certain ought to be its happy ending—this is one of the simple Victorian conditions which De Morgan found it easy to accept. That this kind of optimism is an affair of the artistic sense, and not exclusively of temperament or philosophy, can be deduced from the fact that the one austerely simple tale, *An Affair of Dishonor*, is a terribly somber tragedy.

The other sort of gap, the social, De Morgan crossed, in four of his five great novels, by writing the history of individual philanthropies. Organized philanthropy we are quite confident that he detested; but he found his favorite subjects in kindly individual charities of the well-to-do. *Joseph Vance* and *Alice-for-Short* are stories of adoption. Lizarann and Blind Jim are befriended by great folk; the inhabitants of

Sapps Court, and even old Maisie and Phœbe, are befriended by Lady Gwen; and Dave Wardle, like Joseph Vance, marries upward into the class of his benefactors. What Mr. De Morgan primarily delighted in was to place the social extremes together, to prove not only that they can both be equally human, but also that their humanity is one.

He is master, too, of such tremendous effects of contrast as are implied in his plots. No one ever forgets the dramatic thrill of Mrs. Verrinder's reawaking after her sixty years' sleep, or Fenwick's restoration to his conscious identity, or the recognition by Phœbe and Maisie of their true relationship, or Sally's rescue of Fenwick from a rough sea after he has fallen from the pier, or Adrian Torrens's recovery of his sight. These suffer no loss by comparison with such greatest moments of emotional action as the cave scene in *Old Mortality*, the death of Jean Valjean, the mad-dog scene in *The Amazing Marriage*, the episode of the "Cliff Without a Name" in *A Pair of Blue Eyes*, or Borrow's account of a small boy riveted in wonder and awe by his first pictured glimpse of an ineffaceable footprint in the sand. With the phenomena especially of lost memory or lost senses, De Morgan has done more than any other; and his blind men, Lizarann's father and Adrian Torrens, are the most real we have ever had the luck to know, whether in literature or in life.

V

This same unconquerable and romantic love of life that creates blind and crippled men to be more, not less, alive than others, is not content until it has breathed life into a multitude of mere things. Here again De Morgan harks back to Dickens. Mr. Chesterton was, we believe, the first to point out the thrilling and half-supernatural significance with which Dickens invests certain physical objects. De Morgan has something of the same power. From his world of shades, the shades of persons and places that are no more, certain objects, always unimportant in themselves and sometimes positively trivial, stare with unearthly persistence, and become almost volitional agents, Satanic or beneficent.

The readiest example is the "hinseck" which was prematurely crocked. Without it, the fight would not have happened. Without the fight, Joe's father would not have been laid up for a term, or undertaken the Repairing-and-Building trade which was the means of Joe's meeting Lossie and Dr. Thorpe. And there would have been no story; at least not *that* story. It is a broken beer-jug that introduces Charles Heath to little Alicia Kavanagh, "Alice-for-Short"; and that same hopelessly smashed article sets in motion the whole train of circumstances leading to the dead and buried mystery of Alice's descent. It is a thing that plays the principal part in bringing Maisie and Phœbe to the knowledge of each other; an ingeniously contrived model of the old mill which had been familiar to their childhood reawakens the common memories that are to strengthen and draw them together. And a letter that slips behind the lining of an old wallet, as though possessed of a dæmonic and malignant energy of its own, prolongs the years of Joseph Vance's separation from Lossie.

Such devices are, from the point of view of modern technique, literary rubbish. If one is concerned to palliate them in De Morgan, one need hardly bother to point out that the accidental emergence or suppression of trivial things plays an enormous part in life, or to ask whether a philosophical mind need be above admitting and utilizing that part. The real ground of defense is elsewhere. What we have to note is that, in this lavish world of De Morgan, the presence of a certain defect is not necessarily the absence of the opposite merit. He never puts objects in place of character, or accident in place of causality: he supplies a full measure of both. The physical thing is an agent justified, if at all, because it leads to display of character at the most commanding elevations. We may like Thackeray and not like Wilkie Collins; but we have not comprehended De Morgan until we have seen that he was a man who could be Wilkie Collins without ceasing to be Thackeray.

When one comes to the personæ whom De Morgan projected into action by such capricious and even crude expedients, one's first instinct is to say that he specialized in the abnormal, the eccentric, and the quaint. And then one remembers the placid humdrum quality of quite ordinary types, like Mrs. Heath and Mr. Pellew; and the extraordinary and lovable reality of children such as Joe Vance and Lizarann and Dave and Dolly Wardle, or those two young rascals "Porky Owls" (how many pages we have to wait to find that his name was "Howells") and Michael "Ragstroar," later identified as Rackstraw; and the beauty and grace and wit of young women like Gwen Rivers and Alice; and the serene and ripened perfection of old people like Mrs. Verrinder or Mrs. Prichard or Granny Marrable. Every one of the forty-odd people in *When Ghost Meets Ghost* is real. Taken as a group, they cover the whole gap between criminal and saint, between slum and salon, between the cradle and the grave. There are in De Morgan's books seductive women like Judith Arkroyd, and stuffy, dowdy women like Marianne Challis; there are pairs of young lovers who experience love at its most golden, and prosy middle-aged lovers who are rather ashamed of themselves; there are metaphysical bores like Mr. Brownrigg with his Grauboschian philosophy, and slangy and Bohemian young men like Mr. Jerrythought; there are rectors and policemen and cabbies and artisans and faddists—and for the most part it is impossible to detect that their creator knows any of them less well than any others.

And, lest one jump at the inference that De Morgan mastered only the basic elements of character, the common stock of attributes, there is an individual like Alfred Challis the novelist, one of the most subtle, intellectual, and sophisticated men between two covers. The truth seems to be that De Morgan did not specialize in any kind of character at all—unless one can say that he specialized in every kind. There is said to be a type of half-outlawed physician whom his more professional brethren delight to call the "general specialist." De Morgan is the "general specialist" in character, with the difference that in his portraiture there is no quackery.

If one must assign a preference, and insist on loving any one of his creatures above the rest, we suppose mere man is compelled to pin his faith to Sally, Rosalind's daughter in *Somehow Good.* Modern fiction has not produced her like, and modern life cannot often have done so. Sally is the modern out-of-door girl at her matchless best. Sally could swim; but she was too piquantly of the present to be a mermaid, and De Morgan made her "merpussy." She was wild and womanly; untamable and very demure;

> "Like the swinging May-cloud that pelts the flowers with hailstones
> Off a sunny border, she was made to bruise and bless";

she tantalized her lover, Dr. Conrad Vereker, whom she called "Dr. Prosy"—and she also very happily and sweetly married him. She dived off the pier in most of her clothes to rescue Fenwick, and came herself as near to drowning as one can come and still escape—and then, to the infinite horror of her friends, she talked of "swimming over the ground" if the weather cleared. She was slangy and racy,—her relation with Fenwick, whom she called "Jeremiah," had more of sweetheart than of step-daughter,—and she was wise and rare and sound. Yet she is not an instance of surpassing skill in portraiture, as De Morgan's portraits go. All are treated with the same touch; it is as a person, not as a creation, that Sally deserves perhaps a seat one row above even Lossie Thorpe and Lady Gwen. It is in his best in this province of character, not in more debatable matters elsewhere, that we have the authentic measure of De Morgan and of his permanence.

VI

So much for a few of the respects in which De Morgan was indeed, as he was both praised and blamed for being, the Early Victorian surviving in our midst. Now we are going to venture a rather tenuous speculation that he was something more than that, in a subtle way which we hardly know how to phrase or to test. It is possible for a man to be called a prophet when the truth is merely that he has an extraordinary memory—but it is certainly more than the past in De Morgan that seems new to us. It is also conceivable that we cherish some sneaking preferences for things that we pretend to have put aside—let us say, for the novel according to Dickens. But we doubt that explanation too—and we hunt between the lines and in the margins of De Morgan for some hidden, some easily overlooked but all-important hint of the contemporaneous; something which can stand in the room of a permanent philosophy of life, even though it be too intangible to bear that name.

It seems to us as though we find that something in the materials of the very past which De Morgan revealed with so much apparent fidelity. As we compare the past of his London with the present, we make what seems a startlingly simple discovery. The comparison is easily made, because in *It Never Can Happen Again* he brings his story down to the era of the automobile. The discovery is just this: that, except for minor matters of topography, his London of the past *is* his London of the present. There is no essential difference at all. The people are the same, from the baronet with his landed estate down to the cabman and the police force. All the same fads, the same fashions, the same skepticisms defended with the same arguments, are shown as extant then. Society is neither more simple nor more sophisticated; people are neither better nor worse bred; Adrian Torrens in '53 is neither more nor less advanced than Alfred Challis a half century later. In a word, what De Morgan strikes at, whether consciously or instinctively, is our modern notion that we are overwhelmingly different. We know that there are daring people and timid people; but we think of the timid people now as occupying the position held by the daring people of fifty years ago. De Morgan gives us the lie; he says we are all occupying precisely the same old positions. He does it by inviting us to look at the people that filled the past of his Early Victorian childhood. He shows them to us in goodly numbers; he supplies them with infinite leisure to entertain us and answer our questions. We accept the invitation, we look at them. And behold! they are ourselves.

It would never do, of course, to say that De Morgan intended anything of the sort. We suspect that he cared most for the thing to which he dedicated the last of his books: The Spirit of Fiction. And we doubt whether he cared profoundly about any arguable matter. But the *effect* of his work is somewhat as we have tried to state; and in that effect lies the touch of contemporaneous appeal which the artist must have if he is to seem "vital." In De Morgan the contemporary appeal takes this peculiar form, the form of an assertion that we are all contemporaries whether we know it or not, and that the difference is between individuals, not between periods.

Of course the assertion in its extreme form is not true. People *were* different half a century ago; history and fiction are there to prove it. The intellectual center of gravity was differently located: the same beliefs may have been abroad, but the consensus was not where it is now. The question for the moment, however, is not of historical truth, but of a personal message couched in certain terms dictated not by history but by the spontaneous will of the intellect shaping its substance to a certain purpose. The same result, the same universality, can be achieved, it is obvious, either by modernizing the past or by Pasteurizing, so to put it, the present. We believe De Morgan half consciously modernized the past. If he had done otherwise, the trick would have been too transparent; even we modern folk, hungry for new dogmas, especially of a destructive purport, could not have been taken in. Evidently De Morgan was the sort of humanist who values but little the advancement on which we plume ourselves. Whence his exaggerated commentary that there *is* no advancement, that there is not even any change.

For our part, however much these speculations interest us, they do not long interest us most. If one were ever privileged to meet Mr. De Morgan in some after world of shades where even a critic may look at a creator and find forgiveness for his own sins, the words "Early Victorian" would probably not be among the words which one would wish to address to him. One would be more likely to say something of this sort: "Dear and honored sir, there is one thing for which some of us cannot too easily forgive you. You were one of the very dearest and most delightful of our entertainers, and, in those latter days, perhaps the most heartening of all; for while others chose to rant or fume or doubt or vilify, you chose only to give us much-needed pleasure unmixed with pain. But why, with all your wit and all your wisdom, with all your command over the very founts of laughter and of tears —why, when you were the only man in the world who could justly have dreamed of such a labor of love, did you not finish what your great elder brothers had begun? Why did you not give us the missing chapters of *Denis Duval* and *The Mystery of Edwin Drood?*"

This whimsical wish has lived its precarious and intermittent life among us, never asking to be taken quite seriously, for some ten years. But it has died at last. It has been three days now in a grave which there is no forgetting.

NOVELISTS OF TO-DAY

The Five Counties and the Five Towns

EDEN PHILLPOTTS
ARNOLD BENNETT

VII

EDEN PHILLPOTTS

Mr. Eden Phillpotts, who is hardly a "modern" novelist at all within the meaning of this book, raises nevertheless in a peculiarly isolated and crystallized form the central modern problem of the art of fiction: the problem of raw "realism" versus the creative imagination. Critics are commendably fond of talking about that problem; but most of the talk about it has to be theoretical and *in vacuo,* for the reason that most novelists, even the most professedly "photographic," have not really had the questionable courage to do nothing to life except copy it. In Mr. Phillpotts alone, the presence of authentic data is almost everything and the selection and meaning of the data are almost nothing. The difference between the pure realist and the creative artist who uses the handy realistic method is implicit in the contrast between Mr. Phillpotts and Mr. Arnold Bennett. Both use the factual process, and it may be that both overuse it; but Mr. Bennett is trained in a school that understands what is meant by a principle of selection, and how such a principle operates to give shape and coherence to the work of fiction.

If it seems that, in discussing Mr. Phillpotts, we have put disproportionate emphasis on a failure pri-

marily of method and technique, we can only confess that the connection of that failure with our main theme is indeed an indirect one. But it has a connection. We would suggest part of the definition of what a sound novel is, through some incidental discussion of what it is not. Soundness in the novel is fusion among the parts and subordination of their sum to a worthy unifying purpose. These are the artistic counterpart of that philosophical unity and continuity which, as we have maintained, the modern humanist must search out in the life of man the social animal. Who shall say that there is no connection between these two principles, the artistic need for the unity which is beauty and the philosophical need for the unity which is truth? Now, if ever, he who has one kind of vision is likeliest to have the other. There is more than there ever was to help make the good thinker a good artist, the good artist a good thinker. As, then, we discuss here the failure of a mere agency in art, we would be understood as having an ulterior thought for the end it has failed to serve. In this world of art we get beyond the means to the end only when the means have solved their problem of adaptation. Wherever they fail of a solution, criticism has no choice but to deal with the means explicitly—unless indeed it is to be silent altogether.

I

The signal failure of Mr. Phillpotts as a novelist can be phrased briefly in the assertion that this writer is our most impressive example of the artist who has mistaken his material for his subject. With Mr. Phill-

potts the mistake has been so absolute and, from the first, so hopeless that he has remained to this day a prolific novelist without any subject at all; and, so far from getting the deficiency repaired with time and experience, he has allowed it more and more to emphasize itself. We shall analyse his failure by explaining in some detail what we mean by the confusion of material with subject.

Meanwhile, it is necessary to point out some of the elements of half-success that enter into the failure, to give it its impressiveness, its challenging importance. One can hardly find elsewhere so many different kinds of adequacy assembled with so much conscientious and untiring care into a sum-total which strikes one so exclusively by its inadequacy. Half a dozen superior workmen in as many fields had to be spoiled in order to make of Mr. Phillpotts an inferior novelist, and the half-fulfilled or wholly broken promise of them is over all his pages. His works of fiction are more interesting as almost anything else one likes than they are as works of fiction. Clearly he could have been a literary topographer, like Sir Walter Besant, or an essayist on aspects of nature, like Mrs. Meynell; clearly he could have been an archæologist or an ethnologist, or a genuinely remarkable student and purveyor of folklore and of the general quaintness of English life in the Five Counties—so to summarize his preëmpted region, the south of England. He could have written a book like George Gissing's *By the Ionian Sea;* indeed, in his natural capacity for almost any intellectual career other than that of fiction, he greatly re-

sembles Gissing. In a large expository work of reference, Mr. Phillpotts could have done for Devon what Mr. Hardy did in his novels for "Wessex."

But Mr. Phillpotts could not accomplish anything of the sort in his novels, because in each of them the futility of the whole vitiates whatever extraordinary appeal one deciphers in the parts. One of his books is like the preparation for a beautiful and costly building. The ground is prepared and leveled; the foundation is laid; blocks and girders, all of the very finest substance available, are dumped there in nondescript heaps—and there the contractor complacently deserts his undertaking; there they lie, those helpless materials, pretending to be the finished and symmetrical structure we had been invited to look through. Our cheated and baffled sense of the prodigious waste is equaled only by our amazement at the superlative excellence of the material so unintelligibly squandered.

The natural result of this relation between the potential utility of the parts and the extreme uselessness of the whole is that a critical view is condemned from the first to be almost wholly destructive. But criticism has never liked to be primarily destructive: to be so is both ungracious and, on the whole, profitless. Criticism has battened on the faults of greatness—for example, on the vulgarity of Dickens, the monotony of Trollope, the difficulty of Meredith. But it has been sluggish in approaching the greatness of the faulty, of those illustrious failures who have to be praised extravagantly in detail and rejected on the whole.

The consequence in this present instance has been

an odd relation between Mr. Phillpotts and his critics: a relation characterized on *their* side by immense assumptions and almost complete silence. They recognize the peculiar prestige of their author. They see that the enormous quantity and the regularity of his output, together with the fact of its public consumption, give him a really great importance, if only the importance of a prevalent symptom. They appreciate his consistency and dependableness, his faculty of making every book live up to our expectation of it, his fidelity to what stands in the minds of his readers as a Phillpotts tradition. They understand, too, that his precise fulfilment again and again of our expectation has nothing to do with a desire for popularity: certainly we owe it to Mr. Phillpotts to note that he is one of a very few living writers who have never computed the demands of the commercial market or sold the public "what it wants" without regard to what they wanted it to have. Finally, and most important, his critics understand that he has made himself, by persistent application, the authoritative spokesman of a side of life, the side summarized in the word "Devon" as Mr. Hardy's is summarized in the word "Wessex."

These are the matters that constitute among them the largeness of this author's claim to consideration. The claim is recognized—but the consideration is, nevertheless, mostly withheld. And the reason is, as we have said, the natural propensity of criticism to deal with what *on the whole* most challenges it, in spite of some inherent defects, and its natural aversion to what on the whole disappoints it, in spite of unusual incidental merits. Criticism has probably been less interested in Mr. Phillpotts than in any present writer of corresponding eminence. But, even if it is not interested in him, it has the most important reasons for being interested in the causes of his failure, and particularly in the relation between the assembled material of a novel and the use of that material in the finished organization.

II

We find a recent critic suggesting that the names of Hardy and Phillpotts may presently seem to denote one of the striking dualities of greatness in which English literary history abounds—Defoe and Swift, Richardson and Fielding, Byron and Scott, Shelley and Keats, Dickens and Thackeray, Tennyson and Browning. What that suggestion oddly overlooks is the antithesis and irreconcilable contradiction embodied in such pairs of names. An age gets itself expressed in halves; it chooses a great spokesman for its aristocracy, and an equally great for its democracy, it finds one voice for its humanitarianism and another for its æstheticism, one for its faith and another for its doubt. In this sense, the natural name to be bracketed with Hardy is Meredith; and what we have to note about Mr. Phillpotts is that, leaving aside for the moment all questions of equality in workmanship and in productivity, he is more like Mr. Hardy than any writer of lasting importance ever has been like any predecessor. It is difficult to read his characteristic books without feeling quite definitely that he must once have said to himself: "I will know and 'do' Dartmoor as Hardy has known and 'done' Wessex."

This very fact of similarity in the principal source of inspiration, and the consequent overlapping of substance, destroy Mr. Phillpotts's contribution as a counterpart of Hardy's, and reduce it to a mere imitative supplement or addendum. One feels that Mr. Phillpotts, looking for security in the shadow of the greatest literary prestige of his immediate past, found there only eclipse. One can attach to every enduring name in the history of fiction the label of some distinguished quality that had not existed before; we identify even such lesser folk as Maturin, Godwin, Mrs. Radcliffe, and Maria Edgeworth by the most individual traits which appear in them—traits which they invented rather than copied. But when the future historian comes to the summary of Mr. Phillpotts, he will find that the most striking traits are also the most striking traits of a far greater man—and, furthermore, that the most individual qualities of Mr. Phillpotts are his weaknesses as an artist. This lack in fundamental originality is a serious menace to the permanence of even a very able writer. There is such a thing as the genius that takes its own wherever it finds it. But we can think of no success gained by an author's taking so nearly his sum-total of substance from another.

One need not, however, insist on the mere matter of priority in a certain field,—in this instance the field of rural life in the southwest counties,—for if Mr.

Phillpotts had preceded Hardy, it would still remain true that he failed. The really crushing difference is that in Hardy the various expedients of natural setting and quaint lore and rustic humor are *used*, whereas in Phillpotts they are, as nearly as any things can be in fiction, ends in themselves.

There is no questioning the competence of the younger author as a collector of data. To read him is to see a vision of shelves upon shelves of note-books, all fat and teeming and enticing. There are, there must be, records in them of episodes and chance remarks, tales told in circuitous bucolic speech and otherwise lost to memory, landscapes and the lights that lie upon them, plants and herbs and the dates of their upspringing or blossoming, personal appearances and mannerisms—a thousand charming oddities, all indefatigably noted down, often with a nice exactitude amounting to wizardry. If material could be novels, these note-books would be among the masterpieces. We hardly need to see them to know that one is labeled "Nature," another "Dialect," a third "Episodes," a fourth "Comic Rustics," and that they are all bulging. Everything that research could do has been done—so effectively done that there is perhaps no place in the whole world as completely "documented" by one man as Devonshire by Mr. Phillpotts. But the task of documenting the field, properly the beginning of such a localized fiction, is left as the end and sum of the task. We get no farther, and, for the purposes of the novel, are entitled to feel that we have got nowhere.

The insufficiency of material when used for its own sake will appear more decisively from the contrast between Hardy's settings and those of Mr. Phillpotts. Hardy is a master of the subtle relation between place and character; nature is not only the background, but the producing cause, of his persons. In *The Return of the Native*, character and scene are interwoven threads of the same dark texture of atmosphere. Mr. Phillpotts has tried in the best of his earlier novels to master the same effect and give nature a like importance. In *Sons of the Morning* he sets his stage with the same portentous deliberation, and achieves, by way of mere description, the same immensity. The pretense is that we are to see nature as dominant over human lives; we are being constantly reminded throughout the book of the poetic and inevitable congruity between man and the aspects of his environment. Yet when we have read this book and another of the same period, *Children of the Mist*, the two standing apart as their author's most nearly triumphant works, we can find no reason in art or in probability why a set of characters should not flop out of one into the other. The descriptive effects in *Sons of the Morning* are brave and bright, like the clear fortissimo of trumpets; they rank among the most resplendent things in description of nature. The effects in *Children of the Mist* are purposely blurred and filmed; we move through "a radiance of misty silver." But when we examine the personæ of the two books, we find them strangely similar; in mind and heart, they are all equally "Children of the Mist." Both stories are of disappointment, futility, the injustice and inequality of life, its tragic losses and half-compensations.

And, let it be added, both are equally forced and improbable as to plot. We are invited in each to observe the spirit of place wrought out in flesh and blood, the destiny of the human figures wrought out in terms of fateful character. In reality we observe some very short-sighted people jerked this way and that through the motions of a highly artificial plot predetermined by the author, against a back-drop of amazing and unearthly beauty. We have scene at its incomparable best, character in profusion and variety, and action forced into complicated designs of suspense, coincidence, and mystery—these put together, but in no sense fused. They are pages torn from different note-books, each page for its independent interest, and bound in the same covers, but that is all. They strike among themselves no inevitable harmony: the notes are almost strictly interchangeable from book to book. Thus the mastery of local color, in its proper use a tremendous asset, becomes in Phillpotts simply one more element of the extraneous—the largest element and the nearest to independent adequacy; the most impressive substitute, that is, for a subject.

The lack of centrality in Phillpotts's novels is exhibited through a kind of stratified arrangement of setting and action. Instead of purposeful mingling of the two, we find blocks or layers of each. Chapter after chapter opens with a symphonic prelude of nature; then, enter the human figures with their somewhat irrelevant concerns. This type of chapter becomes a formula, with all the monotony of a formulated thing. Moreover, the descriptions are often in themselves rich, luxuriant, cloying; they need the solvent of action and dialogue, if only because they are too rapturously beautiful to be enjoyed in unrelieved excess. They are all consummate in their way; but the very prose has often a flushed and fulsome quality that needs a less impersonal quality of emotion to support and justify it. Nature itself can be made, as in *Richard Feverel*, to exalt and glorify life; but a novel of life is not quite the place to glorify nature for itself. Mr. Phillpotts has been called, too flatteringly, an analyst of the relation between nature and man. Rather, when he takes into his hand the descriptive pen he simply becomes the rhapsodist or prose-poet of nature, with everything else too often and too long forgotten.

III

If we turn from the backgrounds to the persons, we find a lack hardly so definable. The characters, extraordinarily intense and vivid while we are with them, fade as they recede; or else several of them fuse into a general type, proving so that they were not really individuals at all. It is surprising how often certain personages recur through the books. The irascible and hasty youth who looks only after he has taken the flying leap into trouble; the older, graver, more dependable and kindly man who is always entering, a *deus ex machina*, to save impossible situations, perhaps to marry the desolated heroine; the young girl of extraordinary susceptibility, at first a little wilful, a little capricious, but growing in fortitude and worth as she learns to suffer; the tyrannical and irate father, ruling his children without sympathy, threatening dire things to his daughter's lover; the hard-headed, hard-fisted man of substance, who elbows his passage regardless of others' rights and opinions, and knows no law but his own will, until, hard as he is, life breaks him; the aged peasant whose function is drollery, and who is a fool or a sot, or both, except when he is a sententious wiseacre and storehouse of proverbs—these are the most frequent and, as types, the most distinct. But as one tries to recall the individuals within each type, one finds that they tend to merge; they have not each a distinct aroma of personality. Christopher Yeoland is Clem Hicks grown a trifle irresponsible; Philip Ouldsbroom is Will Blanchard grown up. Myles Stapleton and Martin Grimbal might change places without loss or gain to either of two stories. The heroines of the same pair of books, Honor Endicott and Phoebe Lyddon, are the same person at two slightly different social levels.

Contrast with these two heroines of Hardy, both meant to be somewhat frivolous characters: Ethelberta in *The Hand of Ethelberta* and Bathsheba in *Far From the Madding Crowd.* The two are as distinct, within their type, as two wholly different types. Add a third, Elfride Swancourt in *A Pair of Blue Eyes.* The type remains constant, but there is still no confusing the individuals. The difference is that Hardy creates personalities whereas Phillpotts classifies them. The historian of Dartmoor has a sharp perception of class, and of the traits that are common to all members of a given class; but his analysis is more of human nature in general than of the nature of this and that human being. The definition of types, however capable, is not a substitute for the faculty which must remain, after all, the greatest that fiction has ever brought to bear on life; the creation of striking and unique individuals. Elizabeth Bennet, David Copperfield, Becky Sharpe, Mrs. Proudy, Sir Willoughby Patterne, Eustacia Vye are names of acquaintances that haunt us, or come at our invitation. The names of Phillpotts's characters belong to composite photographs which we once saw but which began to fade even while we were thinking of them. This matter is hardly demonstrable in words; but any reader can test it for himself by comparing his recollections of novels from various hands.

Besides this indistinctness of the characters within their types, there is a certain amount of inconsistency in the behavior of particular specimens, often where consistency is important to the artistic integrity of the story. Mr. Frederick Taber Cooper points out the preposterousness of the "physical bargain and sale"—the sale of a wife by herself—in *The Whirlwind*. Of the same substance is the prolonged series of dilemmas in *Sons of the Morning*, where a woman who appears first as the soul of naïveté loves two men simultaneously, marries each in turn, and is haunted during her life with the second by the fear that the first had not sufficiently believed in her love for *him*. Many of the alleged developments and transformations of character in Phillpotts are inadequately explained or motivated, and have the effect of sleight-of-hand performances which fail to convince because they are executed in the dark. We can take a novelist's word as to his premises; let him begin, we concede, where and with what he likes. But thereafter we demand a grade of plausibility amounting to proof of every stage, every transition. Anything less is imposing on us; and it helps matters not at all if the novelist, being sincere about his work, has succeeded in first imposing on himself.

Our point that Mr. Phillpotts is a master of types rather than of individuals receives some sanction from the fact that his grasp is firmest precisely where all persons are most alike: that is, in the moments of stress or of elemental passion where fundamental humanity emerges above the merely personal traits. We are not given a full and finished picture of Will Blanchard the man of anger; but we are given an irresistible picture of his anger. The things in Mr. Phillpotts's stories that ring truest are the things that have to do with the extremes of emotional experience—birth, rage, the parental frenzy, sorrow, despair, death. One of his strongest single books, *The Thief of Virtue,* is strong because it gives the most opportunity for display of the extremes of feeling—the whole situation from the outset, between woman and lover, between husband and wife, between father and child, being an intensely abnormal one. It is the paradox of human character that we are most alike in abnormal situations, most unlike in normal ones; and no novelist has ever succeeded in giving a rounded version of personality except by including a generous proportion of ordinary placid existence. Mr. Phillpotts, a specialist in the astounding, reaches there his greatest emotional strength; but that strength only serves to reëmphasize his weakness in analysis.

IV

The lapses in our author's treatment of character are no doubt partly explained by a lack of intuitive understanding of the subtleties in human make-up. His major characters read as though he had pieced them together of abstractions—so much sensibility, so much pride, so much self-will, so much fanaticism, and so on. Great literary protagonists, one suspects, are not so conceived: they spring, as though ready-formed, from the quickened intuition. It takes the novelist's intellect to *know* them through and through, but they *make* themselves. There is this magic, this alchemy, that Mr. Phillpotts simply does not have; a faculty that is and must remain, in those who do have it, among the inexplicable miracles.

But there is also a part of his limitation that has almost tangibly to do with his lack of the constructive sense. It takes the form, in the earlier part of his work, of a too heavy insistence on complication of event. The characters, under the compulsion of what they are made to do, become warped and shriveled. Just as Mr. Phillpotts's lavish treatment of nature fails of intimate adjustment to the personæ, so his equally lavish inclusion of events, for plot-interest, fails of adjustment to them. And the consequence is a striking absence of what criticism means when it talks about composition, fusion, and perspective.

It is all but self-evident that a work of art must have a center of some sort, somewhere, and that the center of a realistic novel must be in a given situation of several human lives. The romancer finds himself attracted by a story which he wants to tell; but the realist of life finds himself drawn to a number of persons about whom he wants to tell a story. The problem is to find the right one—the one they would have lived if actuality had thrown them together. It is not enough to choose any events that will serve to exhibit them: that method results simply in a series of character sketches, such as the *Pickwick Papers*, which frankly do not aspire to be a novel at all. The realist *may*, of course, achieve his purpose by finding his story first and choosing the characters to fit it; but there is the danger that, unless it is a very simple, very organic story, they will fail to fit. The trap into which we find Mr. Phillpotts blundering throughout his earlier work is the choice of very complicated stories—so complicated that no set of human beings that ever existed could fit all parts of them. And the human beings labor therefore under the embarrassment of having to become, in various exigencies, different persons entirely. Subsidiary events, excrescences on the plot, have to be dragged in to explain these alterations in the characters; and we see by consequence the unhappy spectacle of action and character repeatedly and fruitlessly adding complications to each other, in a vain effort to keep the interaction explained, and to the destruction of that blending of elements without which the result can have no center at all.

The artistic consequences of this fallacy appear at their worst where the event has nothing to do with the character; where the juxtaposition of the two is arbitrary, coïncidental, and therefore artistically immoral and outrageous. For example, a woman going forth to her faithless lover, who is now dying and repentant, is drowned in a flood; a man bound for a decisive interview with an enemy strays into the line of artillery practice, loses his footing when the first shell screeches over his head, and falls from a high place to his death; a man supposed to have died roams into a wood on the night when his former sweetheart, now a wife, is wandering there, and appears to her so suddenly and spectrally that her child is still-born; one man, a deserter, is robbed of the credit of a voluntary confession, and another man of the legitimate self-satisfaction of having at last forgiven his enemy, by the accidental mailing of a letter left on a desk, and then the tangle is set right by the intervention of the Queen's Jubilee, with its general forgiveness of deserters. What shall we call the innumerable instances of this sort of thing, if not melodrama? Powerful and complex forces are set in motion, such forces as require working out to some definite end in terms of the character which is fate—and then some blind irrelevant intrusion of accident, some caprice of circumstance, is used, not to illustrate a theory of the strangeness of life or the blundering impersonality of things, but simply to dodge the whole problem and substitute an entirely different one. Coincidence, modern technique has come to recognize, is bad just in proportion as it is important. The most tolerable employment of chance in fiction is to give a sort of ironic sanction to that which has already come to pass by other agencies. But this is a lesson which Mr. Phillpotts did not learn until late; and it is doubtful whether he has yet learned it thoroughly.

Through the books of his exuberant period, the late '90's, Phillpotts is also the victim of his own humor. Nothing could be more delicious than the talk of Billy Blee and Gaffer Lezzard, Billy Blee's courting of the drunken Widow Coomstock, and the "Libation to Pomona," all in *Children of the Mist*, or the surreptitious opening of the coffin in *Sons of the Morning;* but practically all such scenes are sheer unbridled self-indulgence. The peasants are portrayed simply because they are *there;* they are made to talk interminably just because their talk is funny. Unlike Hardy, Mr. Phillpotts shows off his rustics for page after page of unutilized gossip, for pure delight in them. It is odd and disturbing that the humor which created or reproduced them should not have been able to methodize their abundance.

It is odd too that the humor which keeps them perpetually delightful, even in their extreme coarseness, should have missed the ludicrous solemnity of another situation in *Children of the Mist:* Will Blanchard's perpetual uneasiness of conscience in regard to the lapse in his past. We see him tortured by something akin to the murderer's guilt; he broods over a wrong and suffers tragically lest his sin come to find him out and demand expiation; he is surrounded with dark hints and lives his life before us under a cloud. Eventually we discover that he has deserted from the Queen's army in time of peace and run away to marry his sweetheart, who was being forced by her parents to marry a rival suitor. This piece of solemn mystification over so small a matter results, not in a conviction of the haunting omnipresence of conscience, but in the suspicion that Will must have been all these years, to have felt so abysmally over such an affair, a bigger simpleton even than we had thought him.

V

If we survey the workmanship of Mr. Phillpotts after 1900, we find it chequered. *The Thief of Virtue*, a novel which we have mentioned as containing his firmest handling of character, shows him startlingly near to simplicity and strength of construction. If by any chance his career had ended with this book, we should have thought of him as having got through his artistic muddle into clarity. Of the later stories, *The Thief of Virtue* does have, by exception, an entirely adequate centralizing theme, a striking situation involving a small group of principals and depending for its effect on a legitimate kind of suspense, happily never resolved.

Philip Ouldsbroom, the bluff, irascible, self-willed, fundamentally generous and warm-hearted dominant figure in the book, is the most fully vitalized specimen of our author's favorite type. Ouldsbroom appropriates, almost by violence, the sweetheart of another man, a younger. When a son is born to his wife, we see him in parental ecstasy—but the father of the child is really the wife's former lover. In the clash of temperaments between Ouldsbroom and the boy, who inherits none of his supposed father's noble weaknesses and all of his real father's niggardly virtues, the story finds its nucleus; and for once Mr. Phillpotts was able to work out his theme to its logical end, the miserable and tragic death of Ouldsbroom, without precipitating the discovery of the secret—though to suppress it he had to resort to some dubious measures, including the violent accidental death of the wife. Here is, at least, a pattern; it is frayed in spots and some loose threads are never caught into place, but the design is recognizable as unified.

The crystallized unity of this theme is the more astounding if we place beside it the extraordinary diffusion of a book published only a few months earlier, *The Three Brothers*. Here again the prime object appears to be a contrast between two characters, the one making a specious display of virtues not really possessed, the other concealing real worth under a grim exterior. But so many irrelevant destinies are worked out by the way that we may fairly remain in doubt whether there is any primary object at all. For a capital example of the difference between art concealed and art lamentably missing, one has only to compare a chapter of *The Three Brothers* with two exactly corresponding chapters of a story of thirty years earlier. Readers of Hardy will remember how, in *The Return of the Native*, Eustacia engineers her first meeting with Yeobright by disguising herself and taking a part in the mummers' presentation of the Christmas play at Yeobright's house. We are given incidentally a vivid and sufficient picture of that performance, with all its crude rusticity; but our attention is focused none the less on Eustacia's ulterior design, her palpitating dread of discovery, her expectancy, the extreme sophistication of her artifice and its ultimate success. It happens that, in *The Three Brothers*, Mr. Phillpotts elected to spend a whole chapter on a rehearsal of the same play, with its traditional figures of St. George, the Turkish Knight, the King of Egypt, the Dragon—and for no constructive end whatever, but solely to display the rustic manners in comic action under the tutelage of a vicar who has somewhat priggishly undertaken to improve them. Between these two versions of substantially the same material, there is the same difference as between a page of the Congressional Record and a page of well-written history.

Against such purposeless and disproportionate compilation, a book like *The Thief of Virtue* stands out as almost symmetrical. But when we look still further, into the productions of the years since, we find that *The Thief of Virtue* represents after all, not artistic clarity after artistic muddle, not a tendency, not even a symptom; for subsequent works, the most recent of all, seem to have abandoned the last vestiges of construction and given themselves over exclusively to exploitation of material as such.

We shall fairly have described *Old Delabole* and *Brunel's Tower*, two very recent novels in which Mr. Phillpotts turns back from Dartmoor to Cornwall, if we say that the stories which they contain are the thinnest imaginable disguise for the author's careful notes on the two industries of slate and pottery. We learn all that moderately untechnical language can tell us about quarrying slate and making pottery. Never before, surely, has the humanity in fiction served so single-mindedly as pretext for the display of particular trades and mechanic arts. A plentiful quantity of realism since Gissing's has had to be described by criticism as muddy with detail; but here at last is detail enthroned and regnant, not illustrating character and place, but calling upon them to illustrate it, and barely tolerating the human figure. It would be inaccurate to say that the number of minutiæ occludes the story: the whole function of the story is to display the minutiæ. It is a show-window for specimens of slate, samples of pottery. And the chief event of *Old Delabole*, an event narrated with effect almost worthy of Hardy's tremendous crises, is a landslip at one of the quarries, watched from a safe distance by the entire population of the hamlet, and innocent of any decisive effect on the people, their relations to each other, or their story. It is in such manipulations that these two books seek their substitute for the history of hearts and motives, the obscure interplay of life on life, the infinite variety of the human drama.

We can hardly affirm too often or remember too consistently that fiction, if it is to contribute anything at all to the criticism of life, must find in these greater and purely human affairs its fulcrum and its center. Its primary task is not cartography of the physical world, nor even the propounding of theories about man's ultimate destiny: it is the revelation of man himself, his hopes and strivings, his failures and triumphs. In it, the work of his hands may find a place, even the quarrying of slate or the manufacture of teapots—but only in so far as these concern his spiritual and moral life. Joe Gargery sweating at his forge, Dr. Manette fumbling at his last in a dank prison cell, Amelia cooking her scraps of food over the kitchen fire while her husband gambles away sovereigns in a gay company—these are human figures who could not be made more human by dissertations on the composition of iron or the grades of leather or the chemistry of cooking. When the novel undertakes to report anything and everything that can be established as factually true, its proper and peculiar function is gone. Mr. Phillpotts's replacement of the realism of life by the realism of things is not only the *reductio ad absurdum*, it is the utter destruction, of the novel. Matter has been allowed, even fondly encouraged, to fill the room of subject-matter; truth is lost in the mob of facts; and just in proportion as the result acquires the value of an expository treatise, it becomes meaningless as an interpretation of life.

VI

There is, of course, another aspect of these later

failures; for no book that bothers to masquerade as a novel can actually let itself off with the assemblage of specialized physical data. Such assemblage is the chief aim of *Old Delabole* and *Brunel's Tower*. They are clearly the work of a man whose ruling incentive is the passion to impart what he knows, and who uses the method of fiction to make it palatable. But we see in them also a large mingling of his anxiety to tell us *what he believes*. There grows upon Mr. Phillpotts a damaging tendency more or less perceptible from the first: the sermonizing or didactic tendency, which evolves gradually until, in the two books just mentioned, the exploitation of local data is first, the declamation of the author's ideas about life and work is second, and the characters and story are nowhere. In other words, the novelist has made his puppets to illustrate and proclaim his philosophy of life, instead of taking them as they might be found and using his philosophy of life to interpret them to us.

This way of allowing the initial impulse of art to become its end results in what is, technically speaking, the most unpleasant phase of Mr. Phillpotts's works: their excess of dialogue. He was always an easy victim to the temptation of overdoing this very subordinate ingredient of the novel; we have already spoken of his earlier chapters as beginning with a set, formal picture, and then proceeding mostly in talk. But there is nothing even in those earlier works to match the amount of colloquy in the more recent ones. Whatever in these is not description of nature or exposition of mechanical processes, is talk; the novelist's prime art, the art of presentation, is not exercised at all. Not even the war, which has drawn from Mr. Phillpotts his best story since *The Thief of Virtue*, has been seriously corrective of this fault. When, in the last chapters of *The Green Alleys*, the author "lets out" the war to his rustics, as a subject for their quaint droning, one feels that he has inevitably belittled it by letting it be handled, or mouthed, as any other subject. In this matter of dialogue and monologue Mr. Phillpotts is not in the tradition of Hardy, of George Eliot, of Jane Austen: he is an odd and quaint survival of an older school, the archaic school of frank didacticism, of which *Sandford and Merton* is the remembered example.

As for the opinions expressed in these endless harangues, they are in themselves distinguished and commanding essay material, modern in spirit but restrained and tempered in their iconoclasm. Nearly every one of the books contains a liberal or radical thinker about religious dogmas, an opponent of ritualism and superstition; Barbara Hext, in *The Thief of Virtue*, represents this type before its lapse into mere garrulity. It is but fair to say that Mr. Phillpotts always presents the other side too, the side of prim orthodoxy, in order that the clash may be tolerably equal and result in sparks struck from the flint of opposition. The trouble is, not that the opinions are unworthy of respect and credence, but that they have nothing to do with the real contest, which is of personalities. The extraneousness of the intellectual element in the stories is clearly enough shown in *The Joy of Youth*, Mr. Phillpotts's excursion into Italy and the plastic arts. Never was there a less intimate alliance between opinions and personality than in the young artist of that book. The real battle, that of temperaments and opposed schools of breeding, is constantly being halted for dissertations on the æsthetic life; the hero is a walking compendium of all the illuminating things which Mr. Phillpotts feels about the plastic impulse and its manifestations. It is all very interesting for itself, but it has only the remotest connection with any story that is being told.

In the two stories of slate and of pottery, the principal idea harped on is the necessity of the worker's identifying himself with his work, in order that toil may be elevated above drudgery. This is a valid truth, of which the modern world stands perhaps in unprecedented need. We shall see that at least one of our contemporaries, Mr. Arnold Bennett, has done something toward a fusion of this truth with artistic method, and given us a fictional world in which work means not less than it does in the real world. But the workman who philosophizes about his trade and invents allegorical explanations of its importance is, we fear, too patently a mouthpiece. Sometimes Mr. Phillpotts almost makes him a megaphone. Thomas Body the "fanatic thrower" and old Mr. Crispin are gushing wells of sententious allegory throughout *Brunel's Tower;* Grandfather Nute in *Old Delabole* is their next of kin. Wherever the story gathers momentum and appears about to assert itself, Polonius enters in the form of one of these greybeards and interpolates a whole chapter on the meaning of life, the importance of humility, the sacredness of work, or some such generality; inspiration withers, and the story expires in its tracks under the baleful eye of homily. There is so much insistence on the author's faith in the basic goodness of life, and so much profusion in expressing that faith vocally, that life itself is reduced to a minimum.

To this last, Mr. Phillpotts has written novels by formula without insisting on any of the real advantages of formula. There could be no more ruinous débâcle of the art of fiction. It means the novel turned into a motion picture theatre with a formidable pulpit cutting off the audience's view of the screen.

VIII

ARNOLD BENNETT

I

"AND when we rolled across the floor of roofs into a London that was not yet awake, I still had the sensation of being on an island insecurely anchored in a great sea. We were all huddled together on that bit of turf that raised its breast from the sea to encounter the winds; and we were doing what we could; and we called the episode life. We called it life, this recurring moment of captivity between vast freedoms. . . . Differences of class, of lot—what were they in the immense perspective? We were all one."

So Mr. Arnold Bennett writes in his more didactic and analytical moments. The passage occurs near the end of a very extraordinary and not very characteristic story, *The Glimpse.* It is the story of a man whose whole intellectual and moral life is wrapped up in his work. His wife is a superb creature of material ambitions and ornamental futilities. In the course of years he discovers what the illusions of a grand passion had earlier prevented his discovering: that her whole nature is foreign to his, that any expectation of her ever understanding him is hopeless. What he fails to discover is that it is equally impossible for him to understand her. They are two human souls who have struggled up together out of poverty into wealth, and drawn apart in the ascent. For it appears, as they approach success, that success means one thing to the husband and to the wife a far different thing.

At the outset of the story we see them inhabiting the same costly apartment, surrounded by the same rare and luxurious articles, eating the same food from the same table—and in all that makes the intrinsic reality of life separated by more than the width of the world. By an odd conjunction of circumstances the husband precipitates a confession that his wife is on the verge of active disloyalty to him, and the shock of the revelation brings on a paroxysm of the heart. This point is the real beginning. So far the tale is conventional to the point of triteness—the neglectful husband, the intriguing wife, the impact of discovery, the solution of the knot by the wife's suicide, the husband's realization that the tragedy has been more the misfortune of both than the fault of either. But all this, the familiar plot of fifty novels in fifty years, is what Mr. Bennett reduces to a few chapters which give the preliminary action of *The Glimpse*.

The body of the story consists of the husband's experience during the three days when, in a state of coma, he hovers between life and death, in a vast intermediate world where the ordinary physical realizations of space and time dissolve into the void, and all the meaning of life is made plain to the soul directly, without the intervention of the bodily apparatus. The two hundred pages of that account are an extraordinary challenge to the impossible; an attempt, more than half successful, to make a sustained record of the cosmic sensations of a soul all but disembodied—such sensations as most people experience under an anæsthetic, when the earth and the heavens unspread as a scroll of simple meanings, and the whole panorama of life seems to be revealed and justified.

That is Morrice Loring's "Glimpse." If it is not a vision, it exerts on him the effect of one. It illuminates the significance of life, of character, even of things; it explains all, even the folly and futility of his wife, whom now, for the first time, he understands. It teaches him the reality and the vivid beauty of every soul's experience. It conveys to him the ultimate word of practical human wisdom: that every existing person or thing has as much right to be what it is as any other person or thing—namely, the right of necessity; that all experiences and all desires are not only willed but fated. His wife had had to live as she was; she had not made herself. Now, for the first time, he understands her as she had understood herself.

What the glimpse amounts to, then, is a revelation of the incurable solitude of individual souls. They are solitary because most of them never see the glimpse. To see our isolation is already to have escaped it. But we are more likely to remain the parts of some stupendous whole too vast and too intricate to be comprehended; and because we cannot understand the whole, we cannot understand the other parts. We are strangers to each other. Every life seems to itself immense and sufficient. The span may be short and the desires may be futile; but they are the limited terms imposed upon us, and our egoism glorifies them, makes them suffice. Every existence is surrounded with a blanket of indestructible loneliness; every soul is locked fast in its own self-sufficiency. This is at once the tragedy and the beauty of life: tragedy, because the failure to understand others as we understand ourselves is what produces such mishaps as Loring's; beauty, because if we were not solitary we should seem to ourselves unimportant, and nothing would appear as of enough consequence to be either beautiful or sad.

Life is, for the individual, in Arnold Bennett's view, a "recurring moment of captivity between vast freedoms." What the freedom is we cannot know. All we are given is the moment of captivity—and perhaps the strength or the imagination to rebel until we learn that rebellion is profitless. Only to a few souls, those who are torn by some great experience, does the revelation of other souls come. We lavish most of our imagination on ourselves; between ourselves and even those who are nearest us we feel a tissue of differences. Necessarily, we live a good share of our days in terms of the things we did not know soon enough. We covet the useless things that never seem useless until we have got them; we long for the beautiful lost things that never seemed beautiful until we had lost them. That is what Mr. Bennett means when he says that romance is always in the past.

II

The first implication of Mr. Bennett's view of life is

his sense of the significance of *things*, the crude material substances of living. Our modern malady is materialism. We are choked and strangled and drowned in things; we express all our values and ambitions in terms of things—things that we have, things that we haven't but want, things that others have, things that we can't possibly do without. It is very largely this disease of things that forms the impenetrable wrapping round each soul, and cuts us off so tragically from each other. The houses we live in, the money we handle, the cars we ride in, the books we read—these are more important to us, and actually more real, than the existence of other souls that have as many and as strong reasons for being what they are as we have for being what we are. The disease is more marked than it once was, because we do not admit that it is a disease at all: we call it Progress. Our ideal is the commercial ideal, which demands our surrender to the fallacy that the more things we can amass the better off we are. No piece of modern art can be effectually realistic unless it shows, among other truths, the immense and increasing part played by the material in modern lives; unless it shows our blind, our childish and sometimes fatuous emphasis upon dead matter.

This emphasis Mr. Bennett does show, as exhaustively as any writer has ever done. In the journalistic knack of reporting surface details and heaping them up into great clots and masses of undeniable reality, he has exceeded even his contemporaries. To choose only a single instance, itself of relatively slight weight, one early chapter of *The Glimpse* consists entirely of description of Bond Street, with its shops of leather, shops of precious stones, shops of cakes and sweets, shops of cravats, shops of gowns, shops of pictures and engravings—Bond Street, with its "equipages compromising with equipages in the narrow defile; and moguls, incas, pro-consuls, eunuchs, usurers, sultanas, houris, mandarinesses and serious ladies getting in and out of the equipages, and in and out of the shops, serene in the consciousness that there was nothing more correct than this, and that in the whole street not a single necessary of life could be discovered!"

But Mr. Bennett does not stop at this grasp of surface aspects. He not only excels in the treatment of things, wherever he finds them: he goes where he can find them most, and where there is least else to be found. He goes, that is, where the commercial ideal is most visibly and exclusively dominant. The central inescapable fact about him is that, of all the endless complicated phenomena of the hurrying modern world, that which most absorbs his attention is the phenomenon of industrial organization.

In specific terms this means, as the whole novel-reading world knows by this time, that Mr. Bennett is a specialist in the Five Towns, great pottery manufacturing communities in the north of England. Hanbridge, Bursley, Knype, Longshaw, and Turnhill—names thinly disguised, as we know if we happen to be curious enough to consult the map—have become within the last decade almost as familiar as Mr.

Hardy's Casterbridge and Overcombe and Egdon Heath have been since the previous decade. The dominant fact about the Five Towns is not that they are picturesque, though they are; it is not that they are provincial, though they are so much so as to constitute a sort of world within and behind the world. Rather, the dominant fact is simply that they manufacture pottery; that manufacturing pottery is what they exist for, and that without it they could not exist at all. The number of inhabitants, the lives they lead, the thoughts they think, the objects they see, the hopes they cherish—all are colored and controlled and, before that, even brought into existence by one elemental and inhuman fact: that the whole region consists of a peculiar kind of clayey soil.

Observe the homely directness, the species of inevitability, in the fact. "Civilized man cannot live without cooks," as "Owen Meredith" said to fill out a rhyme of long ago; cooking cannot do without crockery; and crockery cannot be without clay. That, in a nutshell, is the economic history of the Five Towns. They exist in order to put clay, shaped and baked in a certain fashion, on the tables of the United Kingdom. Thousands of houses and tens of thousands of lives have no other reason for being than that England may dine off a certain kind of plates. You cannot call it exactly a cruel fact. It is true that crockery produces many thousands of lives that we may regard as sordid; but it is also true that it sustains many thousands of lives that might otherwise perish, or never exist at all. Not a cruel fact—but too stupendous and far-reaching to be either cruel or kind. It is a finality, a thing that is simply *so* and no more to be said about it.

The Five Towns present in a staggeringly simple way the whole riddle of industrialism. It is deplorable and indispensable; you cannot get along without it, and you cannot endure the results of it. If the industry were less homely, like the manufacture of silks, or if it were more primitive, like the cultivation of the soil, the case would gain something in dignity and lose something in force. As it is, the case stands midway between the luxuries and the necessities. Crockery is necessary enough to call the whole county into existence without a direct affront to the reason; it is luxurious enough to cause one some disturbance when it defaces the whole county. And it is totally and irrevocably lacking in human dignity. The whole affair is pathetically ludicrous and grimly droll. It is not futile, like the making of trinkets; it is not physiologically ghastly, like the mining of coal. Nothing about it is either tragic or splendid. It is merely dull, in a large complacent way.

Nothing but crockery could have served the purpose half so well. It raises the whole unified problem of industrial organization without any of the special issues, such as unsanitary conditions, extreme poverty, exploitation of one class at the will of another, or actual danger to life and health. The only question one asks is, Can it all be worth while? And that is a question, as Mr. Bennett means it to be, without an answer. This spectacle of industrialism is simply part, a focal part, of the larger spectacle called modern life; and the question insists on translating itself into, Is modern life worth living?

From such great blocks and lumps of reality Mr. Bennett fashions the frame and a good deal of the substance of his typical books. He treats the Five Towns with a prolonged and tremendous series of appeals to the physical senses; he conveys subtly an impression of their effect on the masses of people who dwell in them, and of their importance to other masses of people throughout England. How familiar the author is with his material, even the most trifling details that go to make up his atmosphere, only he can prove. Literature has probably never known a more exhaustive degree of "saturation" with one kind of data, or a more consistent example of "hugging the shore of the real."

III

It is this extraordinary profusion of local color that gives rise to the most frequent adverse criticism of Mr. Bennett: that he is merely the note-book realist, a collector of data and not a composer, an instance of the clever journalist turned writer of novels. Applied at its face value, the term "journalist" means less than nothing, for Mr. Bennett's treatment of detail is of the kind with which journalism has least to do. However, the critics who call Mr. Bennett a deified newspaper reporter do presumably mean something. They mean that his work is overburdened with a sort of detail any one can amass, granted only a pair of eyes and no end of patience. They mean that he makes wealth and authenticity of detail ends in themselves.

Now, one must make a virtue of admitting that there is a danger in this kind of facility—the danger that the novelist will fall a victim to his own skill, exploit his chosen scene, for its picturesqueness or its hold on the public fancy, after he has ceased to have anything to put into it, mistake his material for his subject as Mr. Phillpotts has done, and lose his meaning in the noise of his machinery. *Clayhanger*, one of the four really momentous books, does become somewhat muddy with minutiæ; the design is clogged, and one cannot see the city for the buildings. But even here, where illustration is most profuse, profusion is far from being an end in itself. Things in themselves cannot make up a criticism of life—and Mr. Bennett's novels are just that. They are an adverse criticism of the overwhelming importance conceded by modern life to material things. Thus the critics who charge Mr. Bennett with having merely photographed his scenes for the sake of the scenery are identifying him with precisely the fallacy which he is trying to expose in the modern world.

The real significance of the scene in such books as *Clayhanger* is its causal connection with the characters. That atmosphere of ovens and chimneys, of smoke by day and ruddy glare by night, of mud and packing-straw, of habits decreed and regulated by the laboring schedule, is omnipresent; and it creates the personæ after its kind. It is woven intimately into the texture of their personalities. They bear the stamp of the conditions among which they grew, as Hardy's reddleman bears in the very pores of his skin the ruddy complexion of his trade. Such types are unthinkable, as Mr. Bennett hints, in a region of agriculture. There is no more consistent embodiment in the novel of the doctrine that people derive their temperaments, their outlook, their whole tone, from the source of their livelihood.

If we look for sharply specific illustration, we shall find it in Sophia Baines of *The Old Wives' Tale*, the special poignancy of her case being that, while she escapes the Five Towns physically, their influence continues to follow and dominate her. One may say, if one likes, that it is her character, a thing that transcends locality and environment, that keeps her out of the arms of Chirac, when she is lonely, and lovely, and young, and hungering for sympathy. But what is it that keeps her out of the theaters of Paris? She spends a quarter of a century there, survives her first petty troubles about money, becomes the mistress of a flourishing *pension:* yet never once does she see the inside of a French theater. That small detail in the presentation of Sophia needs her whole youth in the Five Towns to explain it. None of the smudge of factory chimneys touched her soul, which died as it had lived, resplendent, proud, indomitable; but the surface of her temperament, all the habituated part of her life, was glazed with the soot of those same factory chimneys, even after she had half forgotten their existence. She and her sister, two women of utterly unlike and opposed personalities, are yet alike in that, as one critic has put it, they "quietly and proudly starved in their respectability rather than touch a morsel of forbidden food." That undeviating respectability is the Five Towns in them. It preserves them from the irresponsible gratifications; it also denies them the innocent spontaneous enjoyments. They never shake off the commercial distrust of "culture"; the sacred rite of changing window curtains fortnightly will always mean more to them than any romantic possibility of escape. They work ploddingly all their lives, and when they are old women they are not even able to take a vacation or find ordinary comfort in a few days of doing nothing. The Five Towns made them; and they belong to the Five Towns to the end. Atmosphere, if it had nothing else to justify it, would achieve a sufficient importance by its translation thus into terms of personality.

And when Mr. Bennett deals with the Five Towns historically, as he often does, he is still dealing with people. As he traces the manufactures from the era of private and random enterprise down to the period of corporate monopoly, he is really tracing the different products of two generations of men, and hence the differences in the men themselves. Not the spectacle of industrialism alone, then, is the object of his interest and the source of his material, but the definable results of that spectacle on individual and collective life. If his people seem more and more smothered and muffled in things, that is how the author wishes them to seem. He is trying to show character with all the material wrappings round it. On one hand the conditions, on the other hand the human results of the conditions—the conditions illuminate the people, and the two merge and fuse. The folk are almost a translation into compendious form of their environment and history; and in that fact alone is enough justification of the Five Towns novels as pieces of "art." The author has chosen to take people among the massed conditions where souls remain most solitary; and, having taken them, he shows what it is that makes them solitary.

IV

Of course the insistence on things primarily, or even on people as fashioned into a certain mold by things, would result in a whole community of characters indistinguishably alike. Equally of course, individual variation is the core of the social novel. It is the core of Mr. Bennett's novels too; to note this is merely to reaffirm that he is an artist after all, rather than a sociologist.

It is to be regretted, however easily it may be explained, that a large part of what has been written about him has tried to portray him as scientist and thinker rather than as novelist. For example, a controversy rich in points of view, as well as in witty and tart rejoinders, rages about his work in a literary journal, with half-truths uncounted supplanting one another in the center of the stage and each contender insisting that *his* discovered half-truth is ultimate truth. One writer equips Mr. Bennett with a "working philosophy" of responsibility, of tested conventions; a second insists that his philosophy is merely a naturalistic conception of the ultimate futility of human life; a third glorifies him because he has no philosophy at all. Some of the disputants try to deduce his general ideas from his non-fictional books, his criticisms or " pocket philosophies "; their opponents hotly retort that the novels do not practise what these other works preach. In the end a fourth critic rises to point out that after all Mr. Bennett is not the realist he has been called, but an ironist, delicately satirizing his puppets as he exhibits them " in the homely straits of human character and experience."

Of these points of view, the last and most literary seems to us to come nearest the truth—the others falling short of it just in so far as they are non-literary. Mr. Bennett does have an ironic sense of man's littleness, the transient and parenthetical quality of the individual life; we have already heard him defining life as " a moment of captivity between vast freedoms." There is irony in his using all our modern industrial apparatus, the machinery, as we flatter ourselves, of our solidarity and brotherhood, to wall human souls apart from each other, even to make it impossible for the soul to know itself. The celebrated flippancy of his style is a further confirmation of this ironic cast of his mind. His verbal manner definitely repels some readers, who find it unconscionably " smart." His flippancy toward some of his characters is like that of a professional guide hired to conduct a party through scenes of interest and amusing himself the while by poking fun at the ignorance and provincial oddity of the sightseers whose shillings he has accepted. There is no missing Arnold Bennett's vivid and consistent appreciation of how life tricks and cheats the individual. He leaves his people pathetically little human dignity, if dignity depends on self-knowledge and rational hopes. Whatever his people get out of life, they do not get what they are looking for. They remain cooped up in the narrow compartments of their own being, imprisoned by the irony of life in the little cages of materialism and stupidity in which they were born. Almost nothing about them is inspiring; no one of them tempts the reader to envy. One doesn't, in the nature of things, envy the exposed victim of irony.

But even this generalization of Mr. Bennett's attitude as essentially ironic does not take us far enough to do justice to our author. To see how far it falls short, one has only to reflect that irony applied to the whole of life is necessarily disheartening, whereas the general effect of Mr. Bennett's novels is decidedly not so. His work leaves one with an obstinate and perhaps irrational sense that life is worth living even if it does not give what we ask of it, and that our efforts mean something even if we do not know what. The details are tinged with an ironic hopelessness, yet the whole is a message of hope. The author is always seeming to say that nothing very much matters—and we are always refusing to believe him. What is this fundamental paradox that is so often overlooked? Mr. Bennett's theory of the world does not account for the sympathetic and humanistic tone of his presentation of life; neither does his own temperament as reflected in his style. What then does account for it?

The secret is almost too simple to have got itself officially talked about. It lies in the individual character's own consciousness, his way of facing and accepting life. Life is not what our reason tells us as we impersonally survey life: it is simply what it seems to us as we personally live. Each of us creates his universe in his own fashion. We do not have to succeed in order to find living worth while; we have only to hope. One can be happy without being at all important to anything, so long as one feels important to one's self. We constantly hear such lives as Constance Baines's called dull. But it is not dull to Constance. No life is dull as regarded from within; no person sincerely calls himself dull. All the stupidity of stupid folk is in what we perceive about them; the Chinese are not "foreigners" to themselves. Plebeian imaginations are fired with the romance of simple enterprises, patrician imaginations with that of great and complex enterprises. Mr. Bennett's characters, plebeians most of them, live always on the edge of the unutterable. They have the expectation of coming suddenly the next moment on the sack of gold that is always just round the corner. The universe may be making fools of them, they may be making fools of themselves, but they are sublimely unaware of it, and they refuse to feel foolish—as all of us refuse.

For example, a quarreling husband and wife are fools to every outsider in creation—and when the wife gets her own way, the husband is more of a fool than ever. Yet Mr. Bennett makes the quarrels of Clayhanger and Hilda in *These Twain* so inevitable and so deadly serious that the reader knows just how certainly *he* would quarrel with Hilda if he were in Edwin's place, or with Edwin if he were in Hilda's place. At the end of the first volume of the trilogy the reader may see Clayhanger as a timid young man who has wasted his life and his chance, and who is about to consummate the general dinginess of his career by marrying a disappointed and desolated woman; but Clayhanger, we are told, "braced himself to the exquisite burden of life." The circumstances were unheroic enough; but Clayhanger set that all right by being a hero. Printing may be a dismal trade, but to him it was a fine art. His relatives might be stupid folk with a little too much prying and tyrannous curiosity in their make-up, but he shields Hilda from their interference as though he were saving a Christian maiden from the jaws of wild beasts in the Coliseum. In short, he and the other folk live the romance which is of the attitude, let the actualites be what they may. Mr. Bennett, whose vision is most acute where we have seen that Gissing's was most blurred, proves that life is always threatening to become a glorious affair, just because every one who really lives is always tremulous with hopes.

Such is the duality of Mr. Bennett's world. It is an ironic duality, because its emphasis is on the failure of life to gratify our desires or live up to our idea of it. But the irony is rendered heartening by the insistence on man's own incurable illogicality. Hardy shows us a world in which it is insane to hope for anything, because all hope is doomed to disappointment. Arnold Bennett shows us a world in which it is insane not to hope for everything, because hope is the nature of man, one of the conditions of existence. The very fact that life does not give us the substance of our desire proves that the desire alone sustains us. Hardy demonstrates the logic of despair. Arnold Bennett begins and ends with the fact that man is not a logical animal. Where a novelist like Gissing falsifies life by assuming that all poor people feel as poor as they seem to a rich man, Mr. Bennett interprets life as a state in which the thing that may happen is immeasurably more important than the thing that does happen, and in which no man is poorer than he seems to himself. He does not give his characters his own notions about life, he gives them life itself. Which is one reason why they are pretty nearly as real to us as we are to ourselves.

V

If a novelist is to do anything really noteworthy toward conveying this sense of how each of us beautifies his own world by filling it imaginatively with the substance of things hoped for, that novelist must be a master of individual points of view. Most novels exhaust the point of view of a single character and no more, viewing others for the sake of their bearing on that one. We know how Thwackum and Square seem to Tom Jones, but we never know how they seem to Thwackum and Square. If Tom Jones had had a more penetrating insight—if he had had, say, the wit and imagination of any of the characters through whom Henry James reproduced his material—he might have perceived, not only the ridiculous creatures that Thwackum and Square objectively were, but also the importance of each in his own eyes. He might have understood that their pedantic and arid lives meant as much to them as the surging of his hot young blood meant to him.

Now, it seems to us that Mr. Arnold Bennett is the first writer in English to reveal almost all his characters, without ulterior purpose or motive, *as they seem to themselves.* There is no conflict between this ideal and what we have already described as Henry James's ideal, exhaustion of the single point of view. It makes no difference to our present point whether the characters are revealed through the superior insight of one of themselves, or through that of the author. Either way is remote enough from the common system of submerging the lives of all but the most important characters. This latter practice has resulted oftentimes in a feeling that the lesser folk could have had no existence at all except for the sake of the story. When they dropped out of sight, they dropped out of reality. But the minor folk of Mr. Bennett give us vividly the feeling that every one of them has his own story, and that his story, if told, would have the glowing vitality of the story that is actually being told. Even where his people are farthest from understanding each other, the reader is near to understanding them all equally. Like Henry James, Mr. Bennett feels himself driven most urgently, whatever his other motives, by untiring curiosity. It is, to be sure, a curiosity sometimes more impudent than urbane; but we can forgive the tone for the sake of the results. In the objects of his curiosity, the number and range of the points of view which he undertakes to comprehend all at once, Mr. Bennett resembles no one but himself.

Of the four novels that permanently matter, the three which go together as a trilogy are prolonged studies of contrasted points of view applied to the same set of facts. *Clayhanger* is the biography of Edwin Clayhanger, a printer's son of the Five Towns, from young boyhood to the edge of middle life; *Hilda Lessways* is the biography of Hilda through approximately the same period. Hilda enters the pages of *Clayhanger* for a strange and breathless interval—just long enough to win the heart of the young printer and fill his head with flushed and romantic dreams and, as it appears, to return his love. Then, without explanation or even an adequate farewell, she drops out of his existence. Saddened and puzzled, Clayhanger goes on with the humdrum of his printer's life, disappointed in his ambition to become an architect, and thoroughly mystified by the whole episode of Hilda. All he learns for many years is that the woman who had promised to marry him almost immediately thereafter married some one else.

In *Clayhanger* she is unexplained and apparently inexplicable. But in *Hilda Lessways* the author supplies the chain of circumstances which dragged her away from the fulfilment of her promise and bound her to a different destiny. He not only explains, he justifies and ennobles her. This time it is Clayhanger who enters for a breathless interval, presently to drop out of sight unexplained and but half understood. The readers who insist that the two characters are not the same from book to book are, of course, exactly right. In the first book, Hilda is the woman whom Clayhanger sees and thinks he knows; in the second, she is that woman as she knows herself. The Clayhanger of the first book is self-understood; he of the second book is the different person whom Hilda Lessways never knew quite so well as she supposed. To illuminate this discrepancy, we have only to recall how persons change with the growth of our knowledge of them, until we can hardly think back to how they seemed on first acquaintance.

The scheme of these first volumes of the trilogy is rounded out by the third volume, *These Twain*, in which the two previous points of view are combined and superposed. It is the story of Hilda and Edwin during the years of adjustment of their married life. One must say of this book that it is marred by the greatest excess of Mr. Bennett's glibness and flippancy. For several years now we have watched him turn composition into an industry, frankly interspersing his works that count with potboilers of a gifted and facile sort—such books as *Buried Alive*, *Helen With the High Hand*, *A Great Man*, *The Lion's Share;* all of them skilful and diverting, good for an afternoon's lark, well worth doing if their author could do nothing better. We have watched the process, and wondered when the signs would emerge in the pages which Mr. Bennett intended for his best. *Clayhanger* showed no sign; *Hilda Lessways* escaped the taint. Could it be possible indefinitely, we wondered, for a serious worker and an irresponsible worker to inhabit the same body, use the same pen, yet remain, in the words of one critic, "distinct and non-communicating beings"? In *These Twain* we have our answer. Says one observer: "As for *These Twain*, I confess that it seems to me a lame rather than a triumphant conclusion of the matter. I think I find the trail of the serpent here—or, let us say, the Dead Sea fruits of that brilliant incontinence to which, since the appearance of *Hilda Lessways*, in 1911, Mr. Bennett has so frankly yielded himself. Here is not a little of the inconsequent cleverness, of the pursuit of the comic fillip, of the voluptuous cuddling of paradox, which have vulgarized British letters for two decades."

And this is just. Yet it is certainly true that whatever value *These Twain* possesses, it possesses because it is a full and merciless revelation of the pettiest things in marriage; and it is the superposition of the two individual points of view which makes that revelation possible. The wonder is that Mr. Bennett had nothing more or better to reveal. The generally disappointing stuffiness of Clayhanger as he enters middle age, the entire illogicality and unscrupulousness of Hilda, who will use any methods to get her own way, resort to any argument, and justify herself on the ground that whatever she does she means for the good of her husband—this sort of vivisection is the easiest possible task for so facile a pen. The result may be an inimitably close transcription and interpretation of the average well-to-do marriage; and we could be content to take our reward in such terms if there were only something to justify our previous confidence that Hilda and Edwin were rather better than average persons.

VI

There are several reasons for the preëminence of the remaining book, chronologically the first of the four. Unlike *Clayhanger*, it is not overloaded with details that do not bear directly and visibly on the unfolding of story and characters. Unlike the trilogy, it presents a wide range of personality. And in events it runs the whole gamut of human affairs. It omits not one of the fundamental sources of comedy and tragedy that make up our living world. Every momentous happening that can befall man or woman from the cradle to the patriarch's grave is here set down. Yet the action is never hurried or crowded; the people never behave as if they had just stepped into a story or come to keep an appointment with the photographer. The background is one of honest, regular, and plodding work. You regard a workaday world, and regard it long enough so that everything that can happen does happen. There is a good deal of justification for the verdict of one critic, rendered before it was quite fashionable to praise *The Old Wives' Tale*, that in his opinion the book will be read fifty and a hundred years hence as Dickens is read now.

But what we wish especially to emphasize is that part of this preëminence is the result of the two main points of view combined in the one story, on a scale larger than that of *These Twain*, and with a far finer seriousness. What *Clayhanger* and *Hilda Lessways* achieve when taken together, that and more *The Old Wives' Tale* achieves by itself. The story is that of two sisters, Constance and Sophia Baines, daughters of a respectable old-school linen draper of the Five Towns. Constance, the steady-going, solidly dependable, slightly "dumpy" sister, lives the placid yet somehow exciting life of a housewife and mother in the scene, even in the very house, of her birth. Sophia, petted and pettish and a little spoiled, develops brilliant initiative and a contempt for the stuffiness of Bursley. She marries in haste; her husband, a worthless scamp, deserts her in France. She does not see him again until, a woman far on in years, she stands by the bed where he has died in miserable squalor. Meantime she has learned a deal about life. She has fought a bitter fight for bare self-preservation, against the rapacious Paris of the 1870 siege and after; she has succeeded, not in the way of her girlish dreams, but in the average human way; and after thirty years she has gone back to Bursley and to her sister, who is now a widow. And the two finish out their lives together.

In a superficial view, Sophia is the one who lives, Constance the one who vegetates. But what Mr. Bennett makes clear beyond mistaking is that *both* live, and that those two different careers are equally triumphs of fortitude, of womanly courage, and—yes, even of imagination. Constance, wondering whether she shall wear her best or her second best to honor the return of the sister whom she has not seen for more than a quarter of a century, and pathetically undecided between the tram and the train, is as momentous a figure as Sophia caught in the Paris of 1870 and earning her little fortune while others starve. She is as momentous because she is as fully and as faithfully revealed. To us her life may seem gray; but to her it is scarlet.

We are made to understand every one of the characters nearly as well as we understand these two. Gerald Scales, the rascal who marries Sophia, is after all more a weakling than a villain; he is even a pathetic and persecuted weakling, with an opinion that life has not been quite fair with him. Daniel Povey, who killed his wife, was a murderer by the law of the land—but very few men would have done differently. Chirac, with his naïve Continental code, his complete lack of moral sense and his pagan goodness, is at once fantastic and likable. The son who steals from his father's till is never understood by that father; but we understand him, and do not have to wait until we have forgotten the theft before we forgive it. There is even an amazing attempt to admit us to the mysterious and innocent mind of a ten months' baby.

Not only are we made to understand the characters: in rare moments, or after unusual accumulations of experience, it is given them to reach something like understanding of each other. The understanding does not always come in time to make broken lives whole, or to heal wounds of misunderstanding; but it does sometimes come, as earlier in *The Glimpse*. Constance enters into the fullest comprehension of her own mother's grim and silent character, long after that mother's death, when Constance herself has to bear a loss that cuts off half her domestic world. Sophia, looking down on the emaciated body of Gerald Scales, whom she had last seen young and proud and pitifully sure of himself, has part of the answer to the tragic riddle of youth and age. Constance and Sophia, reunited after thirty years, find themselves infinitely closer now by understanding than once they had been by blood. As girls they had quarreled pettily; as aged women, coming together from widely sundered lives, taught by suffering and loss, they are strangely though not sentimentally near each other.

It is this aspect of *The Old Wives' Tale* that expresses the point of last importance in Mr. Bennett's philosophy of life: his insistence on experience as the only teacher of the meaning of life. Other matters have a high critical importance, which we mean not to belittle. But one may push them aside in order to reëmphasize finally this note, the comprehension of life through the experience of it. Dissonant personalities, like those of Constance and Sophia, can come together at the end, however different their lives; they can come together because each has learned what life is. And the last and crowning experience is the mysterious discovery that somehow life has meant the same thing to both, that it means the same thing to everybody. They have separately learned, even if they cannot define, the meaning of existence. That is the whole story. We all do learn what life means, if we live it honestly, without shirking. That is the whole meaning of the story. It is everywhere the best meaning of Arnold Bennett. He is often made the target of adverse criticism, some of it closely and justly reasoned; but not the most malevolent of his critics can justly refuse him one word of praise. He does sanction and fortify the natural human passion for believing that life can somehow, behind all the miseries and the mysteries, mean something profoundly worth while.

The Beauty of Order and the Beauty of Freedom

H. G. WELLS

JOHN GALSWORTHY

IX

H. G. WELLS

I

WHAT all of us most admire in Mr. H. G. Wells, both those who oppose and those who applaud, is of course the unmatched versatile intensity which he has always applied, and still applies, to the process of being himself. Hardly ever, if at all, have we encountered in fiction so pronounced an example of the author frankly identifying himself with the thing written, using the thing written overtly for self-revelation and self-transmission, making himself as a whole the message. The novelist usually presents himself to us under masks and disguises. He expresses himself here a little and there a little, by implication and innuendo, after some elaborate pretenses of denying his own existence. The artist's impersonality takes at its extreme, as in Shakspere, the form of withholding from us entirely the artist as a person, and giving him to us only as a will, through the triumph or certain qualities or attributes, and the emotions evoked in us thereby. Mr. Wells, on the other hand, has no artist's impersonality at all. His impersonality is of the thinker only; and he gives himself over to us precisely as our friends do in frank and frequent intercourse. The disguises which other workers in fiction interpose between the public and their private selves exist in his work just sufficiently to turn his mental history into a story—so that the slightly uncharitable reader may wonder why he bothered with the disguise at all.

The answer to that possible question seems to be that Mr. Wells, being essentially a polemical and propagandist writer, inflamed by the sense of having a large burden of truth to acquit himself of, feels the need of the largest possible number of hearers, and chooses to exert his unquestioned gifts as a teller of tales in order to make his kind of truth the more palatable. We leave aside for the moment the problem of whether he does not make it so palatable with romance that readers refuse to take it seriously as gospel: the present point being simply that he uses fiction as a teaching agent, and that to do so is an inevitable consequence of his flaming personal sincerity.

The second consequence of it is a queer sort of continuity—queer because it has almost nothing to do with consistency as ordinarily conceived. However much of the charlatan there may be in him, there is very little of the dilettante. The proportions of romance and of realism in his work may constantly shift; he may find his interest now in the future, now in the past, now in passionate first love, again in some terrible mechanical engine of destruction, presently in a new gospel of good-will;—but his general meaning is always the same. In the course of ten years he may altogether renounce his view of science, of the importance of individual revolt, of war, of religion, of half a dozen other components of life; but he never even revises his general view of life itself, as something which has got somehow to be changed. He is several novelists successively, but always the same man. Telling stories as unlike each other as *The War of the Worlds* and *Marriage*, he tells them, for exactly the same purpose, a corrective purpose. And this continuity that runs through all his work is everywhere so insistent that we wonder how he can have registered so many changes with so little change.

When we speak of Mr. Wells as being always concerned with expressing himself, his own sum-total of experiences and aspirations, we are very far from wishing to belittle him by comparison with the impersonal novelist who tries to be everybody in turn. If Mr. Wells chooses to stick to himself, as he incorrigibly does, even his enemies must admit that he has a wonderful and enchanting self to stick to, and that companionship with his own mind must very greatly resemble commerce with a multitude. For, next to our first fact of his intensity and continuity, the uppermost claim of his work is its multitudinousness. His mind is such a compound of contradiction and paradox, of logic and illogicality, that he quite escapes the monotony and reiteration of the propagandist to whom life is an affair of a simple formula or two. Just at the instant when one is prepared to utter a final and crushing objection to some one of Mr. Wells's ideas or interests, one finds that Mr. Wells himself has uttered a final and crushing objection to it.

No art so completely didactic as his has ever achieved so complete an escape from the usual indictments against didacticism in art. For example, he usually exhibits a certain testiness against the slavery of sex-passion: yet several of his most commanding men are obsessed through many years with a particular passion, and the author does something like justice to the haunting and mournful beauty of such desire. Another object of impatience for Mr. Wells is the general stodginess and stuffiness of what he calls Victorianism: yet every Victorian childhood recorded in his books is seen through a glowing mist of romance, the romance with which each of us invests his past. In a word, Mr. Wells has so just a perception of the half-truth in everything that the mind registers, that we have to look twice before we can be sure of having disinterred what he means for truth. When one turns back to the closing chapter of *The New Machiavelli,* prepared to contest Remington's desertion of his wife for his mistress and of his public position for obscurity, one finds all of one's objections to his course stated by Remington's friend Britten in that very chapter, and on the whole much more cogently than one knows how to state them.

In short, Mr. Wells has the grace—partly intellect, partly a sense of humor—to see that very few things are ultimately and always true or right, and to subject even his most ardent convictions to the test of renewed and challenging experience. He does not criticise life by a set formula: therefore, it is futile to try to summarize *him* in a formula. Criticism of

Mr. Wells always finds itself anticipated by Mr. Wells himself; he is as baffling to the critic, through his variousness, as life is to him, through *its* variousness; and, like life, he is always shifting his attack, changing his plan of battle, now beating down opposition frontally, now outflanking it.

If we look for the center in which his various ideas and convictions most coalesce, we shall find it in his peculiar species of hard modernity. We were just about to cite him as an example of the "tough-minded" man, in William James's phrase, when we found him quoting, on the title-page of *The New Machiavelli*, our very sentence from *Pragmatism*. "It suffices for our immediate purpose that tender-minded and tough-minded people . . . do both exist." It is quite clear that Mr. Wells is ultra-modern in his tough-mindedness; and he gives the fact a considerable poignancy by his frequent and contemptuous exposure of tender-mindedness—with him, almost a synonym of Victorianism. But there is nothing specially heroic in that, since we are all tolerably inexorable with what we regard as the illusions of other folk. The great value of Mr. Wells's toughness of mind is the merciless rigor with which he applies it to his own illusions.

For nothing is clearer about him than this: that, with all his toughness of intellect, he has an unusual sensitiveness of temperament, and even (shocking as the fact must be to him) a capacity for sentimentalism. The result of this contradiction is that he is always scourging himself, preaching to himself a hard gospel of discipline and austerity, demanding of himself sacrifices to truth. He reveals in one episode after another the beauty of pain when pain helps to self-knowledge; he even preaches the duty to do the wrong thing—that is, the conventionally wrong thing—when the right thing is only a safe, timid, and unthinking submission. However unsparing his tough-mindedness may be in exposure of others, it is always most ruthless in self-exposure. There is a perverse quality in his personal revolt that always draws him toward pain, a kind of Nemesis of the personal conscience that makes him take the way of greatest hardship. He finds duty in infidelity, in betrayal, in dishonesty—that is, in the appearances that we call by these harsh names. "Directly a crust forms on things," Margaret says to Remington in her last recorded letter, "you are restless to break down to the fire again." And she describes him as one who goes "deliberately out of all the decent fine things of life to run dangers and be singed and tormented and destroyed."

This is the peculiar mettle of Wells's modernity. It is an instinct for the truth that can be had only through sacrifice of safe things, the tried conventions; only through adventures and wounds. The ascetic and the voluptuary struggle together, and the ascetic always conquers. "Break me, O God," is Wells's characteristic prayer, "disgrace me, destroy me as you will, but save me from self-complacency and little interests and little successes and the life that passes like the shadow of a dream."

II

This, it will be seen, is nothing if not a modern spirit: and this ruling spirit is equaled in modernity by Mr. Wells's materials and methods. It is to be presumed that his contemporaneity needs little emphasis. His work is a concrete embodiment of much that the age had long darkly intimated. The man himself is so unequivocally of the present that he seems almost of the future; his work is so strikingly a fulfilment that it has the ring of a prophecy. Every one will have noticed the rapidity of his composition, the appearance in it of references to political events or social movements that are in process even while he is writing, his leaps from one intellectual position to another still more advanced, his impatient discarding of one interest for another. Not, perhaps, since Defoe have we seen a large body of serious production that bears so impressively, even while it is being brought forth, the stamp of the *new*. Quite clearly Mr. Wells is a person with whom we shall never catch up. No sooner do we think we have overtaken him than we discover that he is up and off again, leagues away, swift and unattainable as ever. He restores something of the original derivative meaning of the word "novel": his novels are almost literally *news*, as journalism is. Where other writers make literary capital of the sociology of the day before yesterday, Mr. Wells invents the sociology of the day after to-morrow.

The spectacle he presents is that of a tireless, impatient, and inexhaustible energy, such as that of Benvenuto Cellini. He gives us the latest thing in flying-machines, in destroyers; he ridicules the latest thing in fads. And he is master of all the involutions of our machine-ridden political life, of our commercial life since the advent of the big "combine," and of the era since the conspicuous interlocking of politics and commerce. An insignificant detail in illustration is his literal reproduction, in text and sketch, of the advertising matter which was used to boom the patent medicine called "Tono-Bungay." In all this there is perhaps a large element of charlatanry; but it is charlatanry of the most brilliant sort, irresistible and infectious through pure impudence. Mr. Wells is so much the child of his age in the purely material sense that he seems to anticipate the next age. His face is the face of the Future.

The reason why the operation of Mr. Wells's mind gives us so strongly this effect of prescience is that he has really a forward-looking mind. We are not thinking now primarily of his prophetic romances, his Utopias of society and of science. For even when he writes about literal realities of the moment, he is always most interested in the problem of what they are to lead to. Readers of *The Future in America* will recall their first feeling of vague disappointment at the author's failure to prophesy. That book is simply a literal description of our vastness, our ramifying complexity, as Mr. Wells saw it in 1906. But it is far from being an exhibition of immense material achievements for their own sake, a panegyric of "Bigness": under all the exhibition is the question as to the worth, the direction, the destination of the spectacle, so that we understand the title as *The Future in America?* This forward-looking habit is so vividly a part of Mr. Wells's equipment that we can think of no large display of the material reality of civilization in all his pages that is not accompanied by the note of interrogation, of wonder. Ponderevo, driving his newly conceived destroyer down the Thames on her trial and seeing England drift by him as a pageant, sounds that note again and again. "Light after light goes down. England and the Kingdom, Britain and the Empire, the old prides and the old devotions, glide abeam, astern, sink down upon the horizon, pass—pass. . . . We are all things that make and pass, striving upon a hidden mission, out to the open sea."

It is this blend of extremely modern material achievements with the extremely modern questioning and doubting mood that results in Mr. Wells's principal characters, the central men of his books. Granted the few necessary alterations in detail, these are almost indistinguishably alike. They are real enough as persons, for Mr. Wells incessantly pours his own reality into them, making each a replica of part of his own moral history. But their reality as individuals is as nothing to their composite reality as a group—which is their identity with their maker. Anything that he has felt as important, he puts into them. For example, his own scientific education is utilized in the manufacture of such men as Ponderevo in *Tono-Bungay* and Trafford in *Marriage;* his own pursuit of statecraft and sociology is repeated through Remington in *The New Machiavelli* and Stratton in *The Pas-*

sionate Friends. Mr. Wells makes all these except Trafford write their own history, in the first person singular.

Incidentally, the style in which they do it is the style of Mr. Wells, the style he has made us familiar with in books which are not novels at all. He gives his men in each case a utilitarian reason for pouring themselves out; a reason that is always something more than the artist's itch for self-communication. For example, Stratton writes his life that his son may presently read it and use its warnings in his own career. And not only does the author provide his men with his own didactic sense: he conveys into them his own impatience with the conventional limitations of the novel. Ponderevo, beginning his record, says: " . . . most of whatever artist there is in me has been given to turbine machines and boat-building and the problem of flying, and do what I will I fail to see how I can be other than a lax, undisciplined story-teller. I must sprawl and flounder, comment and theorize, if I am to get the thing out I have in mind." As a matter of fact, Mr. Wells has an expert proficiency in the technique of story-telling; but since it does not comport with his simpler purpose of writing out what is in him he throws it uncompromisingly overboard.

For a variety of such reasons as these, we may assume the practical identity of Mr. Wells's chief persons with Mr. Wells's own personality and views. And, to state the importance of this fullness and directness of self-surrender, we have only to reaffirm the multiplex and versatile modernity of Mr. Wells's own mind.

His mind has been the battle-ground of some of the most important conflicts of our age, a laboratory for the working out of countless social experiments which must still look to the future for their conclusion. There is probably no man living who could express so large a part of what is newest in the world, by the simple process of expressing himself. We do not raise yet the problem of whether the novel is the proper place to express what is newest in the age, or the other problem of whether Mr. Wells's expression of it is adequate as fiction. But at least all of us must concede that fiction, unless it is more and more to become the property of the æsthetic few and lose gradually its leverage as criticism of modern life, must draw more and more of its substance and its appeal from the spiritual history of such representative individuals as Mr. Wells. It is very difficult to discuss the "art" of a writer who pretends to none, and whose importance is simply that he has shown us with unfaltering courage and a passion for truth all the most significant things that are going on in the world of the present.

III

These generalizations about Mr. Wells's men characters leave out of account approximately the first ten years of his work in fiction, the ten years from 1895 to 1905. As we know, he filled those years with romances: prophecies of the future, in the vein of such works as Bulwer-Lytton's *The Coming Race*, Hudson's *Crystal Age*, and Bellamy's *Looking Backward;* imagined reconstructions of society in some Utopia out of the real world; or fantasies based on the development of machinery in application to traffic and domestic life—such tales as *The War in the Air, When the Sleeper Wakes, The First Men in the Moon,* and *The War of the Worlds.* In these the creation of character, if it were attempted at all, would be of negligible importance to the whole; and the realities of human nature as treated by Mr. Wells are naturally confined to his period of pseudo-realism, the period since 1905. But in all other respects the Wells of the mechanistic romances is the Wells already described. His passion for truth is the same, however fantastic its garb; his ruthless acceptance of unpleasant facts about the world receives the same emphasis; above all, the sociological purport of Mr. Wells's thinking is clear, even in those early extravaganzas. In short, Mr. Wells is the same tough-minded person. It is not necessary to give a detailed account of this first phase; but it is desirable to trace in it the first vestiges of the kind of truth on which presently Mr. Wells was to put all his stress.

Politically speaking, we can describe the central paradox of Mr. Wells as the twofold insistence on (1) a kind of modified Socialism,—the general diffusion of equality and well-being,—and on (2) an enlightened aristocracy, the most intense possible exertion of the high individual virtues of responsibility and courage. He cannot tolerate widespread misery or poverty among masses of people; and he cannot tolerate what in his view makes misery or poverty possible, the timidity and fatuous blindness of the governing classes.

Consequently, the more impassioned he becomes for the democratic equality, the more insistent he becomes on the aristocratic nobility—the nobility which the aristocratic class as constituted woefully lacks. The only possible triumph of democracy for Mr. Wells, then, is through the nonconformity and revolt of the individual aristocrat, the man who feels surging in his veins a contempt for littleness and personal safety, for class consciousness and the world's accepted injustices, for muddled purposes and blind appetites and power without imagination. Mr. Wells's uppermost desire is clean civilization, liberty, and equality; his agent, his hero, the *bona-fide* aristocrat, is the individual rebel. It is significant of the tenacity with which he holds these two ideals of the emancipated democrat and the inflamed aristocrat, that he gives them a sharp imaginary embodiment in just those early works where he comes nearest to telling the story for the story's sake.

When the Sleeper Wakes (1899) exemplifies these two ideals. It is the story of a modern young Englishman who falls into a cataleptic trance and, waking after two hundred years, finds himself owner of half the world, through the multiplication of his own fortune and the use of his name in many devious financial transactions. He opens his eyes on a world of new marvels, of life apparently revolutionized. But as he becomes acquainted with his knowledge and his power, he finds that everything is a logical extension of its prototype in his own Victorian world. The laboring class has become merely a race of machine-tenders. "In the young cities of Graham's former life, the newly aggregated laboring mass had been a diverse multitude, still stirred by the tradition of personal honor and a high morality; now it was differentiating into a distinct class, with a moral and physical difference of its own—even with a dialect of its own." A third of the population is reduced to economic slavery. The religion of the churches has become simply a matter of noisy "competition for attention"; the church advertisements read: "Salvation on the First Floor and turn to the Right"; "Put your money on your Maker"; "The Sharpest Conversion in London. Expert Operators! Look Slippy!" "Be a Christian —without hindrance to your present Occupation"; "All the Brightest Bishops on the Bench to-night and Prices as Usual"; "Brisk Blessings for Busy Business Men." Motherhood has become a question of scientific incubating; newspapers are supplanted by Babble-Machines that bawl into the public ear whatever those in power wish the public to believe; literature is supplanted by the phonograph and the motion picture; London is a mammoth hotel, and no longer a swarm of houses; all life is reduced to mechanical terms of the utmost efficiency.

But under the splendor of this machine-made life hundreds of laborers are toiling in grime, breathing powdered felspar, poisoning their blood and making their faces repulsive as they work over a certain purple enamel much affected in the decorations of the city, clubbed into submission when they break into song or when they seize their bread before their work is finished. It is to these people that Graham's heart goes out, for them that he wills to use his power. The autocratic Council, with its frank contempt of the lower orders, has been overthrown; the present governing power is vested in the demagogue Ostrog, who rules the people, as the saying is, "for their own good," making them fair promises and letting them believe they have self-government. Really, Ostrog thinks of the people as "swarming, yelping fools." "Suppose," he says, "they get the upper hand of us, what then? They will only fall to other masters. So long as there are sheep Nature will insist on beasts of prey." But Graham is not satisfied: what 19th century man would be satisfied two centuries hence, if he could live to see the logical outcome of the civilization he once proudly helped perpetuate and extend? In the upshot Graham gives his life to save the general mass of humanity from a fresh oppression by the governing class. He is one of the earliest examples in Wells's work of the perfect aristocrat doing sacrifice to the humanitarian ideal. It is not preposterous to rank the book as a whole with Swift's *Gulliver* and Samuel Butler's *Erewhon* as a satire upon the form of civilized institutions.

In *The War of the Worlds* (1898), a story of the subjugation of the human race by a visiting horde of Martians, Mr. Wells includes a panegyric of what is to him the all-important aristocratic virtue, courage—the courage of revolt, of desperate non-conformity; the personal courage that makes its possessor dare to put himself in an insignificant minority against man, almost against fate. To the monsters from Mars, human men and women are simply "edible ants," to be exterminated in the unsparing way of the biological war among species. But a few hardy human men and women survive, hide, conspire, and plan a revolt. Of these, the leading spirit is the old artilleryman—a plebeian, for Mr. Wells hardly ever finds the aristocratic virtues in the aristocrat—a plebeian, but fired with a vision and the courage of it. He rants against the timidity of the men who submit to be tamed and fattened for slaughter, who accept the life of the cage and make sport for their captors; and in so doing he is of course ranting against the general human servility that makes men surrender their initiative, give their lives and destinies into the hands of some governing power that has only itself to be responsible to.

The old artilleryman draws a graphic picture of the inert mass of mankind, and then he goes on: "Well, the Martians will just be a godsend to such as these. Nice roomy cages, fattening food, careful breeding, and no worry. After a week or so chasing about the fields and lands on empty stomachs, they'll come and be caught cheerful. They'll be quite glad after a bit. They'll wonder what people did before there were Martians to take care of them. . . . There's lots will take things as they are—fat and stupid; and lots will be worried by a sort of feeling that it's all wrong, and that they ought to be doing something. Now, whenever things are so that a lot of people feel they ought to be doing something, the weak, and those who go weak with a lot of complicated thinking, always make for a sort of do-nothing religion, very pious and superior, and submit to persecution and the will of the Lord. . . . It's energy in a gale of funk, and turned clean inside out. These cages will be full of psalms and hymns and piety." All of which is surely a vivid enough picture of man in the mass celebrating his own disinheritance, making, as is his wont, a religion of his impotence. It provokes the old artilleryman to contemptuous impatience. His way is to form a band—"able-bodied, clean-minded men," "able-bodied, clean-minded women," who shall learn the secrets of power and eventually overthrow the Martians with their own weapons. They must learn, they must store away books—"not novels and poetry swipes, but ideas, science books." In the end, man will be ready to make off with the aerial fighting-machines of the Martians, their deadly Heat-Rays turned against the aggressor —"*swish* comes the Heat-Ray, and, behold! man has come back to his own."

This insistence on man's mind as the culmination of all created things, and on the necessity of man's dignifying his position in the world by using his mind, is the basis of Wells's naturalism, his democracy, his sociology, and his humanitarianism. Man's failure to use his mind is, conversely, the one object of Wells's satire. It is this insistence on the value of science, the impersonal and self-forgetful use of mind, that more than anything else binds together the scattered parts of his extraordinarily versatile genius and the work of his two distinct periods. The old artilleryman with his vision of man coming back to his own through convictions and the courage of them, one of the earliest embodiments of Wells's doctrine, is an exact prototype of Benham, one of the most recent, facing the tiger in the jungle with the words: "I am Man. The Thought of the World."

IV

Benham's story, *The Research Magnificent,* Mr. Wells's formal attempt at the epic of the individual aristocrat, shows best the continuity of this writer's mind from the first or romantic phase to the second or realistic. William Porphyry Benham's "Research" is for the noble or, as he calls it, the Aristocratic life. It begins with an attempt to shake off the limitations of the selfish man; it ends in a quest. The quest is for a Noble Society; for, Benham discovers, "one cannot be noble, so to speak, in vacuo." But the emphasis of the book is all on the limitations. First Benham rids himself of physical fear, the "comfort in a crowd, in support and in a refuge"; he tears himself away from "pitiful temporary shelters." Then he sets himself to the task of overcoming desire and indulgence, which involves the attempt to free himself from sex. Jealousy draws him back into sex-slavery, and he declares war on jealousy. Finally he adds prejudice to the list of his enemies: and his death in a street riot is the final gesture of his openness of mind.

The trouble is that Benham, in the course of his self-emancipation, emancipates himself so thoroughly from life and the actual human world that his aristocracy has no more social significance than the piety of a hermit in the desert. In losing his weakness he also loses his contacts. But he is a direct and unequivocal version of the qualities that Mr. Wells, in his romances, had indirectly praised. He is a sublime fool who comes very near to being, as Mr. Wells points out, a great prophet, the prophet of individual nobility. Given a genius for the warm and ingratiating human appeal, he would be Mr. Wells's ideal of the Superman. As it is, he is one of the most fantastically unreal of Mr. Wells's creations; and the book as a whole is not so much a novel as a tract, a fluent and florid gesture of discontent. It is almost as though the author had turned back fifteen years, into the capricious world where he could make anything exist by a stroke of the pen; but *The Research Magnificent* is awkwardly hampered, as those earlier works are not, by the tyranny of the realistic method.

As a fact, it is in less extreme cases of revolt, where the emphasis is on society itself rather than on the social anarchist, that we find the realistic Wells at his best—in *Marriage* his study of the domestic life, in *Tono-Bungay* his study of the business life, and in *The New Machiavelli* his study of the political life. Here we have protest rather than panegyric—and it is Mr. Wells the protestant, the fighting man, who most captivates us. The protest is against society and in behalf of the exceptional individual—for without this double emphasis the author would not be himself. But the protest is something more than mere empty denunciation, the crying out of the individual because he is hurt. It may not be constructive, but at least it is somewhat patiently analytical.

Bluntly and inelegantly, the principal fact about Mr. Wells's typical men in these books is that they are forced out of their jobs. They are, as we know, men who have a special predilection for some definite achievement in science or in public life: they are such men as perform the intellectual work of the world, the creatively executive type. The stories make a large collective story in illustration of one theorem: that the constitution of society is such as to force the man of executive or creative energy out of the one thing he can do most serviceably, into something else—or into nothing at all. In *The New Machiavelli* the statesman just at the threshold of a great future is forced out of public life by a private entanglement; in *The Passionate Friends,* a similar entanglement produces much the same result. In *Marriage* the scientist of genius is snatched out of his laboratory and forced into trade by the need of money. In *Tono-Bungay* the designer of submarines and flying-machines is tempted into a peculiarly tawdry business life, his only possible escape from poverty. Always the individual is crowded and mastered by the pressure of conditions, the conditions produced by the collective will of society, and too thick for him to evade or resist. The trouble, according to Mr. Wells, is with the contradiction between man's nature and society's conventions and prohibitions. Man is so constituted that he needs above all else to work out what is in him: but society is so constituted that it will accept his gift only if he obeys a set of laws that have nothing to do with his serviceableness, and allows himself to be inhibited by every Pharisaical Thou-shalt-not of the unthinking majority.

This is the cruelty of the world as Mr. Wells sees the world. It wrecks a man's public usefulness because of something irrelevant in his private life—usually passion. The life of the character becomes a conflict between the need to give society his best work, his self-expression, and, perhaps, a passion which society refuses to countenance but which is nevertheless a condition of his usefulness. The issue, from the point of view of the character concerned, is fearfully simple. Society is saying to him: "You must sacrifice everything to giving us the best you are capable of." The immutable law of his own nature is saying to him: "You must be yourself at all costs." And, unless he is born lucky, there comes at length the situation where he knows that the second and, as he thinks, higher law clashes irreconcilably with the first and lower; his process of being himself makes him, in some respect that seems to him trivial, a person whom society will not countenance: and thus his potential greatness as a servant of society is wrecked by the demands of his selfhood. The ultimate indictment of society, then, is that it is a wastrel of its human products and of their unusual abilities. It cares more for its dead rules than for its living men.

This deplorable result Mr. Wells sees as the outcome, not at all of malevolence, but of "muddle." Like Mr. Bernard Shaw, he is always talking about the muddle-headedness of the British world. The purpose of life is lost in the war of parties, each with its "interest"; it gets itself achieved, if at all, "as a bye product of the war of individuals and classes." Remington, thinking in impersonal terms just before the hour of his fateful decision, sees most of all "the heated disorder of contemporary things." "Before mankind, in my vision that night, stretched new centuries of confusion, vast stupid wars, hastily conceived laws, foolish temporary triumphs of order, lapses, set-backs, despairs, catastrophes, new beginnings, a multitudinous wilderness of time, a nigh plotless drama of wrong-headed energies."

Muddle! Part of the confusion is the incubus of the past, of "Victorianism": the conditions change but the ways of thinking do not change, and we have to cramp ourselves to precepts that were never made for us. A still greater part of the confusion is our artificial sex-morality—the most important thing in our lives overlaid with pruderies, pruriences, concealments, cowardice, false shame, cant. "We weren't taught," says Remington—"we were mumbled at." "Neither of us was ever given a view of morality that didn't make it show as shabby subservience, as the meanest discretion, an abject submission to unreasonable prohibitions! meek surrender of mind and body to the dictation of pedants and old women and fools." "This is a dirty world, Britten, simply because it is a muddled world, and the thing you call morality is dirtier now than the thing you call immorality. Why don't the moralists pick their stuff out of the slime if they care for it, and wipe it?" There is more of the confusion in the inequality of the sexes, the clash between the supremacy of the mother in nature and the supremacy of man's possessive instinct in man-made law. And on the political side there is the confusion in the state between its natural function as a public servant and its actual operation as a servant of those who can profit by the safe *status quo*.

These are Mr. Wells's principal kinds of muddle. It is simple justice to him, whatever one thinks of his ultimate philosophy, to indicate that his objection to them proceeds from a high sense of order and of social economy, and is only the obverse of the great positive modern force upon which he depends for any good that may come out of the confusion—the will to think in unselfish terms of the social order, rather than in selfish terms of personal expediency; the instinct of solidarity, or, as he calls it, the "state-conscience."

V

Thus far we have been too preoccupied with describing Mr. Wells to find much room for criticising him. His faults are so many and, on the whole, so obvious that it takes an invidious mind to add to their number: yet that has been done, at least once of late, by a critic of no little authority who calls Mr. Wells an "advocate" of "loose fluent sensuality." "Advocate" of sensuality he certainly is not, any more than Fielding was. He understands, as Fielding did, that sexual irregularity is a characteristic part of some lives; and he tells the truth about the passions, without in any sense advocating them. Also he seems to share with Fielding an honorable belief that passion accompanied by honesty with one's self, in the face of threatening society, may be cleaner than the chastity that results from timidity or witless conformity or Pharisaism. That lawlessness is better than open-eyed and courageous self-mastery, he has never even hinted. Even the physical indulgences of his men and women are more ascetic in their moral purport than the restraints and inhibitions of the bloodless folk whom he satirizes.

Coming to the faults that do patently exist, we trace them both on " low technical grounds " and on high intellectual grounds. Technically Mr. Wells is not open to criticism for pouring himself out through his principal characters: because in the truest possible sense he *is* his principal characters, and his own moral history is part of their story, part of the illusion. But when we take his books collectively, we may with some justice criticise him for inordinate repetition and consequent monotony. He simply does not know how to be dull: he is one of the extraordinary and brilliant persons who are interesting even in their fatuities. But he certainly never passes the infallible test of absolute greatness in fiction: variety, truth, and power in creation and depiction of character. His very fluency and prolific haste have defeated this achievement—for great new characters mature in the novelist's leisure and reflection. And it is not an injustice to Mr. Wells to say that his extreme facility has betrayed him, at times when he was writing too fast to think at the rate of his productivity, into a good deal of gasping, ill-considered utterance, a kind of verbal gesturing. More serious than this is his too frequent resort to melodrama when he has supposedly committed himself to realism. Episodes such as the stealing of the "quap" in *Tono-Bungay*, the whole Labrador postlude in *Marriage*, and Benham's confrontation of the tiger in the jungle belong in another *genre* altogether. We understand that Mr. Wells is a virtuoso of many instruments, but that is not a reason for playing on more than one of them at a time. Partly because it is most homogeneous and least subject to romantic aberrations of plot, *The New Machiavelli* remains by all odds his one nearest approach to supremely great realism.

The intellectual objection to Mr. Wells's principal point—his point about the wantonness with which society casts off useful men for irrelevant reasons—has to do with a deplorable shortcoming of the modern spirit in general: its contempt for "common sense" (too sweeping a consensus to be flippantly ignored) and for the non-spectacular virtues; for the courage that inconspicuously endures, the patience that waits long for a desired end, the charity that suspends judgment; for these and a dozen other attributes that can help hold the balance of life true—life being, when all is said, a balance and not an absolute finality. We do not accuse Mr. Wells of pretending that life is simpler than common experience finds it: rather, if anything, we must accuse him of finding so great complexity in the clash of grand and overwhelming issues that he sometimes misses the simple principle which might bring order out of the chaos. Principles, we realize, are among the least real things in Mr. Wells's cosmos: he sees them only as rules that interfere with temperament and produce tragedy. But the fact remains that, because he is so eager to frame his indictment against society and to inaugurate the romance of revolt, he often misses the logic of society and destroys the romance of self-abnegation.

The great trouble with his sort of iconoclasm—a trouble from which one can invent no way of escape—is that it shoves off on to the shoulders of society the burden of responsibility which belongs to the individual. Trafford's inability to get on happily with Marjorie is laid at the door of the institution of marriage. The author says that marriage itself is a muddle: the reader can only answer that that particular marriage unfortunately was. The first point of view goes on a sociological tear and pities the poor dupes, the victims of fate. The second point of view admits the pathos, but says it is the result of individual blindnesses of exactly the sort that society as an organization cannot cure. The romance of the case is all in the adjustment wrought by patient love, the growth of mutual understanding; and the romance happens to be the strongest part of the case. But Mr. Wells is too busy declaiming to see that: and when the adjustment comes, it comes through pure melodramatic accident. In general, we think we see that the tragedies are such as no reconstitution of society could prevent.

Never has Mr. Wells achieved anything more strictly in character than his voicing of precisely this objection to his own earlier logic. In *Mr. Britling Sees It Through*—of course Mr. Britling's other name is Wells so far as the spiritual adventure is concerned —our author ceases to damn the world for its refusal to let its brilliant wayward men do exactly as they please, without penalty, and begins to damn their own waywardness. Mr. Wells is being very much himself here, where, suddenly discovering the popular morality, which multitudes have always preached better than they practised it, he offers it to us as a brand-new and copyrighted religion of the future. There had been a point where he idealized hate as one among many forms of creative energy; now there is a point, after his glimpse of "blackened ruins in the town behind, the little grey-faced corpses, the lives torn and wasted, the hopes extinguished and the gladness gone," where he idealizes love as the sole agent of beauty and order, and can even whisper: "Father, forgive them, for they know not what they do." It is very much Mr. Wells's way to look backward and downward upon so large a part of himself; it is also very much his way to undertake, even in his first hour of confession and penance, the task of teaching the world how to think, how to behave, what God to worship.

Many readers of *Mr. Britling* will understand our wish that almost any one but Mr. Wells had written it. The book is important as a picture of England learning to know war and, through war, itself; and it is far more important as a forecast of how multitudes and millions of consciences are to grapple with hate and love on the largest, most impersonal scale. Yet those are precisely the things we find it hard to think of, in reading a book by a man whose effort has been to get outside everything by occupying successively all the intellectual positions there are—a little like Mr. Dooley's politician who " *ought* to know the most about it, be raisin iv havin' been on the most sides." " Mr. Wells is now having a *liaison* with God," says one critic, with a slightly too harsh felicity—the charge being, not that Mr. Wells is by ever so slender an allowance insincere, but that it is so abnormally easy for him to be sincere. His truths have always come so easily, and he has always been so expressively facund about them! Whereas these present truths, to be efficacious, ought to be hard-won truths, wrung by the unbearable pressure of things from the dry-throated inarticulacy of the simple and silent. Mr. Wells is a trifle too much like a professional conscience. Truth is truth whoever tells it—that indeed: but there are truths that come with a peculiar flatness from some sources. And Mr. Britling's truths are discounted, however inevitable and however genuinely of the folk-conscience, by the fact that Mr. Britling's creator, having expressed and doubted every other kind of truth, must sooner or later duly come to this kind. Besides, who shall escape a lurking wonder what other religion he may find, as soon as he has caught up with this new future of his? Is it not almost a condition of growth with such a man that, having signed his *Pilgrim's Progress*, he must turn round and write his *Hudibras?* Or is *Mr. Britling* really a destination and a haven?

In any event, Mr. Wells has always impressed the necessity of the large impersonal view, of trying to plan and build a clean civilization for the future instead of worrying along with makeshifts—the lesson of the state-conscience. He has invented a powerful dialectic for his belief that right thinking, not a majority vote, makes rightness of conduct, and that "bad" conduct with the right motives is better than "good" conduct with the wrong motives, or with none at all; so that "morality" may be more deadening to the soul than "immorality." The net result of his writings must be, we should think, to set the individual reader to examining his own heart, scouring his own motives, and sparing insincerity in himself no more than he spares it in his neighbors; setting a standard for his moral life, and then living toward it even at some cost to his bodily comfort and with some sacrifice of the approval of others. The necessity of this, whatever we may say of other and lesser aspects of Mr. Wells's doctrine, is a profound moral truth, of which Mr. Wells has given us half a dozen strikingly new and impressive versions.

X

JOHN GALSWORTHY

I

THE social philosopher who has but one large thing to say usually says it over and over again in a voice which becomes at length a shout or a frenzied shriek. Mr. John Galsworthy stands practically alone among latter-day novelists, as the social philosopher who, however often he delivers his one message, repeats it in a voice of astonishing quietness and clarity. Of all the qualities that make up the rich timbre of that voice, it is surely this trait of quietude, of coolness, that impresses the hearer first and haunts him longest. In a decade when most art has been noisy, and when especially the art of iconoclastic thinkers has treated itself liberally in the matter of rant and gesticulation, the art of Mr. Galsworthy has remained serene. The thing said is so simple, and withal so comprehensive, that the most casual wayfaring reader can hardly miss its purport. But the voice in which it is said is so exquisite in its modulations, so very unperturbed among the various shouting, screaming, or wailing voices of our time, that to hear it justly requires some intentness in the listener. And this is the excuse for postponing the message a moment in order to describe the inflection of the utterance.

One can best summarize the style of Mr. Galsworthy by saying that no single quality of it has the dubious distinction of calling attention to itself. It is a style that wins without arresting, and persuades without ever having challenged. It is quite without self-assertiveness, yet it is charged with individuality. Its frequent brilliance of phrase is simply the maximum of fitness and neat condensation—the brilliance that comes from self-discipline and long apprenticeship, not from the paroxysmal cleverness of particular moments. Without the crackling smartness of Mr. Chesterton or of Mr. Bernard Shaw, without the mannerism of the later Henry James, without the flippant facility of Mr. Arnold Bennett, it manages to become a profoundly personal means of expression. There is nothing meretricious in it that one can identify it by—no hysterical violence, no sacrifice of sense to sound or of truth to wit. Where many an artist has lost himself in self-assertion, Mr. Galsworthy has evidently found himself in self-effacement.

For it is quite clear that he *has* found himself. His calm assurance is essentially that of the sure touch. It is possible for the worker in prose to be carried away from truth and sincerity by giving the public more and always more of what it has first applauded in him, as a speechifying demagogue responds to the popular acclaim by going with every sentence farther and farther beyond what he means. It is also possible for him, if he finds himself ignored or derided, to lash himself into an infuriated utterance in the attempt to win a hearing at any cost. But Mr. Galsworthy has neither the insincerity of the spectacular success nor that of the desperate failure. We find thriving more and more in his pages, as the number of them grows, what must surely be called the finest flower of artistic experience —artistic self-knowledge and self-command. Academically, Mr. Galsworthy would be a writer of importance if he had nothing of unique impressiveness to communicate, simply because, through this distinguished restraint of his craftsmanship, he has proved more conclusively than any one else now writing fiction that English prose can be unmistakably modern without having to be either ugly or cold.

The fine fusion of Mr. Galsworthy's narrative manner as it appears in the ripest of the novels has obviously something to do with his apprenticeship to the stage and his other apprenticeship to the study. The artist who wrote *Strife* and *Justice* and *The Pigeon* was proceeding in the opposite direction from the modern "talky" play, the drama according to Shaw or Brieux; he was practising the most exigent selective sense on the masses of words, most of them waste, that make up the exchange of even very silent lives. That kind of discrimination is the uppermost quality of the dialogue in the novels, where every word, however aimlessly spoken, figures demonstrably in the march toward a predetermined effect. Shelton of *The Island Pharisees* uttered a heedless ironic laugh in the presence of Antonia, and would have given, the next instant, anything to recall it; but it had gone from him irrevocably, it had been written black in the history of two lives, it was "a little bit of truth." Every speech in the best of the novels has that character of profound and irrevocable importance. Little impulsive utterances betray the secret direction of a whole life. In his dialogue Mr. Galsworthy shows himself the dramatist incarnate.

No more has his training as essayist and critic missed transference to his fiction. The same kind of condensed emphasis that gives so much meaning to the tiny and fragile miniatures in such volumes as *A Motley*, *A Commentary*, and *The Inn of Tranquillity* appears in the chapters of *The Man of Property* and of *Fraternity*. It is partly what enables the author to make his larger canvases accommodate so many figures without the appearance of crowding; and it is what enables him to practise on the redundant form of the modern realistic novel that sort of rigid selectiveness which we associate with the short story. The play and the sketch (one the poster, the other the pastel of letters) make equal war on waste; and a pen trained to their type of compression will be able, in the wider area of the novel, to make little stand for much, for everything.

II

Both halves of this double training appear in Mr. Galsworthy's special contribution to the form of the novel: his perfection of the separate chapter as a unit in mood, in episode, and usually in scene. His composition in the novel is essentially dramatic rather than epic; it consists of a series of dramatic nuclei or kernels, careful foreshortenings of the subject-matter. He does not so much try to give the history of his personæ in a continuous line or curve as to plot it by a dotted line. Each dot is a chapter dedicated to one episode, the episode so chosen that it implies its own past and future, as a figure in paint or stone may imply in one frozen attitude the action of preceding and succeeding moments.

Henry James, practising his invariable motto of "Dramatise, dramatise!" achieved somewhat the same form with his chapter; but he never fully escaped the necessity of filling in the gaps. He sketched the connection between one chapter and the preceding, and then elaborated his central episode. Mr. Galsworthy elaborates his central episode and leaves out the connection—which means that the episode is in itself more decisive, more crowded with self-explaining relations. Each of his chapters has its own unity of mood, its exquisite symmetrical finish, with an almost complete freedom from the extraneous—the preparation and exposition, the backing and filling, which we are accustomed to think of as the necessary evils of the fictional art. Each episode has the singleness of effect, the "dramatic crystallization," of a short story by de Maupassant; it is like a skilful and separately complete sketch.

We are familiar elsewhere with chapters of all sorts, their structure determined by a crucial event, by pure chronology, by pure caprice of the author, even by the most tawdry exigencies of serial publication; and most novels remind one, in their succession of chapters, of a serried and irregular chain of mountains. Mr. Galsworthy turns the chain of mountains into a chain of beads, all of them strung on the invisible thread of the story and all consisting of a skilfully manufactured alloy of setting, action, character, talk, and dominant mood. The units are much the same in size and contour. What saves the succession of them from monotony is that the artificer, a master of color and contrast, has given each its own tint of mood, so that, although they are alike in form, no two are the same in effect.

We look also to Mr. Galsworthy's training, his mastery of the drama and of the short narrative sketch, for the explanation of his fundamental difference in method from both Mr. Wells and Mr. Bennett, his nearly exact contemporaries. Mr. Wells offers with the freest, most open-handed generosity the acceptable gift of his experiences, his versatile mind, his views, himself; Mr. Bennett holds out, in the same amazing and inexhaustible quantities, his preëmpted property the Five Towns, their characteristic life cut out for us in great segments and slabs of actuality. Both writers stand as exponents of the artistic theorem that the whole is equal to the sum of all its parts; *Tono-Bungay* and *Marriage*, *Clayhanger* and *The Old Wives' Tale* mean simply what they are. The worth is in the mass or bulk; we evaluate quantitatively. The question is, How *much* life? or, How wide a range of life?—never, What does it mean? Not so with Mr. Galsworthy. What he gives us is not so readily reducible to a summary. But it consists, one can say with certainty, of something which is other than it seems—some phase of life first carefully isolated, then colored and displayed in the light of an artistic purpose and left to explain itself, not as so much human experience transcribed bodily, but as a representation of something outside and greater than itself.

Mr. Galsworthy stands, then, as an instance of the opposite theorem, in art equally valid, that the whole is *not* equal to the sum of its parts. What he means is to be sought outside, not inside, what he says. He has learned to a nicety the art of making all that he reports far-reaching in its power of suggestion. The reported spoken word or physical act, the glimpse of truth or of passion, represents or illustrates something not directly expressed at all. We do not mean that Mr. Galsworthy falls short of having mastered the external or factual truth of the social order about which he writes: one always has a comfortable enough sense of his safe clutch of the real. But familiarity with the facts is not everything; the amount of truth is not to be measured by the amount of material. Galsworthy chooses details, not to be added up into the sum-total of his meaning, but to point in the direction of it; and he needs no more of them than will serve to point unmistakably. One has in reading him a distinct impression of the mass from which his comparatively few details are sifted. He possesses, it may be to an extent never before seen in the English novel, the power of making a few deft and insignificant touches suggest a whole picture of mood or of character, a whole philosophy of life. If he has any rival in this respect, that rival must be Stevenson, a romancer—between whom and the avowed realist of modern social living, any comparison is intelligible only in so far as it is purely technical and academic.

III

The meaning or message of Mr. Galsworthy we shall have summarized if we call him the critic of the static element in society—that is, of the aristocracy and the upper bourgeoisie—from the point of view of the dynamic or revolutionary element. Mr. Galsworthy writes of the aristocracy which is founded not on bestness but on badges—all the insignia of class which exert a restraining force on the individual, the badges of property and social rank and family which apply to the grandson an enormous pressure toward the ideals and instincts of the grandfather, and which make the man of the younger generation more responsive to the dictates of his own kind than to the urgency of shifting conditions in the world. In other words, Mr. Galsworthy is the analyst of the ornamental and property-holding classes and of the forces that keep them within their own social and intellectual fences. He sees them trying to solve new problems with old formulæ that no longer fit, and imposing on the individual the unyielding ideal of conformity, at whatever cost to the individual's own instinct.

Thus he presents both the strength and the weakness of material aristocracy in England. Its strength is that it nearly always triumphs over the waywardness of the non-conforming individual, breaking his will, and sometimes his heart, as it draws him back within the safe barriers of class. Its weakness is that it is based on conventions instead of on needs; the instinct of conformity means simply that aristocrats must stand together in order to stand at all. The aristocrat as Mr. Galsworthy pictures him is the blind mouth of society; the revolutionist or radical democrat is the hungry eye. The one keeps what he has, assuming, just because he has always had it, that it is what he wants; the other wants the truth, and wants the aristocrat to have it too.

Perhaps indeed the weakness of the revolutionist's case is his insistence that the aristocrat shall throw away something he already has for the sake of the truth, whereas the revolutionist himself, having nothing, is already free for service of the truth. Certainly this disparity does its part toward explaining the inability of the two classes ever fundamentally to understand each other. Unlike the professional reformer, Mr. Galsworthy sees the disparity, and sees it as tragic. And if he depicts the aristocracy as a system of limitations, inhibitions, blindness through the will not to see—a system fostered by heredity, by tradition, by self-interest, above all by the tremendous force of inertia—he also depicts revolution as a force constantly overleaping itself, and losing all because it demands more than is in the nature of things.

For an exposition of Galsworthy's general doctrine, his definition of the aristocrat, one should read the introduction to his first novel of some permanent importance, *The Island Pharisees*, a document in which he describes his view of the social unrest, the central and all-important conflict of which all other conflicts about particular issues are simply the less important phases. That unrest means, to him, the clash of two temperamentally dissimilar beliefs about society: Whatever is, is right, and Whatever is, is wrong. The conflict is always waged about the *status quo* of the given moment, the aristocrat fighting to maintain and the revolutionist to abolish.

The battle is first of all one of temperaments, as we have said. The aristocrat loves safety, the approval of his own sort, the straight walled road laid for him even before he existed, the regularized, shielded life of convention and formula. The radical loves danger, swimming against the stream, the life of the free body, with no responsibilities except those which seem at the moment to exert the strongest claim. He is always responding to something obscurely present in his make-up that compels him to hate and fight whatever is conceded without argument or by majorities.

Secondly, the battle is of the intellect; and here the revolutionist has all the advantage. He can see what is wrong with the world, and he can see that the aristocrat will never do anything to diminish the wrong. For the aristocrat is so preoccupied with the means of keeping what he already has, that whatever imperils it seems to him irrelevant. Things are as he wants them, and a number of dangerous malcontents are trying to upset his security and take away the world he has always helped to govern, in order to substitute a different world in which he will be a man like any other, only more helpless. Therefore he sets his jaw against every malcontent, clings tenaciously to everything that reminds him of his own difference, his superiority, the safe and ordered beauty of his world; and he convinces himself that it is the best possible world. His only real argument is that he likes it best—but he does not feel the hollowness of this.

Intellectually, he is on the losing side, because he only thinks that he thinks. But he has on his side, first, an enormous majority, being tacitly supported by the passive, non-thinking, non-dynamic mob; and, secondly, he has all the machinery of finance and commerce, of law and government, of institutions and religion, to help him win. Against these, the intellectual minority of rebels can urge only the logic and courage of its convictions. And in battles of ideas, the side that is numerically weak never wins—at first. The truth has not prevailed until it is everybody's truth, even the aristocrat's; but by that time it has ceased to be urgent, and the battle begins all over again on more advanced ground, over a new idea of which the aristocrat has, as ever, the safe or accepted notion. Thus the rebel thinker becomes at last the accepted prophet of what everybody believes; but meanwhile the rebel himself has gone on into the future, shaking from his feet the dust of the present. He is the creative element, the leaven in society; aristocracy is the resisting mass which he leavens. The aristocrat is always coming to the position which the radical has lately abandoned; the two are always a generation or more apart in belief and instinct, and the day of mutual understanding never dawns.

Some such relation as this between the creative and

the sterile elements in society is what Mr. Galsworthy perceives and uses as the nuclear principle of his social philosophy; and, *as* a principle, leaving aside for the moment his particular applications of it, it is one of the eternal verities, tritely fixed in the saying that the world always crucifies its Messiahs. The world embraces the gospel its Messiahs once preached, without stopping to reflect that if they should come again they would preach a quite different gospel, equally remote from anything that the world is ready to accept.

Of course Mr. Galsworthy is not offering either himself or any one of his imagined revolutionists as a Messiah: we only state his doctrine, in paraphrase of his own general terms, in order to show that his work has an unshakable foundation of important truth, the truth of how light is propagated, society leavened. The more practical question for criticism concerns the superstructure which Mr. Galsworthy raises on that foundation. Meanwhile the wonder is that an art based on so vast a truism should be in its detail so free from grandiloquence, the large gesturing and the mouth-filling words of the enthusiast; that it should never fall short of sobriety and symmetry. For it is not every philosopher who, having declared war on exaggeration and distorted emphasis, knows how to pay the truth the high compliment of simply telling it.

IV

Mr. Galsworthy states his large truth, as a fact, in terms of workably small and quite usual social problems, mostly of the sort that involves the members of a single family. The struggle takes place between the aristocratic forces that tend to hold the given family together as a unit and the democratic forces that tend to break its organization and throw the individual members on their own resources. The representatives of those forces make up two of the three groups of Mr. Galsworthy's personæ; the human prizes for which they contend, usually members of the younger generation, are the third. On one side are the exponents and apologists of conservatism, of the established order—men of substance, fathers and mothers who have forgotten the stresses of their youth, uncles and matchmaking mammas, clergymen, society matrons, and a few persons of the younger generation who were born old in spirit—such folk as Old Jolyon and Soames Forsyte in *The Man of Property*, Pendyce père in *The Country House*, Lady Casterley in *The Patricians*, Frances Freeland in *The Freelands*, and Antonia in *The Island Pharisees*. Opposed to them are rebels against their way of thinking and of living, the intruders and upstarts, dangerous and unsettling folk—persons such as Ferrand and Courtier and Derek Freeland among the men, Mrs. Bellew and the obscurely dangerous Mrs. Noel among the women. Between these, allied by birth and training to the aristocratic order but blown upon by new winds of doctrine and caught in the surge of young individualism, are the youths and maidens whom we see drawn in two directions, until finally they are forced back into conformity or, by rare exception, thrust beyond the pale—such protagonists as Shelton, George Pendyce, Irene Forsyte, and Lord Miltoun and Lady Barbara, these last in *The Patricians*.

It is significant of Mr. Galsworthy's rather somber sense of what it costs to see the truth without having the courage or the genius to follow it, that the persons of this third group, who are the heroes and heroines, are almost invariably the victims. They *have* seen the truth, in glimpses, but the truth has not made them free. Whichever way they go, they leave more behind than the heart and the intelligence can spare. If they return to the fold, they have given up the captaincy of their own destinies, the thrill of adventure which turns existence into living; if they leave the fold, they are wholly lost and incapable of grappling with life, they cannot do what they have never done, or do without what they have always had.

This is the principal indictment of the aristocratic formula: it procreates beings who are capable of seeing its limitations but incapable of overcoming them—sons and daughters who crave adventure of the mind and heart, yet have no strength for the ways of adventure. The outcome is always tragedy, if only the tragedy of self-fulfilment denied and thwarted. The plight which Mr. Galsworthy most often analyses is that of the person who wants more than he can get and dreams more than he dares. Condemned by his own nature to hunger for the untrammeled life, such a person is condemned by his environment to act as though life were prearranged for him. He takes the paved road, with chafing and discontent. And he does not see how surely another thirty years will find him helping to reënact his own tragedy in his children, wrestling to hold their bodies and incidentally losing their souls just as his elders had done with him. For there is no reactionary so rigid as he who has once been an insurgent.

This theme, the impingement on each other of two opposed doctrines and temperaments, is what Mr. Galsworthy works out in four of his most significant novels. These four taken together, each of them presenting a separate phase of the general conflict, complete the pattern of Mr. Galsworthy's satire. In *The Island Pharisees* he satirizes the aristocratic class through what it believes; in *The Man of Property* through what it possesses; in *The Country House* through what it does; and in *The Patricians* through what it inherits. These are the four phases of the aristocratic limitation—inability to believe any truth except that which is palatable and flattering; inability to part with anything that is one's own, even if one no longer seriously needs or wants it; inability to act outside the limited field where one's reputation is safe among one's own kind; and inability to escape the predestination in one's blood, the still voice of elders and ancestors inexorably ruling one's life. By his philosophy, his property, his conduct, and his heredity, the four fences of his narrow predetermined square, the aristocrat is cut off from the mass of mankind, the large "community of hopes and fears" which merges the solidarity of tribe or clan or class in the solidarity of nation or race or, at the largest interpretation, of mankind.

In each of the four books, all these instincts are present and potent; for Mr. Galsworthy is too great an artist, and too well aware of the complex of human emotions and motives, to interpret any single group of lives as ruled exclusively by one impulse. But he makes one of the four impulses visibly predominate in each of his four groups. Antonia breaks with Shelton because it is impossible for her to agree with the young revolutionist Ferrand, Shelton's protégé, with whom she sees Shelton more and more agreeing. Ferrand is to her like a destructive principle, the Nemesis of the class she represents. She does not see how Shelton can find any light or truth in him; for to her he is darkness. Antonia's instinctive hatred of the truth, her Pharisaical assurance that any light she does not see is darkness, is Mr. Galsworthy's kind of evil. In *The Man of Property* it is Soames Forsyte's habit and need of ownership that makes him regard his wife as essentially property. She never means much to him until he faces the prospect of losing her; but then he holds her with all his ruthless strength, wounded, full of hatred, yet unable to forego the long habit of mastery, of possession. In *The Country House* it is the fear of losing caste, the dread of what people will say, that eventually drags George Pendyce back to his family and Mrs. Bellew back to her husband. And in *The Patricians* it is the austere claim of an inherited something in the blood that, more than any other cause, separates Lady Barbara from Courtier and makes Lord Miltoun renounce Mrs. Noel for his career.

These four groups are enough alike, as types of the aristocrat, to be caught in the same mesh of impulses and traditions. They are different enough so that to each group one particular strand of the mesh seems stronger than the others. It takes the four together to provide Mr. Galsworthy's full documentation of the reactionary class, the class that possesses the material power of the world. Each of the books is a finished and vivid picture of personality. The four together have the strength and the impersonal logic of a *composite* picture—a definition of the type from which the several individuals derive their being.

V

We have not meant, even by implication, to present Galsworthy as being, like Shaw, a destructive critic of the family as an institution. He happens to choose the family as the fighting ground for the two extreme social doctrines in which he is interested; and in every instance the triumph of the doctrine which he regards as relatively right would involve the disorganization of a certain kind of family. But his attack is not against the idea of the family: it is against the principle of solidarity on which that one family is based. Mr. Galsworthy does not see how two loyalties that conflict can both be right; and he is always interested in the larger loyalty. He attacks the solidity of the family group when it interferes with the solidity of mankind. The ruthlessness of his gospel that the individual must be free for humanity is the ruthlessness of Christianity, which requires that a man hate his own flesh, his own kindred, or anything that blocks the larger outlook.

This ruthlessness is of the intellect; for after all the unique trait of Mr. Galsworthy—unique, we mean, among adverse critics of the aristocratic system—is his tenderness for the helpless individual aristocrat. The trouble with the folk in his world is not the presence of vices, or even the absence of the mild negative virtues. The trouble is their lack of the positive and courageous virtues—the power to think, to grow, to give themselves, to act outside what they have been taught. It is as symptoms that these persons are terrible; for as persons many of them are lovable enough. Antonia and Lady Barbara among the women are great in their capacity for personal sacrifice: it is when called upon for the impersonal sacrifice of prejudice that they neither hear nor answer. Old Jolyon Forsyte and Mr. Horace Pendyce are lovable figures, with all their old-school crustiness; Old Jolyon's tenderness for June is as Mr. Galsworthy's tenderness for *him*, and one does not soon forget Mr. Pendyce's acute suffering for the beasts which perished before his eyes in the burning barn, or his appreciation of his friend of many years, the Spaniel John. In his wife Margery we see the mother quite turning the aristocrat out of doors: she wants her son to have what he wants, whatever it does to the family and the system—because she cannot bear to see him suffer. Her one charming insurrection against her husband shows us plainly enough the source of the rebellious streak in George Pendyce. Lady Casterley in *The Patricians* has every kind of greatness except the ability to see that other people's concerns are as important and as real to them as hers are to her. It is only when her plans for the well-being of others are thwarted that she becomes hard, unsparing, inexorable. These are all good folk, most of them gentle and engaging folk, spoiled for the larger purposes of the world by the ineffaceable imprint of class and class limitations.

There is something in Mr. Galsworthy's make-up, a kind of gentility, which prevents him from being a satirist in the vindictive sense. It has to do with his philosophical belief in the community of all living things, his perception that what hurts one hurts all, so that to hurt anything is the only real crime. That belief prevents him from taking, with even the unloveliest of his characters, the tone of scorn. The unloveliest of his characters, we suppose, is the Rev. Hussell Barter, a sample of the modern hide-bound ecclesiastical Pharisee; yet the Rev. Hussell Barter is shown at least twice, despite his innate caddishness, in circumstances where he appears as human and rather admirable. And this general diffusion of tenderness, the substitution of sympathy for scorn, accords with Mr. Galsworthy's temperament as well as with his philosophy. It is difficult to call to mind another artist who unites so critical a sense of the disastrous and deadening results of class blindness with so much solicitude for the blind individual. That solicitude reaches downward to the lowliest of living things, upward to the exalted and lonely. Rigidly controlled by the reason, it is one great element of beauty and strength in Mr. Galsworthy's work. Not so controlled, it makes for beauty and weakness—as it does in *The Dark Flower*, Mr. Galsworthy's one attempt to show the intimate life of a man's heart in no light but the glare of its own emotional intensity. There, where inhibitions are in abeyance and sensibility rules unchecked and uncriticised, Mr. Galsworthy is only a part of himself—the most lovable part, not the most permanent.

This solicitude needs to be distinguished with some care from a soft and shallow humanitarianism much in evidence during the last hundred years. For the dominating quality of this novelist's art is after all, as we have said, impersonality, restraint, a kind of austerity which one can only call Greek. He is neither satirist nor sentimentalist; his irony is not a lash for the individual soul in its moments of inhumanity, but only a sense of the strangeness of the world's contradictions, and especially of man's inhumanity to man. There is something in all cruelty that faintly puzzles him; his indignation is provoked, but it is the patient indignation of high courage. There is a sympathy which is pure self-indulgence. Mr. Galsworthy's purpose is too inflexible for anything of that sort. Like Mr. Wells, he will have the truth at whatever cost; like Mr. Wells, he shows that its cost is sometimes prohibitive. But he differs from Mr. Wells in that he does not make an insistently selfish personal necessity of the truth. He keeps himself and his desires out of the actual spectacle; his personality is present only as the interpretation of the spectacle, the conclusion we are forced to draw. The result is a number of lives that seem to live themselves intensely in our sight, quite unconscious that they are there for a purpose. The purpose is outside them; their very blindness helps us to see their significance more clearly. Mr. Wells's characters act more in terms of ideas, Mr. Galsworthy's more in terms of temperament and desire. One puts all his ideas into his books, usually into the mouths of his personæ. The other leaves his ideas to be gathered by us readers if we want them; and the result is that the ideas seem, not like one side of an argument, but like an inevitable part of the nature of things. This security of Mr. Galsworthy in the possession of a kind of truth so irresistible that it proves itself gives his work its restraint, its air of calm and impersonal conviction—the Greek austerity and something of the Greek sense of inevasible Fate.

VI

It is rather difficult, in the face of these gifts of sound thinking, fine workmanship, and still finer conscience, to state the reason why Mr. Galsworthy has not also more of the Greek immensity and grandeur. For after all the chief limitation of his work—a limitation none the less felt because indefinable—is a certain slenderness of effect. It has every attribute of fine imaginative literature,—excellence of style, consummate mastery of formal technique, an adequate purpose, fervor and intensity, a sympathetic appeal to the most different types of readers,—and yet it achieves on the whole less than we should expect of the elemental bigness which we feel in the great Victorians, in Balzac, in Hardy and Meredith.

This feeling that the great enduring masterpieces leave with us has no necessary connection with mere bulk or largeness of scale, for we feel it in a chapter of *The Pickwick Papers* just as much as we do in the whole of *David Copperfield.* All one can say is that it is the most elemental type of creativeness that gives this feeling, and that probably nothing else can give it. It takes its shape usually in the creation of characters who are intrinsically great, even if they are only great villains like Iago or great clowns like Falstaff or great fools like Micawber. It is a lawless faculty, or at least it is a law-making rather than a law-abiding. It creates out of the void, reproducing whenever it drives the pen something of the original cosmic creation.

This thing, whatever its name and composition, Mr. Galsworthy does not have in the most eminent degree. His novels are almost certainly better literature than those of any one else now writing novels, if one judges them apart from this triumphant greatness which belongs to the immortals. In artistic dignity, in the author's attitude toward his subject, in the worth of that subject, in knowledge of life and the philosophy of it, every one of them since *The Island Pharisees* is a masterpiece, and in some ways the latest of them, *The Freelands,* is greatest of all. Yet we doubt whether any reader marks an epoch in his intellectual life by his discovery of Galsworthy, as many a reader does by his discovery of Hardy, of Meredith, of Dostoievsky. One speaks of this undefined lack with some hesitancy, just because it is and shall remain undefined: yet speak of it one must. So far as we can lay a finger on the lack, its secret is that Mr. Galsworthy applies the exquisite tracery of his workmanship to characters who are essentially little. Perhaps there must be a glorious unreason in the creations of genius at its most splendid; perhaps Mr. Galsworthy is too completely and sanely master of himself to be the father of a Tartuffe, a Père Goriot, an Uncle Toby, a Becky Sharpe, an Evan Harrington, a Tess. There is everything in Mr. Galsworthy to make us wish his novels came oftener, provided only they could do so without suffering in quality; but there is nothing to guarantee that readers of fifty years hence will turn to him as readers now turn to Dickens. In him the epic sweep is replaced by the lyric intensity.

Nevertheless, it is true that his is one of the most needed, as well as one of the most gracious, voices that speak to this generation. The aristocratic prides and the aristocratic fears, they are a part of nearly all of us; they are no more the limitations of one small class than the aristocratic virtues are the advantages of one small class. Pendyces and Forsytes lead the way, set up the ideal—and the whole mass is infected with "Pendycitis" and "Forsyteism." For the average man and woman, of America as well as of England, there is plenty of need for self-examination; we are all in some degree Island Pharisees, creatures of the narrow and selfish outlook.

Against these limitations of the mass of us, only reason can prevail. And it is the voice of reason that Mr. Galsworthy raises. He assails the convention that destroys, not the convention that builds and protects. Unreason, blindness, excess, these are the real enemies. Some of us are idle, others overworked; some are voluptuous, others ascetic; some have useless wealth, others only grinding poverty; some are brainless, others fanatical;—these excesses, fruits of unreason, are what must be destroyed. Mr. Galsworthy happens to believe that the really crucial trouble with society is at the top of its organization, in the land-holding, money-spending, governing classes; but he never goes at the question in a blind iconoclastic fury. His aim is to make those who are blind see the tragedy, and the humor too, of their own blindness—for to him the most grotesque tragedy of all is not to know one's self and what one wants, to pass perhaps a whole lifetime without ever having been on speaking terms with one's own heart. "From your heart," he apostrophizes Fashion, the Figure Without Eyes, "well up the springs that feed the river of your conduct; but your heart is a stagnant pool that has never seen the sun. . . . *You have never had a chance!*" That is the position of the unhappy majority in his books. The only free, happy, and enviable people in them are the few who have self-knowledge, convictions with the courage thereof, work, and little or nothing else. In these is the hope of the world.

And hope is the one note that becomes more and more insistent throughout Mr. Galsworthy's work, emerging strongly at last through his characteristic melancholy. The failures he records are uncompromising; and so too is the failure of youthful and eager iconoclasm in his latest story, *The Freelands.* But the failure there, we are made to know, is less irretrievable than the others; more wisdom comes out of it for those who fail, and we read it as a preface to hope. "Was that defeat of youth, then, nothing? Under the crust of authority and wealth, culture and philosophy—was the world really changing; was liberty truly astir, under that sky in the west all blood; and man rising at long last from his knees before the God of force? . . . The world is changing . . . changing!"

The Realistic Spirit and the Ironic Spirit

EDITH WHARTON
JOSEPH CONRAD

XI

EDITH WHARTON

I

Popular and non-technical discussion of Mrs. Wharton—most of it conducted, fortunately or unfortunately, from *The House of Mirth* as an accessible point of departure—has agreed that this author writes, of all women, most like a man, or at any rate least like a woman;—disagreement beginning as a usual thing at the question of whether she deliberately tries to do so. Criticism, more or less professionally interested in the same points, has contrasted her with all manner of women writers from Jane Austen to Mrs. Humphry Ward. Like all such popular judgments, this dictum is empty or significant according to what one means by it; but at least we find it significantly ratified in the remark of a critic of keenest sensibilities, himself among those least likely to be swayed by catch-words. It was in speaking of *The Custom of the Country*, in an essay lately much quoted and referred to, that Henry James summarized one effect of Mrs. Wharton's temperament as "the masculine conclusion tending . . . to crown the feminine observation."

We may catch up here the popular saying and this

its specialized variant as helping each other point toward the central and definitive quality of Mrs. Wharton's realism. It seems to us that her writing is fundamentally sexless, as that of few women and of no men has been. Fundamentally, we say: for her superficial qualities are on the whole of a masculine order. We would be understood here as assuming no deep-rooted and inalienable difference between the minds of the sexes: it may or may not exist. For the momentary purpose, let the masculine qualities be those which men have most commonly exhibited, and the feminine those which women have most commonly exhibited. Speaking, then, in these conventional and provisional terms, we think we discover this about Mrs. Wharton: that in some superficial ways she achieves masculine qualities of mind and art, not primarily to escape the traditional limitations of her own sex, but to escape those of both sexes, of sex itself. We leave aside the important question whether in escaping the limitations she may not also risk losing some of the possibilities. We leave it aside to report the simple fact, that her peculiar way of writing like a man is a species of protective coloring adopted in order to escape being obviously a woman, and that the balance of sexual qualities results in an actual approximation of sexlessness.

This, if a dark saying in itself, is easy of explanation. The masculine quality of Mrs. Wharton, her protective coloring against the merely feminine, is her tone of irony; that fine "asperity" toward her characters and toward all her material, which the criticism already cited has named the "masculine conclusion"—a little oddly named, we think, asperity being in itself so inconclusive a quality, and Mrs. Wharton's habit of thought having so little to do with conclusions of every sort. Now, it is our general point that this masculine tinge of irony or asperity, this habitual and determinate skepticism which refuses to court illusions on any terms, is with Mrs. Wharton a secondary and incidental quality, not a primary or essential; and that when we look for her primary quality we must find it in her balance, her detachment from points of view, her very inconclusiveness. In other words, her rôle of ironist is her way of escape from the tyranny of intuition without criticism; it is an agency and not an end. Essentially, she is an ironist not at all, and still less is she a satirist or a sentimentalist. Essentially, she is a votary—among Americans the first, the most consistent, and by all odds the most important—of the realistic spirit. Her irony is a more or less conscious rejection of false gods and half-gods; but her full spiritual allegiance is to something beyond, that denies irony even as irony denies sentimentalism—the scientific spirit of modern realism.

This truth about Mrs. Wharton, provided only one keeps it on the plane of her single-minded purpose and unconfused by considerations about her method, answers a multitude of questions or makes them irrelevant. The freshest possible example comes to our notice in one critic's speculation whether *Summer*, our newest experience of Mrs. Wharton, has or has not a "happy ending." *Summer* is the story of a low-born

New England girl who, in spite of a vicious heritage, feels in herself something that rebels against soddenness, something that thirsts unquenchably for life. Deserted by an attractive weakling after her self-surrender to a torrential passion, left tragically alone to face motherhood, she turns back in her helplessness to the community of backwoods degenerates in which she was born. Better the filthy animalism of their outlook on life, she thinks, than the patronizing kindness of the decent stupid little country village in which a broken-down lawyer has reared her. She has missed the stars: better the pit than the plain. Yet something in her feels the impossibility of bearing her child in the moral squalor of her ancestral surroundings, which she has hardly seen before since her babyhood; and when her elderly guardian, whom she has always despised as futile, comes offering rescue through marriage, she numbly allows him to take possession of her life. Thus she returns to the stodgy mediocrity which she has always hated. Her future is neither the scarlet triumph of her dream nor, failing that, the black tragedy which she had thought to invoke: it is a gray makeshift life.

Is this a happy or an unhappy ending? Both and neither; the question is simply non-existent in Mrs. Wharton's purpose. She neither despises Charity Royall for relinquishing the dream nor applauds her for escaping the penalty. She seems to be actuated by no consideration other than simple fidelity to how things happen. She is neither the ironist insisting on the gap between human hopes and their fulfilment nor the sentimentalist proposing repentance and sympathy as remedial of all human ills. She offers the people and the facts for what they are in themselves and in representation of life. The truth of life is there, but not the meaning of the truth. *That* we must find for ourselves; or perhaps it is not to be found; or perhaps it does not exist. Such is the inconclusive conclusion; and it is strictly typical of Mrs. Wharton's scientific ruthlessness of purpose, and of that modern impersonality which escapes all prejudices by renouncing all opinions, all points of view.

II

How account, then, for the extraordinary vibrancy and tenseness of Mrs. Wharton's novels, their complete freedom from insipidity? Novels so impersonally conducted ought, we tell ourselves, to read as though written by an automaton. Like instruments tuned to the "well-tempered" scale, they ought to be flat, uniform, standardized—whereas they strike us with the poignant and acid tang of the full orchestra, an instrument which owes part of its effectiveness to the fact that it can never be ideally in tune. *The House of Mirth*, *Ethan Frome*—these are orchestral in their richly subtle clashing of overtones, a sort of infra-discordance which is among the rare improbable finenesses accessible to the artist, on condition of his readiness to take infinite pains for infinitesimal effects.

Among the subtle discords which make up the resultant harmony of Mrs. Wharton's art, the asperity of her personal tone has of course its effect; and the impingement of this tone upon the impersonality of her main design is a constant excitation to the ear that listens finely. A second part of the secret is the tensity of her style—a style that combines eagerness with discipline, poised perfection of phrase with entire lack of mannerism. It is as though the softest and richest of gold were hammered down to the hardness of steel, the hardness almost of the diamond. Here again is "the masculine conclusion tending to crown the feminine observation."

But we shall not have come to the pith of the secret until we have indicated the still more important and more general ways in which the impersonal work contains and expresses the personal workman. It is only as a thinker about ultimate meanings that Mrs. Wharton renounces, as we have said, all standards and points of view: in the immediate things which make up the tangible substance of her art, she exerts a critical sense all the more rigorous for being partly intuitive. And in this critical sense she is, in a most decisive and constructive way, the cosmopolitan, the world-citizen. She understands America through France, through Italy; and without France and Italy, her peculiar way of understanding America would be impossible.

The word "cosmopolitan," left undefined, can mislead and belittle. Used of Mrs. Wharton, it means the crowning attribute of the older civilizations, that asceticism of taste which runs to fineness rather than to muchness. The cosmopolitanism, let us say, of Mr.

George Moore is characterized by some arbitrary preferences of the undisciplined to the disciplined, of the lavish to the ordered, and especially of the exotic to the indigenous. Mrs. Wharton's cosmopolitanism is, finally and essentially, the faculty of discrimination working in a rich field. She is the critic of American materialism because she is bred by a standard which subsists on ideas, using mere things sparingly and subordinately. She is the critic of that subtler American materialism which consists in having ideas only to let them tyrannize over one and drive one to preposterous lengths. Because our civilization is young and, as Matthew Arnold would have said, "raw," it is difficult for ideas to circulate freely and naturally among us; either we have them not, or else we have a few of them madly, ungovernably, to the pitch of obsession. Mrs. Wharton is the satirist both of our materialism and of our freakish and faddish emancipations from materialism. For both are products of excess; and the asceticism of fine breeding is the enemy of all excess. It appreciates fineness in things and fineness in ideas, and works out the ideal adjustment, for urbane living, between ideas and things. Qualitatively, it is Epicurean; quantitatively, it is Stoic.

This is the explanation of Mrs. Wharton's vibrant intensity of effect, so far as the full explanation lies in any one statement. Familiar with many things, she rejects most of them as not quite good enough; and the few that she keeps gain immensely, in vividness as well as value, because they have survived the test of such selectiveness. In other words, Mrs. Wharton's work is so searching and so trenchant because it tacitly involves so many standards of comparison. She is equally different from the naïve cosmopolitan who accepts everything in the world and the naïve provincial who accepts everything that he happens to know. When she writes about the smart society of American cities or the impoverished society of run-out New England villages, her intimacy with the physical material is equaled by the detachment of her point of view, her complete refusal to identify herself with the material. The eyes that see are American; but the discrimination that criticises is Continental. Her stories of New England in decay are utterly different in this respect from, say, the stories of Miss Alice Brown. Miss Brown personally sympathizes with her characters as human beings. Mrs. Wharton sympathizes with them artistically as objects, while knowing them no less well; and her study of them resembles, comparatively, that of the pathologist. One has, in reading her stories of America, the feeling that she is really writing by indirection about the urbanity and the balance which we lack. In *Ethan Frome*, in *The House of Mirth*, she sees us in microscopic detail from a telescopic distance. Other and more provincial writers have missed the perspective; the transatlantic spectator nearly always misses the characteristic minutiæ. Mrs. Wharton, missing neither, knows us as we know ourselves, yet feels us without self-interest, as we might feel the members of some quite different order of creation. It is in the clash between her artistic nearness to her material and her intellectual aloofness from it that her work becomes vibratile, resonant, orchestral, each separate note intensified as though by a sounding-board.

III

The provincial's way of knowing a thing is to live it until, through saturation, he is unconscious of it; and his gain is largely the moral and emotional leverage of the artist's self-identification with his material. He knows one set of data so thoroughly that he needs no other, and is half unaware of knowing even that one set. For better or worse, the provincial attitude of mind is being replaced in art by the cosmopolitan attitude, which insists that the way to know anything is first to know everything else. Our tendency is away from the thing as it is in itself, shorn of its relations, and toward the thing as a compound of relativities and contacts. So it must evidently be in a world which seems hourly to grow smaller for us through our perception or desire of new unities in it. There remains, to be sure, the great question whether the cosmopolitan gain in a new kind of disinterestedness—disinterestedness being the very kernel of the realistic spirit—can ever make up for the loss of the old emotional energy and immediacy. The doubting critic raises this question about Mrs. Wharton when he speaks of her lack of vision and moral ardor—meaning that, for him, passionate truth in art counts for more than dispassionate. Whether it is so for mankind remains to be seen; only the future can really know. It is futile to indict, and unnecessary to defend, a world-tendency; one is part of it even while one does so, and the tendency goes on anyway. But at least we can see that the tendency toward impartial truth, and away from self-interested and emotional conviction, does exist in art, and that this tendency does give Mrs. Wharton, as the most inflexibly disinterested of novelists in English, a moral recency which equals, say, the material recency of Mr. H. G. Wells.

A good example of her absolute modernity is *The Valley of Decision*, a long novel published before *Nostromo* and *The Old Wives' Tale* were written, and actually before either Mr. Wells or Mr. Bennett had found his direction. We have noted the way in which Mrs. Wharton, when she writes about the America of the present, surveys us with critical aloofness, as from some Old World capital. In *The Valley of Decision* she reverses the process, and surveys an Italian principality of the eighteenth century from the angle of America to-day. There could be no more definitive example of the modern realistic spirit and its disinterestedness, or of the insistence on knowing things in terms of other things. In *The Fruit of the Tree* or *The Custom of the Country* the best in Europe analyses the less good in America. In *The Valley of Decision* the best in America takes its turn as critic of the less good in Europe, and the present becomes the critic of itself as reflected in the past. Only from the outside, it would seem, can such criticism as Mrs. Wharton's operate at all.

The contemporaneity of *The Valley of Decision* will bear some explanation, for its author is far too restrained an artist to make it obvious, and far too sure of her method to sink to the low estate of a mere symbolist. This novel, considered as a piece of pure historical scholarship set aglow by the imagination, is as remarkable as *Romola* is said to be by its kinder critics; and in one respect it succeeds where *Romola* failed, for its scholarship is less obtrusive and considerably less literal. The book is thoroughly adequate as interpretation of a rich and little known past, a crowded page of history read with social insight. But it is a past made to reach forward and comment on the present; and its record deals with precisely the social phenomena in which Mrs. Wharton specializes when she is most patently of the present.

Let us see. In any society in which great wealth or great power is concentrated in few hands, there is always generated an idle and parasitic class which reaps where it has not sown. It is a class conspicuous without greatness and ornamental without beauty; with abundance of leisure it produces nothing, and all its intelligence is directed toward making the producers work for it and serve its ends. The wives and children of the rich are natural candidates for this class; the social adventurer and adventuress, and all climbers and fourflushers generally, belong to it. It consists of the spoiled children of power. Mrs. Wharton has constituted herself its American historian; and in the futility of its members, the tragic inequalities engendered by their very existence, and their pitiful attempts to escape from idleness into freedom, she has her chosen field.

The House of Mirth is the tragedy of the woman

who is a little too weak to do without money and what it buys, or to earn it for herself, and a little too good to sell herself. Lily Bart is one of the gayest and saddest of the spoiled, and she is predestined to tragedy. Poor, she is a fragile butterfly whose wings crumple at a touch. Rich, she would be hard and cynical, graceful and useless and obscurely unsatisfied. *The Fruit of the Tree* proposes the old problem of wealth trying simultaneously to satisfy two contradictory demands—the demand for its creative use in industry and social amelioration and the demand for irresponsible and parasitic retention. The book adds the highly special problem whether it can be right for the doctor or the nurse to help a sufferer die when there is no hope of recovery; but this is a side issue, Mrs. Wharton's one lapse into artistic disintegration. *The Custom of the Country* treats the marital adventures of a much-married lady; but the question asked is not so much about divorce as it is about the parasitic marriage—the marriage of the woman who, by the very unpleasant "Custom" of the title, uses instead of helping her husband, and casts him off when he is no longer useful. These are the typical themes of Mrs. Wharton. They are themes natural to a society in which wealth is made as conspicuous by its useless by-products as by its legitimate fruits. Incidentally, it seems to be the society she treats, and not her personal point of view, which explains why most of her women are unconscious cynics, and why so many of her men are unconscious idealists.

IV

Now, these are also the themes of *The Valley of Decision*, spread on a canvas broad enough to include them all. The drama of wealth and power is vast and slow-moving enough to include the life of a whole Italian principality during a generation of the latter eighteenth century; but the struggle, translated partly into terms of politics and the state, is still between the parasitic and the productive.

The story is the life-story of Odo Valsecca, first an obscure lad, heir at several removes to the duchy of Pianura, then through a series of deaths the reigning duke. The young manhood of Valsecca, the period of his education and travels among the courts of other petty principalities, each under its tyrant, provides a view of all Italy in a time of aspiration and of change. A new leaven is at work in Italian life. Strange ideas of the rights of man and the responsibility of princes have crept over the mountains from France, and "The Old Order" is being insensibly undermined. The people are beginning to groan under a system of too many taxes and too little bread; they begin to regard their rulers as oppressors; and the Church, for ages the most powerful oppressor of all, is becoming powerless to uphold longer the mediæval tyranny of princes.

Odo Valsecca is in many ways at the forefront of his age. He is one of the first to welcome "The New Light." First he sees the helplessness of the Church and of the official religion; for a priest-ridden people there was no hope; the mystical side of religion had become simply a drug to make the great mass of people forget its misery. Valsecca turns to the humanitarianism of the French philosophers, reads the books that the Church has banned, and becomes the friendly pupil of savants and humanists whom one government after another has hounded into exile. When, at the turning of his life, he has to choose between the great woman whom he loves and the throne of Pianura, he is ready to renounce the succession; but her vision is brighter than his, and she sends him back "to serve liberty on a throne." In the suffering of his loss of her, he speaks bitterly of her readiness to dispose of his life. "'It is not mine to dispose of,' she caught him up, 'nor yours; but belongs, as much as any slave's to his master, to the people you are called to rule. Think for how many generations their unheeded sufferings, their unrewarded toil, have paid for the pomp and pleasure of your house! That is the debt you are called on to acquit, the wrong you are pledged to set right.'"

He returns sadly to the palace that has come to seem so empty, and takes up the burden of a prince who has seen the light. But there are strong forces of reaction against him—all the forces of the old order, represented by a scheming prime minister; by the widow of Valsecca's cousin, the late Duke, whom he has been compelled to marry for the safety of the state; by the Church, which looks upon him as a dangerous atheist; finally by the very people whom he has pledged himself to serve, and whom centuries of tyrants have rendered so lethargic that they can bear anything rather than change. As he uproots one after another the old abuses, governing for the welfare of the governed and regardless of his own, his enemies and those whom he is trying to befriend unite against him, against liberty; and on the very morning when he was to have promulgated a new charter of popular liberties his rule begins to crumble. In this smaller scene beats the ironic heart of the French Revolution: "Man was free at last—freer than his would-be liberators had ever dreamed of making him—and he used his freedom like a beast. For the multitude had risen—that multitude which no man could number, which even the demagogues who ranted in its name had never seriously reckoned with—that dim groveling indistinguishable mass on which the whole social structure rested. It was as though the very soil moved, rising in mountains or yawning in chasms about the feet of those who had so long securely battened on it. The earth shook, the sun and moon were darkened, and the people, the terrible unknown people, had put in the sickle to the harvest."

With Valsecca everything has failed—his love, his labor, all the dream of justice, of restoring to the people what his ancestors had taken from them. There is small kindness in the fate which spares his life, for as he goes forth into the daylight and rides away toward the frontier he is a man without a home and without a task—a victim of the age that was not ready for him, a martyr of the invincible conservatism and inertia of things as they are.

In many ways this panoramic study of a past civilization has the effect of prophecy. The conflict between reaction and a new idealism, because it is an eternal conflict, seems oddly local and present, as direct in its bearing on us as anything Mrs. Wharton has ever imagined. It is surprising how the life of Pianura duplicates, without anachronism, a thousand phenomena of our own near past, all the way from so general a symptom as the contemptuous patronage of the arts and philosophies down to the woman who takes her pet monkey with her on a journey but leaves her child at home. In not a single page is the author's purpose of strict objective and historical truth vitiated by any ulterior design: she is faithful to the letter and the spirit of her chosen period, and if she kills two birds with one stone, it is because the second happens to be in the line of her aim at the first. This is in fact precisely what the novel makes us feel. If any one can read it without feeling that its inner truth focuses sharply on the problems of our own cisatlantic age, he must think and read within a strangely narrow intellectual horizon. *The Valley of Decision* has more of America in it than *The House of Mirth* has; and for that reason it serves to crown the paradox that Mrs. Wharton, who is most European in spirit and technique when she writes about America, is most American when she writes about Europe.

V

It is impossible to discuss the purely technical side of Mrs. Wharton's work without some mention of her obvious discipleship to Henry James. Henry James's Prefaces to the New York Edition are beginning to take their place as the best existing handbook about the art of narration on its technical and constructive side. Perhaps it is enough praise of Mrs. Wharton to say that, through experiment and self-criticism, she had read the purport of those prefatory essays before they were written. It is certainly no dispraise if we note that she seems to have written the short tale as it could hardly have been written had not Henry James discovered some new possibilities in it and given it a new bent.

Mrs. Wharton's own early work in the short story was relatively slight for its strength, and in one sense arid. Nothing in such a volume as *The Descent of Man*, definite and positive in flavor as that volume is, seems quite so worth while as the author's skill and her own delighted preoccupation therewith. One form, the very short story told in crisp dramatic dialogue in a single scene, she made perfectly her own, using it again and again with a deft strength new in English, or at least never shown in so many like performances from one hand. But the greatest stories are longer and later ones in which the workmanship is less obtrusive—not because there is less of it, but because there is more to carry it. In *Tales of Men and Ghosts* (a title often misunderstood, by the way: the men and the ghosts are in the same stories, not in different ones of the same volume), lately in *Xingu*, and much earlier in *Crucial Instances*, a volume which appeared before *The Descent of Man*, the stories are far better worth telling—and perhaps one might say that they are better told, too, since one can so easily forget how they are told.

It is in these more generous stories that Mrs. Wharton proves herself the discriminating—never, we believe, the slavish—pupil of Henry James. Her situations are as highly specialized as his, and in very much his way: that is, they nearly always consist of circumstances ordinary enough in themselves but made extraordinary by the unexpected and unique element in one of the personalities concerned. For example, a woman taking her sick husband home, a long journey by rail, finds him dead in his berth. There is nothing in the event itself to interest either of the story-tellers here compared; it could have happened to anybody. But the woman in Mrs. Wharton's story finds herself unable to disclose the death of her husband; and for the rest of the journey she keeps up a lamentable pretense that he is too ill to be disturbed. She does this because her imagination revolts against the outcry, the fuss, the impertinent solicitude of strangers, which are sure to follow, and because she needs to be alone with that queer blend of callousness and sensibility which is herself. Here, in an odd and uniquely twisted relation between what happens and the person to whom it happens, lies the nucleus of any story that either of these two writers could take serious interest in. And the development follows the suggestion of the theme itself; for Mrs. Wharton resembles Henry James again in her discovery that the way to tell such a story is to use the consciousness of the person concerned as a standard of reference, and to study the event solely in terms of what it means to a principal actor.

The bearing of all this on Mrs. Wharton as a novelist is as simply stated as it is important. At a certain point in her development she made the one great technical discovery that the later work of Henry James had opened to his juniors: the discovery that the very short story—"the short-story with a hyphen," as they say who love to formulate its rules—was dead as an important form of literature almost before any one had bothered to define it, and that, economically speaking, it came into existence for the sole purpose of suggesting a new kind of novel. The novel as it is best written to-day has the sharp focus, the unity in purpose and point of view, of the short story. The change came about through the invention of an intermediate form, the kind of two-hundred-page narrative which results, not from foreshortening the novel into the novelette, but from expanding the short story into the "novella." Examples of it are Stephen Crane's isolated masterpiece *The Red Badge of Courage*, Mr. Conrad's "Heart of Darkness," James's "The Spoils of Poynton," and—strikingly like James's story in the number of persons and the perspective of the whole—*Ethan Frome*. Nothing that Mrs. Wharton has done has quite the hard shapeliness, the smooth enameled finish, the exquisite inward adjustment part to part, of this tragic idyll of New England. If the tale told is sterile, as some have called it, then at worst one is left to wonder how sterility can be so perfect.

Mrs. Wharton when she writes *Ethan Frome* is living a chapter, the very most recent of all, in the history of the novel. When fiction discovered the possibilities of the short-story unity in works of length approaching the novel's, it was only a step to the discovery that the longest possible stories were reducible to the same unity; and the novel began promptly to re-create itself out of the new intermediate form. "The Spoils of Poynton" in one decade means *The Awkward Age* in the next, and *The Golden Bowl* presently. The longer works have exactly the organic oneness of the shorter; in them, the phases of life treated may be of dimensions to suggest the novel, but the treatment is, in a new way, selective and climactic. Events multiply, but they multiply for the sake of some effect which can be sensed all at once, cumulatively. The older novel was a chain. The new novel is a wheel, every spoke going straight to the hub. We hope it is not too fanciful to suggest that this unifying tendency in the novel is a pretty close parallel to the unifying tendency in everything else. In every phase of existence, and among all the phases together, there is a strong inherent trend toward order, toward symmetry and centrality: how could it not be so in the arts, this fine free art of fiction among them?

At all events Mrs. Wharton has retraced in her own career these steps through which a great master of technique had gone immediately before her, through which the novel itself is going. *The House of Mirth* was a novel struggling for, and barely missing, the new organic roundness; *Ethan Frome* reached perfection in its kind, a smaller and more special kind; and now—if we may judge a direction by a present attitude—the lesson is applied, the severer unity carried forward from the shorter type into the longer. The result is *Summer*, a story by no means so great as its author's greatest, but in this constructive sense the most strictly modern of her longer works, and a logical completion of the parallel between her artistic evolution and that of her time. If anything may be added to make this completion more complete, we think we find it in a softening of her former asperity—some slight sacrifice of the irony which is a personal tone, without any relaxing of the irony which is fate. If we judge *Summer* not by what it says but by what it makes us feel, it is Mrs. Wharton's nearest approach to a quality which ranks among the perils of the artist only because he has so often not known how to control it or what to do with it—the old and new and always supremely modern quality of compassion.

XII

JOSEPH CONRAD

I

If Mr. Joseph Conrad appears at first glimpse as a romancer,—and it is certain that to many readers he does,—the explanation is simply that he is a deeper realist than is commonly perceived. There is a truth outside of truth which is romance; there is a truth within truth which is the living heart of truth. Romance is a vision; but this heart of truth, the objective of the greatest realists, of whom Mr. Conrad is one, is a patient discovery.

These matters can be made clear if we regard each living organism, from the individual life up to the mass of collective lives, as being an affair of circles within circles, spheres within spheres, from an outermost layer of superficial reality to an innermost core or principle of reality in which all that envelops it is implied, explained, and justified. The truth about life is like (shall we say?) a series of Chinese dolls, each fitting inside a larger until a largest contains them all. The romancer looks at the outermost one and imagines still another outside that; his truth is in the similitude of life viewed in the large, but grander, more free in perspective, fitting reality as a garment fits the body, not as a glove the hand. But the realist's quest is inward. His inspection of the single life takes him beneath the outer husk of act and habit, expression and gesture, to the stratum of emotion and fancy where these have their root; and perhaps under that to the substratum, made up of heredity and environment and pure accident, which we call character. But he has not really acquitted himself until, beneath the last wrapping of all, he has uncovered some inmost kernel of truth, some such secret dream or frozen despair as obscurely rules every life, giving to all the outward manifestations a logic and a legibility not otherwise theirs. And if he confront the medley of lives which makes up the general spectacle of life, his concern is still with its hidden center, the secret aspiration of all mankind—the dream of brotherhood.

As a result of the inward bent of Mr. Conrad's mind and interest, it follows that no one else has written with so profound a sense of the awful privacy of the soul, the intense palpitating secrecy which underlies even the most placid phenomena of the every-day world. Every one of his stories, properly understood, is a story of mystery, though with hardly anything of the conventional machinery of mystery. Readers will have noticed the extraordinary number of passages in his work which involve the physical presence of somebody or something hidden: evidently the bare fact of concealment fascinates him. But the whispering intensity of such passages is only the reflex of Mr. Conrad's general feeling that everything in the world is in thraldom to secrecy, that secrecy is almost the law of life. Every being is at bottom inexpressible and trying to express itself, every truth is in essence a paradox and struggling for consistency. The "Secret Sharer" haunts the captain's cabin and the captain's thoughts until he seems to have become the captain's other self; but the unearthly and dreamlike reality of the whispered consultations of those two is as nothing to the reality of secrets buried in the consciousness too deep for even whispered consultations. That young rebel stowaway is the negation of tranquillity in a stolid and respectable ship's company; it is an outrage upon all fitness that he should be there and they innocently not know. But he is only an obscure symbol of rebel man precariously living on his pin-prick of lighted dust in space, a negation of the serene immensity of the cosmos which mocks him.

It is important to understand this about Mr. Conrad, for it is the heart and marrow of his kind of irony. Even his verbal irony is only a way of reminding us of the paradox of outer and inner, the incredible gap between the appearance and the reality. In *Nostromo* his account of Señor Hirsch's tortured and horribly violent end is sprinkled with reminders of the utterly commonplace facts of Hirsch's previous life and occupation. The tragedy of an old man whose world has dropped to pieces round him is described in these terms: "The enthusiastic and severe soul of Giorgio Viola, sailor, champion of oppressed humanity, enemy of kings and, by the grace of Mrs. Gould, hotel-keeper of the Sulaco harbor, had descended into the open abyss of desolation among the shattered vestiges of his past." Thus, even as a stylist, Mr. Conrad is occupied with the ironic or tragic unfitness of things. He reminds us by a system of allusions that the strange and sinister things that people do are never so strange as what people are; and he makes the secret inner reality throw a somber or a shimmering light outward over the plain coarse texture of the dullest lives and occupations.

This primary interest of Mr. Conrad in the inmost verity of things, and the subordinateness of his interest in their external appearances, are the prevailing notes in all that he has to say of his own art. "Art itself," he says, "may be defined as a single-minded attempt to render the highest kind of justice to the visible universe by bringing to light the truth, manifold and one, underlying its every aspect." The artist must "reveal the substance of its truth—disclose its inspiring secret: the stress and passion within the core of each convincing moment." If he succeed, "you shall find there . . . all you demand and, perhaps, also, that glimpse of truth for which you have forgotten to ask." The emotional side of life will not suffice for him, as it does for the sentimentalist in fiction: "His aim is to reach the very fount of laughter and tears."

Mr. Conrad has no lack of the modern realist-reporter's facility in transcribing minute surface aspects of life; indeed, his notation of them is eminently firm and sharp. But he transcribes them only as indices of the moral life which at once implies and transcends them; and he penetrates further into the dusky hinterland of character and motive than any other modern "historian of hearts"—the more remarkably, it seems to us, because quite without the apparatus of the "psychological" novelist.

II

To be a historian of hearts, in the sense of feeling the isolation and secret mysterious beauty of each individual adventure, is to be almost necessarily a historian of the lonely. Mr. Conrad speaks somewhere of "the indestructible loneliness that surrounds, envelops, clothes every human soul from the cradle to the grave, and, perhaps, beyond." And instinctively he chooses from the medley of lives those that are most detached from "the community of hopes and fears," most cut off, by some agency of race, of inheritance, of character, or simply of chance, from participation in the life of civilized and social man. In the earlier stage of his work his bent was toward the man cut off by his own act; in the later stage it has been toward the man cut off by his own nature. But whether he writes about a disgraced man outlawed from society, or about a profoundly individual and solitary man locked in the unlighted cell of his own temperament, the meaning is always that there is a tragic beauty in our secret process of being ourselves; that the indestructible barriers of self are the most inexorable things in the world. And so, not only does he become very definitely and specially the spokesman of the outcast, but he also perceives that, in some intangible and spiritual sense, every one in the world is an outcast.

The first barrier that Mr. Conrad studied was that of race. The central character of *Almayer's Folly* is the isolated white man stranded in a back-water of life among brown men. *An Outcast of the Islands* presents the sharper issue, the more relentless tragedy, of the white man's infatuation for the brown woman. In the two novels about revolutionists, *The Secret Agent* and *Under Western Eyes*, Mr. Conrad comes a step nearer to Western civilization. Haldin, the anarchist murderer in *Under Western Eyes*, condenses in one laconic utterance the whole burden of the antisocial life and conscience—" Men like me leave no posterity." Here again the theme is fundamentally racial. The characters, both anarchist and autocrat, are alike victims of the deep unconscious irony of the old Russia; that irony which expressed itself in the sterile violence of anarchist and autocrat against each other, while between them the real Russia was gored and trampled.

But neither of these types of fiction, where the action turns on tragic mischances of race or of interracial contact, is the true quintessence of Conrad. For he is most himself where he explores the purely individual solitude, probing, not the mystery of racial difference, but the intricate laws of the individual variation. When he does that, he comes even closer to the meaning of spiritual solitude as a universal reality: because he studies solitude, not through the nature of race, a mere circumstance, but through the nature of the soul itself, or through some physical event that has left its impress indelibly on the soul.

The soul that was born aloof may be represented by Captain MacWhirr, the stolid and unimaginative master mariner of *Typhoon.* The clue to MacWhirr's identity, his unspeakable remoteness from the hearts and lives of common men, is his utter incapacity for fear, even for ordinary caution. It is not that he has courage: it has simply never occurred to him that there could be anything to require courage. Fear itself is actually more social than his kind of immunity from fear, for fear at least rests on the constructive imagination of things to be shunned, and such imagination drives men together. But MacWhirr "was unable to discover the message of a prophecy till the fulfilment had brought it home to his very door." He had "just enough imagination to carry him through each successive day, and no more." Similarly, Lord Jim is rendered solitary by his romantic self-loathing, "Il Conde" by his instinctive horror of all human brutality or extreme self-assertion, Nostromo by his colossal vanity, Mr. X. in "The Informer" by his skepticism, Heyst in *Victory* by his distrust of spontaneous action, and a dozen other characters by a dozen other such qualities as make every individual unique and incommunicable.

The soul that has become unapproachable through the effect of something accidental in its past may be studied in Falk, who has become monstrous and inhuman in his own eyes because he has once eaten human flesh; or in Dr. Monygham, who has lashed himself into misanthropy by constant self-torture with the thought of his ancient betrayal of a trust; or in

Captain Whalley, in "The End of the Tether," who has severed himself from the tradition of seamen's honor by sailing his ship after his eyesight has dimmed. All these are so near to being ordinary folk that we see ourselves reflected in them; and this nearness to common life is half at least of Conrad's strength in treatment of character. The other half is his perception of the strangeness which underlies the familiarity; the strangeness which comes from the something inexplicable and nameless at the center of every soul, making it eternally foreign to every other.

Thus Mr. Conrad reproduces in the individual the mystery of race. He deals, not only with a world in which East is East and West is West, but also with a world in which every man is a foreigner to his neighbor. The secret and invisible thing that renders us alien to each other is the thing that Mr. Conrad is always trying to disentangle; nothing less will suffice for his insistently humane and tender curiosity. When he has traced that thing to its source, and shown how it expresses itself in all the groping and baffled actions of the outward life, he has done his task. What we do and say and strive for may be the necessary means and materials of the search; but its end is always the tragic beauty of what we are. The outward wrappings, however grotesque or trivial in themselves, are suffused with this light from within—a light other than the glamour of romance as we commonly understand romance, because that glamour is an illusory flicker thrown from without over the mixed spectacle of reality, while this inner glow is the radiation of the deepest reality itself.

III

It is legitimate and helpful to indicate at this point that Mr. Conrad himself is, for one inescapable reason and another, among the loneliest of mortals, and that underneath his inspired and almost unprecedented gift of comradeship there exists a melancholy sense of his own isolation. To this extent Mr. Conrad has generously violated his own privacy in *The Mirror of the Sea* and *A Personal Record.* The fact puts us at once in touch with his largest aspiration, the meaning that he draws even out of the things that in themselves make for despair. If he writes about the man fallen out of his racial background, or cut off from his safe and sheltered past, or rendered inscrutable, even to those nearest his sympathy, by passions or memories that cannot be shared, the reader may be very sure that he is only writing about a fraction of his own experience.

Racially, his position is of course anomalous. Of the language in which his books are written he learned the first words in his twentieth year; and there is a dumb eloquence in the simple fact that in the twenty years of his following the sea he never encountered a man of his own nationality. To every faculty except faith, his Poland was long a lost cause; and there was a species of bitter irony in the fact that the soldiers of the autocracy which had hunted his parents into exile became the allies of the nation which has received his fervent loyalty. How wistfully his memory reaches out toward the scenes, the happenings, the personal presences of his lost past, only the chapters of *A Personal Record* can adequately unfold; but it is clear that all these things are most vividly present in the hinterland of his imaginative life. If a great-uncle of Mr. Conrad had not helped devour a Lithuanian dog in the retreat from Moscow, Falk might never have eaten his grotesque meal of human flesh. Upon all the great women of Conrad's books falls the shadow of his mother, tenderly pictured for us in *A Personal Record*. These earliest things are beautiful, and they are gone beyond recalling.

The second of Mr. Conrad's three lives, his score of years filled with "the voices of rough men now no more, the strong voice of the everlasting winds, the whisper of a mysterious spell"—that life of the sea, too, is irrecoverably gone. These losses—each of them the loss of an immense slice of physical existence without any corresponding loss in the accompanying mental and emotional life—account for the vague melancholy of everything that Conrad writes, the melancholy of a man whose worlds crumble away round him and leave him to construct other worlds from the remnants. In one sense he has had everything, in another sense he has lost everything. It is the paradox of these two facts, the physical loss and the spiritual retention, that leaves him alone, in a world where the immediate realities are but seemings, and the true realities are things that have well-nigh "perished out of mind."

It is through this paradox of Mr. Conrad's life and temper that we can understand the full moral import of his work. He has lost and he has retained; in the midst of crumbling and disintegration he has achieved continuity; he has found the way to turn every kind of failure into some kind of success. He stresses the solitariness of his own heart only in order that he may prove how the faculties of hope, of courage, of imagination struggle against it and, reaching beyond barriers of space and nationality, recover old contacts or replace them by new ones. And in his tales, similarly, he stresses the solitariness of men and women, with a kind of inverted emphasis, to show the desperate ardor of their struggle for fraternity. In other words, his mode of arguing the supreme worth of human solidarity as an ideal is to exhibit the whole array of difficulties which tragically interfere with that ideal, sometimes turning the pursuit of it into appalling disaster. Writing about the terrible loneliness of expatriates, he is really celebrating the indispensable security of home and country. In fact, his consistent way of affirming anything is to deny its opposite. His outlaws and anarchists prove the beauty of law and of the civilized conventions; his impractical dreamers exist for praise of the practical life; his skeptics and men of lost honor imply the need of faith and of fidelity. And always, while he portrays the forces of dissolution, the forces that sunder lives, his insistence remains indirectly on the ideal of brotherhood—"the latent feeling of fellowship with all creation—. . . the solidarity in dreams, in joy, in sorrow, in aspirations, in illusions, in hope, in fear, which binds men to each other, which binds together all humanity—the dead to the living and the living to the unborn."

So vivid is Mr. Conrad's sense of "the latent feeling of fellowship with all creation" that if he were to make a formal definition of his personal system of ethics he would probably make it in some such phrase as Royce's "Loyalty to Loyalty"—devotion to whatever fosters the idea and the practice of loyalty in men's lives, hatred of whatever defeats the idea and the practice. Not being given to formal definitions, Mr. Conrad phrases his ideal in a few words which recur with unconscious frequency throughout his books, such words as Conscience, Service, Fidelity, Honor, Solidarity—Loyalty itself among them. These are all intensely social words; no one of them means anything except to the individual whose imagination gets outside the crevice of individual sufficiency and becomes aware of the mass of mankind. The ideas in such words are necessarily the basis of society; and any group of lives largely ruled by them is a society in the most intelligible sense.

It is probably because the life of the sea rests on such simple and unshakable ideas, and is in fact a brotherhood of unwritten law stronger than law itself, that Mr. Conrad finds on the decks of ships so much to affirm his faith in solidarity and so little to deny it. It is only in his tales of the sea that tragedy does not predominate. The life of sailors is a life of invisible loyalties. They feel, not only the obvious loyalty to each other, to their officers, to their code of honor, but also, obscurely and beautifully, to ships, "the creatures of their hands and the objects of their care," and to the tradition of the sea as it has come to them from remote and forgotten generations—generations of seamen that were, Mr. Conrad says, "like stone caryatides that hold up in the night the lighted halls of a glorious and resplendent edifice."

IV

If we have measurably succeeded in expressing the reality and the intensity of Mr. Conrad's faith in the social instinct in man, and the obstinacy of its fight against the forces of dissolution and anarchy in man's own nature, we have expressed what is by all odds his supreme claim as a social philosopher addressing the modern social conscience. But there is another conflict of the social will, against another and larger opponent, not inside but outside man; and this still remains to be described before we can deal with our author simply as the artist speaking to "our capacity for delight and wonder."

Briefly, man triumphs over his individual differences so far as to conclude that fellowship must be the supreme logic of creation. Then, having to that extent learned the lesson of brotherhood, man looks outside the immediate world of his own kind, and discovers that fellowship is not the logic of creation at all—that in the chaos of warring species and mute constellations there *is* no decipherable logic. And again he despairs of the frail human sodality. If the universe is framed for lawlessness, if disaster is as natural in it as triumph, and war as inevitable as peace, why should man take the trouble to invent loyalties and organize brotherhoods? Why should not the individual assert himself and get what he can for himself out of a precarious existence, let what may happen to others?

These are, of course, the questions raised by such pessimism as that of Heyst in *Victory*, or by the despair of such disappointed optimism as that of Martin Decoud in *Nostromo*. One logical outcome of a desperate world is despair in the individual; and to a temperament such as Hardy's, despair is the only possible outcome. But there is another logic, the logic of a different temperament, which answers that, if the universal affair is desperate, it is so much the more necessary for the human affair to be hopeful, and that men's standing together against the universal threat is one way to cheat adverse destiny. This is in fact Mr. Conrad's answer. And it is characteristic of his inexorable love of truth that he draws the answer, by another of his paradoxes, out of a dark view of the world-purpose—a view which is dark because it is negative, blank, entirely non-ethical.

"The ethical view of the universe involves us at last," he says, "in so many cruel and absurd contradictions, where the last vestiges of faith, hope, charity, and even of reason itself, seem ready to perish, that I have come to suspect that the aim of creation cannot be ethical at all. I would fondly believe that its object is purely spectacular." The cosmos is "a spectacle for awe, love, adoration, or hate, if you like, but in this view . . . never for despair! Those visions, delicious or poignant, are a moral end in themselves. . . . The unwearied self-forgetful attention to every phase of the living universe reflected in our consciousness may be our appointed task on this earth—a task in which fate has perhaps engaged nothing of us except our conscience, gifted with a voice in order to bear true testimony to the visible wonder, the haunting terror, the infinite passion, and the illimitable serenity; to the supreme law and the abiding mystery of the sublime spectacle."

In other and less eloquent words, the fact that the world has no meaning does not prove that what we feel about it has no meaning; and it is futile folly to renounce the natural and spontaneous emotions in order to hope exorbitantly or to despair about a mere assumption. This is the logic that drives us back to the soluble problems of our own tangled world, the microcosm of purposes which do exist and in accordance with which we do act—the world in which the various private dreams and the collective dream of brotherhood are sufficient moral ends.

This, too, is the logic, expressed as usual by indirection, which comes out of Mr. Conrad's tragedies of intellectual men. Heyst, in *Victory*, is the modern man who asks so little of creation that he does not even reach out his hand for what life offers him. He has schooled himself to "a full and equable contempt." To a really lucid mind, action, from whatever motive, is a defilement; and love is only a stratagem "to bring out of the lightless void the shoals of unnumbered generations." Men and women are the least substantial part of the general nightmare: Heyst sees them as "figures cut out of cork, and weighted with lead just sufficiently to keep them in their proudly upright posture." But, through a temperamental accident which contradicts his deliberate choice, he commits himself to life, to love; and when he suffers the normal human loss, having only the negation of his abnormal philosophy to help him to resignation and readjustment, he can but cry in despair, "'Ah, Davidson, woe to the man whose heart has not learned while young to hope, to love—and to put its trust in life.'"

Thus, as in other stories of Mr. Conrad, the meaning of failure is less tragic than the physical fact. Heyst dies, but in the moment of his death his heart beats for the first time with the heart of humanity. The story ends with a dead woman's triumph over his paralyzing skepticism.

Against such a negative case as this of Heyst, one may set Conrad's affirmation of a robust working philosophy of life. That affirmation comes to us, as from an artist it should, in the form of an image: the little ship's company in the forecastle of the *Narcissus* on her interminable and timeless voyage from Bombay round the Cape of Storms and homeward to a port of England. In that forecastle there is no forgetting of either nature or man. Round the ship is the unchanging circular emptiness of the horizon, never free from the veiled menace which is part of the life of the sea; within the ship is the vivid realization of the only practical answer to the menace, a comradeship of choice cemented by necessity and the hostility of the common foe. The pressure of the immense nothingness outside is only a pressure of men together. It is a pleasure to think that in this first of his pictures of the working partnership of a few lives regulated by a common bond of service, and strong in a conscious fidelity, Mr. Conrad may have intended a half-symbolic image of man's part in his world of space and time.

V

Mr. Conrad's use of conscious artifice in his writing is so exclusively determined by his general ideas—especially by this general idea of man's relation to the universe of which he must be, for art, the focal point—that it is exceedingly difficult to separate the novelist from the thinker. That Mr. Conrad is indeed the conscious artist one may deduce from his style, which in every phase, from its somewhat too flushed and rhapsodic beginnings to its carefully disciplined later developments, is marked by care for the fitly chosen word, the rhythm and cadence of sentences. Or, if other proof is needed, let it be sought in the arrangement of the effects of light and shadow in the story "Youth," or in the purely decorative opening and closing formula of "The Brute." Such matters are important, and they have something to do with Mr. Galsworthy's professed belief that Conrad's work is likely to "enrich the English language."

But it is more immediately desirable to point out the exact and inevitable correspondence between art as this author defines it and his account of the relation of man's consciousness to "every phase of the living universe." We find him declaring that the truth of the objective world is in the emotions evoked by it; that the moral worth of a phase of the cosmos is in direct ratio to the moral or social feelings stirred in the beholder. And art he defines through exactly the same relation of the phase of reality to the mood in which the artist receives it. In his own words, "To snatch in a moment of courage, from the remorseless rush of time, a passing phase of life, is only the beginning of the task. The task approached in tenderness and faith is to hold up unquestioningly, without choice and without fear, the rescued fragment before all eyes and in the light of a sincere mood."

If we accept his definition as sincere—and there is no evidence to indicate that he has ever followed any other—we find him taking in the presence of an artistic "subject" the same posture he recommends us to take toward the incomprehensible whole of things, and cherishing no purpose beyond the moral sensations evoked by his lesser spectacle; there being in fact, between the greater cosmic affair and the lesser artistic, no difference at all except the artist's necessary care for communication of what he has experienced. It is worth while to note in passing that this is among the most acceptable definitions of art that have ever been framed, in that it falls between the acceptance of art as purely decorative and unmoral and the opposite requirement of a didactic and utilitarian value.

One or the other half of this general definition, or the combination of both halves, will be found to account in minute detail for Mr. Conrad's artistic process. If the value of life is to be defined in terms of the emotions evoked by it, then there can be no curtailment of the phase by arbitrary "technique," with its different, its unmoral and abstract notion of relevance. As a fact, Mr. Conrad's practice of inclusion and exclusion is based on the moral values of the given case, quite in the sense of his definition. He leaves out ruthlessly, even to the sacrifice of just the type of narration which he executes with most overwhelming effect, wherever exclusion prospers his larger purposes. And he rounds out his "phase of life" by inclusion of much that the most rigid economy would discountenance. "The End of the Tether," his story of the master mariner going blind, begins, on the orthodox formula, "near the crisis"; but it loops backward and still backward until it has become the comprehensive story of a life. And, like most of its author's work, it achieves its crisis in such a fashion as to shed relevance backward upon all that momentarily seemed irrelevant. There *is* ultimately no irrelevance in Conrad, because everything that he admits into the chosen subject is fused at last in the heat of his unifying purpose, the evocation of a special mood.

An interesting extension of the novelist's art, so defined, occurs in *Chance,* where even the duality of phase and mood breaks down and the two coalesce. There is more than a casual fitness in Henry James's comment on *Chance:* ". . . the whole clutch of eggs, and these withal of the freshest, in that one basket." Briefly, Mr. Conrad presented the mood of the beholder as an integral part of the subject itself; he put it explicitly into the story, instead of merely so organizing the story as to conjure it into being. *Chance* is the story of a romantic love affair which a first person singular, the author presumably, pieces together from Marlow's account, after Marlow has pieced it together from several other accounts. It is not grossly inaccurate to say that *Chance* is the author's reëdited version of Marlow's interpretation of Fyne's and Powell's not too skilful summaries of what they saw happen. Now, on the supposition that Mr. Conrad wanted only to tell the story of Flora de Barral, her convict father, and her quixotic and impetuous lover, his machinery is cumbersome and formidable. But there is every reason to suppose that what most interested him was the sight of Marlow's eager and humane inquisitiveness at work upon the complex materials of that story. In other words, *Chance* is a sort of apotheosized detective story, in which Marlow is the principal detective, and the thing detected is the exquisite and incredible happiness snatched by two people whose understanding love triumphs over every obstacle. It is no more the story of the love affair exclusively than a detective story is the recital of a crime exclusively. *Chance* is primarily the account of a beautiful if somewhat inquisitive *sympathy* at work upon a phase of life which exists to invite sympathy. Considered as such, it adds a cubit to the stature of that Marlow whom we know in *Lord Jim*, in "Heart of Darkness," in "Youth," and almost certainly, though by no name, in "Falk." Also, it adds a cubit to Mr. Conrad's stature as one more disciple of Henry James, for it obviously practises Henry James's favorite device of tincturing the story throughout with the finest, most responsive consciousness present or available.

VI

We have seen that Mr. Conrad sacrifices economy and swiftness of movement to mood: it remains to add that he sacrifices chronology to the same governing principle. Mood and chronology cannot both be supreme, for to enforce mood any given piece of material must appear where it weighs most in terms of character, not merely where it serves a narrow constructive expediency. Whence innumerable events in the remote past, suppressed only to be revealed at present crises; whence the looping, intersecting construction of *Lord Jim;* whence the odd lapsus in *Under Western Eyes*, so contrived that Part IV shall begin where Part I leaves off. It is relatively unimportant, except as one of several evidences of a purely technical ambidexterity, that these affairs set themselves right by the calendar once the book is laid down; so that, however sure one may be that the tale is incoherent as Mr. Conrad tells it, one invariably recalls the events in strictly chronological sequence.

Nostromo utilizes more than any other of the tales, and to a greater end, this trick of chronology thwarted in the service of a higher coherence. What this novel develops, so far as a very succinct statement will suffice, is the idea of avarice as a force dominant over a large community of lives, until at last it crushes out the few lives in which we have invested the most of our sympathy, including the one life, that of Nostromo, which we had thought most immune from the corrosion of greed. The story rambles in wide loops and circles over a stretch of years; but through it, from the opening chapter, in which two legendary gringos perish in a vain search for gold, until the closing page, in which Linda Viola throws herself into the sea for a lost love, the idea of avarice sweeps evenly on to its sinister triumph, drawing after it with a powerful suction the litter of individual lives, wills, and actions. At the outset we see that idea of avarice embodied in Charles Gould's silver mine, the pivot of the economic and political life of Costaguana, a semi-tropical state of South America. Presently avarice takes the concrete shape of a particular quarterly load of the mine's output, a single hoard of silver ingots which Nostromo, the captain of the Navigation Company's longshoremen, and the young patriot Decoud receive into a cargo-lighter and secrete by night in an island ravine, to save it from the hands of revolutionist bandits. At last, when the revolution has been put down and Decoud has gone mad on his island and killed himself, Nostromo, who alone knows that the treasure is still accessible, resolves to "grow rich slowly," and abstracts the ingots one by one, under cover of night. Thus avarice lays its shriveling finger on him, the selected victim of its irony; and thus the design is rounded out.

It is here, for the only time on a large scale, that Mr. Conrad begins, not with the struggle of the isolated outcast, but with the whole panorama of civilization from which he falls. The rôle of outcast here is played by avarice itself, the *proscrit* of moral qualities, rather than by any individual. Costaguana, the imagined seaboard country of the tale, a republic lying between mountains and gulf, is of course the modern world in little. As Mr. Conrad depicts it, it is complete enough to revolutionize, among other things, one's idea of South American revolutions. It furnishes successive pictures of civilization in different eras, from the old days of free-handed governmental cessions down to the modern days of exploitation by foreign capital and increasing industrial unrest. After the civil conflict is over and the incalculable wealth of the Gould Concession is preserved intact to its owner, one whose vision is of the clearest says to Mrs. Gould: "There is no peace and rest in the development of material interests. They have their law and their justice. But it is founded on expediency, and it is inhuman; it is without rectitude, without the continuity and the force that can be found only in a moral principle. Mrs. Gould, the time approaches when all that the Gould Concession stands for shall weigh as heavily upon the people as the barbarism, cruelty, and misrule of a few years back."

And reverberating through the book, literally from the first page to the last, haunting every chapter like the wandering echo of some lost truth, is the suggestion that the world's problems are more than economic, that national identities must not be tampered with from the outside in the name of progress.

This tale of lives ruled by a precious metal is winning unstinted praise from more and more authoritative voices. It remains thus far, to our thinking, the one work by which Mr. Conrad would stand if he were to fall by every other. There is certainly nothing else in English like it; indeed it is obvious that its author, even when so profoundly original as here, has worked under Continental influences—those of the French and Russian masters, with whom we must include Henry James, whose avowed discipleship is to Balzac and Tourgenev. But from whatever quarter Mr. Conrad's own influence a half-century hence shall appear to come, one feels more strongly with every re-reading that it must come *as* an influence, acknowledged and far-reaching; for he is one of the three or four enduring beacons of our generation. Both as man and as artist he is too great to be comprehended in any one glimpse. And his service, to letters as to life, has been the unfalteringly good service which he has but lately commemorated in *The Shadow-Line*, a tale of devotion and self-command beautifully worthy of its own dedication to a son at the front, and to "all others who, like himself, have crossed in early youth the shadow-line of their generation."

THE YOUNGER GENERATION

XIII

THE YOUNGER GENERATION

I

If we consider the reputations in fiction which have been won mainly within a decade, together with some which are even now being won, we deal with a heterogeneous spectacle in which it is difficult to trace the working of any very specific law. One might be tempted to say that the novel has come into an era of crumbling and dissolution, were it not for the extraordinary diffusion of merit which is among the chief symptoms of the moment. That diffusion of merit through fiction from half a hundred pens, with or without the presence of enough concentrated genius to make a golden age, is a sign of re-creation rather than of dissolution. And the promise of re-creation is supported by the very lack of continuity in the present history of fiction. What is decadence if not the mastery and glibly accomplished repetition by little people of a formula which has been successful in the hands of great people, until at last the formula has been run into the ground? Decadence might almost be defined as excess of continuity in literary tradition. The present interest in a great variety of means, and the disposition to forsake old formulæ for new experiments, are among the most hopeful of signs. So long as the quest of newness is a result of energy and not of weariness, we are entitled to look forward to great fulfilments, not merely back upon them. Even apart from the quickening and revivifying effects which we dare ask of the war, there is enough to justify a belief that the novel is going through a process of self-renewal. Certainly it is remaking itself among us, as the drama remade itself before and during the first half of the life of Shakspere. We may be the pre-Shakspereans of this century.

There is more than a figure of speech in this comparison, and more than a casual fitness. Not only is the novel attaining its new shape, as the five-act romantic drama did in " the spacious time," through the excellent individual contributions of many writers less great than the greatest, but it is also attaining that new shape through about the same balance of native elements supplied and foreign elements assimilated. The splendor of the Elizabethan time in literature is its effective union of some old and alien things—the tradition of Aristotle and the tradition of Seneca, the Italian *novella* and the Italian lyric and dramatic forms, the rescued heritage of the Renaissance and its humanism—with some indigenous and relatively new things: the self-evolved types of morality and interlude, of mystery and pageant, the lore of native kingdoms Welsh and English, and the magically rapid evolution of blank verse;—the old shaping and sifting the new, the new revitalizing the old, and the whole fired by a new local enthusiasm based on solidarity and national self-awareness. It was an age of copying and it was an age of re-creating. The first without the second is void: witness the "heroic romances" of the seventeenth century, all the voluminous futilities of the Grand-Cyrus school. The second without the first is less than it is privileged to be: witness our grand, yet strangely insular and one-legged Victorian novelists from Dickens to Trollope. The Elizabethan dramatists, like Chaucer, like Spenser and Milton, like the Romantic poets, were national in their feeling and international in their knowledge and taste; they must be studied as matters of comparative literature if they are to be understood, not merely worn as feathers in the national cap. And what is true of them is also true, it seems to us, of novelists in English to-day: they are busy making the novel, in form and content, more international than it has ever been, by uniting some Continental traditions evolved in France and Russia with some British traditions of our grandest period in the novel, the period of Dickens and Thackeray.

There are other matters that could be cited,—lesser matters mostly, outcroppings of influence in this author or that,—but this trend toward internationalism in form and feeling is the nearest approach to an inclusive and adequately descriptive law. Other symptoms are definite enough but non-typical: for example, the recrudescence of the "problem" novel; the rise of the trilogy; the influence of the late Samuel Butler; the tendency toward more and more minute specialization in local color; the opposite tendency toward the globe-trotting international novel; the pursuit of Henry James into salon and studio; the pursuit of Gissing and Arnold Bennett into the slum and the shop; the study of abnormal types and experiences; the study of humdrum and average types and experiences; the devotion to minutely photographic realism; the revolt against photographic realism and the insistence on the representative value of the material used; the reappearance of the very loosely strung biographical novel; the simultaneous development of the novel which is like the short story in its unity and focus. These and other symptoms do exist; and one could convince one's self by a specious array of evidences that any of them is *the* tendency of the hour. But all of them, contradictory as they are, are included within our broad generalization, the force which is at work to Continentalize the fiction of England and America.

II

Some of the ways in which that force has changed the architectural method of the novel we have already discussed in connection with Henry James, Mrs. Wharton, and Mr. Conrad. The technical preëminence of these three writers, and especially of James and Conrad, will have been phrased in historical terms if we say that they were abreast of their time in acquiring the nicety which is French, and decidedly ahead of it in acquiring the intensity which is Russian. For these are, we take it, the distinguishing marks of the French tradition and the Russian: the nicety of finish which comes of infinite care for details, and which has to be described in terms of the process; and the intensity which comes of stark isolation of the theme from all the rest of actuality, and which can be described only in terms of the result. The French temper has a finer selectiveness, concerns itself more with exclusion of the non-essential and nice etching of the essential: the Russian temper is more inclusive, also more capable of obsession, and it reaches unity in the result through a passionate unity of purpose more than through exquisiteness in the process. The last decades of the century just gone were the time when the influence of France came belatedly into our fiction; the Russian influence, anticipated by the individual authors just named and by one or two others, is largely of the present and the future.

In some such matters of chronology we have the explanation of the partial chaos which the twentieth century finds in our fiction. Because the French influence came to us so belatedly, we had not assimilated it before we began to feel the Russian forcing us in quite another direction. The spread of internationalism in taste was much faster than the power of artistic forms to grow; a single decade, the decade in which British novelists began to be fine artificers according to the cross-Channel standard, brought the discovery of what Slavic Europe had done and was doing for the novel in the direction of scope and power; and fiction, by trying to be tremendous before it had completely learned to be skilful, suffered the growing pains proper to extreme youth. Indeed, it still suffers them, principally in the form of size without shape, abundance without method—faults of the realism which is indiscriminately interested in everything.

For this lateness in discovering the importance of narrative method, we have of course to thank the insularity of our own masters of the novel in the mid-nineteenth century. Method involves before all else the problem of what elements can be done without in order that the most may be made of what remain; and this, the first concern of the Frenchman in any form of art, was a matter of the least possible concern to our grand prodigal indispensable sainted Victorians. The challenge they spectacularly rose to was to get everything done, somehow, anyhow, before the sudden curtain descended, the whole bagful of tricks poured out in the one short entertainment—the enchanting mystery and the sublime helplessness of the situation being the bag's inveterate fondness for getting itself replenished from the bottom while the conjurer poured from the top. Neither Dickens nor Thackeray could ever thinkably have bothered much to produce a perfect novel: they were both too much occupied with doing every single thing that could be done. In a very real sense they left all their works as unfinished as their last; it was as though they were always being reminded of some forgotten engagement to dine at seven with a group of boisterous immortals who wouldn't take no for an answer. What they left unfinished was, of course, the outpouring of the inexhaustible reservoir of themselves, waters too tumultuous for any filtration by method. Dickens's novels, says Mr. Chesterton, are simply " lengths cut from the flowing and mixed substance called Dickens." This entire absorption in the question of What, and the corresponding freedom from questions of Why and How, this unregulated identity of the writer with the thing written, is pretty characteristic likewise of pre-Victorian novelists from Aphra Behn to Scott, with the single illustrious exception of Jane Austen, working out for herself, under a beneficent compulsion of circumstance, the lesson of the small fruitful field well tilled. Jane Austen achieved a sort of brilliant false dawn of narrative method, reflected pallidly by Mrs. Gaskell in *Cranford*, and hysterically by two of the Brontës. But the equals of Mrs. Gaskell in and after her time—Bulwer, Disraeli, Reade, Kingsley, Trollope, Collins, Mrs. Oliphant—open the lavish Victorian purse and fling out sovereigns as though they were pence; and on the whole with more waste than that of Dickens and Thackeray, whose gift is after all but the expended interest of an endless fortune. The true modern economy of the novel may be said to have begun in English with George Eliot—economy here taking the form of Jane Austen's microscope applied to a small and homogeneous group of interlocking destinies, wrought out in terms of fateful character upon a small and thickly atmospheric scene, to a greater end than Jane Austen had consciously in view.

Now, the history of the Victorian deficit of method, when it appears in the full record, will have to be put in terms of comparative literature, and most of all in terms of one negative force, the long suppression of Balzac. Balzac was the one influence which could have methodized without seriously curtailing the Victorian largesse. Trollope and other masters of plenitude stood much in need of Balzac, who left them cold and incurious; George Eliot, with her natural gift of intensiveness, stood in far less need of George Sand, to whom she warmed instinctively. It was part of the rich Victorian insularity to accept nothing but more and always more of what it had. George Eliot herself was recreantly to become an exponent of waste, through pushing analysis farther in the direction of the diffusely sermonic than analysis can profitably go. Thus it remained for Meredith to clear the ground and lay, for a more modern refinement of method, his foundation of Comedy. The Meredithian doctrine requires economy both in characters and scene and in analysis of them; and, as we have noted, Meredith's own economy after *The Egoist* becomes more and more intensive. *Lord Ormont and His Aminta* and *The Amazing Marriage*, books which stand at the end of the Meredith shelf, are among the very earliest in English to give the impression of being as thoroughly done as the best novels of Balzac, without that of being thoroughly overdone.

III

The danger of so long a suppression of a great force is that eventually one will receive the dregs of it and mistake them for the good wine. Balzac ignored in one generation, by those who could have copied him creatively, means Zola accepted at his face value in the next, and by those who could copy him but slavishly, with special reference to the worst of him. When a great period refuses to be greatly cosmopolitan, it prepares the way for a little period to be pettily cosmopolitan. This is in fact what threatened, and came partly to pass, in our fiction at the beginning of the new century. The French skill in handling details in composition began to appear in the form of masses of details without much composition; anything that was "realistic" would do. The French scientific curiosity about odd and exceptional phases of life began to show itself in our bent toward morbidly specialized phenomena, treated with nothing of the cool French impersonality to justify the treatment; and this sudden attempt to reach novelty through abnormality threatened to send our whole fiction off at a tangent from the socializing direction it had begun to take. It lost its new typicality and its interest in the broad natural laws of society, of civilization; and for a time Paris meant to us, not Balzac, not even Flaubert, but the dregs of Zola and the experimental novel, the mere technique of Maupassant and the short story.

It was then and there that the English novel was saved by Russia—the Russia in the best work of Hardy, James, Conrad, and the Russia which our novelists began to discover at first hand for themselves. The Russian novel had been social in its import, and its influence tended to resocialize the English novel. The Russian novel had been lavish of detail; and in this respect it led us straight back to our own Victorian tradition. The Russian novel, unlike the Victorian, was invincibly, almost violently and fiercely, unified—not because it selected its material with artful narrowness, but because it brought tremendous areas of experience into the focus of a single mood, point of view, or purpose. The Russian novel, like the French, often dealt with the abnormal, the ghastly; but it did so with a passionate sense that it *was* abnormal, and neither unmorally nor cynically. The result was that we learned the lesson of artistic unity as we could not then have learned it, save in the short story, from Paris; and the novel, with a new intensity and a new skill in minutiæ, attained at last the integrity as a form of art which had been its missed privilege a long generation earlier.

We see the effects of this superposition of influences in some recent stories which, ten years ago, would probably have become just French realistic novels written, with arid skill, in the English language, but now compelled by force of history to be something much better than that. To take a single illustration, *The Devil's Garden,* by Mr. W. B. Maxwell, seems to stamp our two European traditions together in an entirely new type of construction, gaining a real thrill by technique alone, and at the same time turning a mockingly light treatment of sexual adventure into an honest study of life. The book has two peaks of interest with a long dead level between them. William Dale, a rural postmaster, incurs censure for an official indiscretion; then he discovers that his wife, to get the influence necessary to his reinstatement, has sold herself to a lecherous old man. The scene of this discovery, after which Dale goes away in rage and humiliation, is the first crisis. Unaccountably, he returns and takes up the broken relation; the Dales go into the country, buy a farm, and live a placid life full of kindnesses to those less well off than themselves. They adopt a homeless young girl. Dale's paternal love for her, his occasional fits of moroseness and despondency, and his somewhat neurasthenic religious experiences form together the dead level of the story. As Dale grows older, and his young protégée grows into the first beauty of womanhood, he comes sharply face to face with the hideous fact that all his senses covet possession of her, that he is all but on the point of reënacting the part once played by another toward his own wife. He struggles, he is horribly torn; and at the supreme point of his moral agony it is divulged to the reader, through Dale's own self-torturing memories, that long ago, at the time of his disappearance, he had killed the man to whom his wife had sold herself. In this second ironic crisis of the book, then, Dale confronts the fact that he is about to commit the same wrong for which he has murdered a man. The revelation is so placed as to reinterpret his whole previous life and character. It is more than a trick of suspense: it is an example of technical adroitness as nearly sufficient in itself as it could well be, yet rigidly subordinated to a purpose which is other than technical.

Here, then, is a thing with a recognizable shape, a triumphant identity. And it is secure in possession of its kind of truth—an unpleasant kind, perhaps, but that is only to say that the tragedy is of nature and not merely of circumstance. Moreover, it chooses its facts generously, cutting out a broad strip of life; its unity is not so much of selection as of interpretation. Herein it is most Russian: where the French novelist rules out everything that does not visibly bear on his subject, the Russian chooses a subject on which everything can be brought to bear. *The Devil's Garden* seems to us a striking example of what can be done for the novel by the presence of happy auspices and combinations of tradition—the more striking, for this purpose, because the whole performance exacts of its author more of sensitiveness, adaptability, and perception of which way the wind is blowing than it does of the arrestingly brilliant genius which, whether it can afford to or not, often laughs at such lesser things.

IV

What, conversely, shall be said of Mr. Theodore Dreiser if not that he has fallen behind the times precisely through failure to perceive which way the wind is blowing? Not in this context need we bother to raise a serious issue with Mr. Dreiser's philosophy—which, for all we could guarantee to the contrary, may in the end dispossess every other. That philosophy is arrived at by a kind of brutally naturalistic biologizing; it is based almost altogether on the predaciousness of the human animal, in sex, in finance, even in art; and its worthy image, to be found in an early chapter of *The Financier*, is the lobster devouring, with a leisurely ruthlessness, its natural victim the squid. Much could be said against this reading of life, particularly on the score of what it elbows out. Moreover, it seems to us that it is a purely negative view, arrived at by too easy a series of negations. Is the Anglo-Saxon a superficial prude about love? Then Mr. Dreiser will be cosmopolitan and modern by showing that under our skins we are all beasts. Are our finance and our politics infested with sentimental illusions? Then Mr. Dreiser will make war on sentimental illusions by portraying, not folk who have got beyond illusions, but folk so elementally organized that they are incapable of sentiments. It is like denying bipedality by insisting that hands are only forefeet highly evolved. Perhaps they are—but that does not destroy the bipedality, which consists just in the height of the evolution. Mr. Dreiser likes to remind us that man at his best is only a beast: we like to answer that man at his worst is still man—that is to say, a creature better potentially than he is actually. What we see almost equally in the Financier, the Titan, and the Genius is their infra-humanity. And the women of Mr. Dreiser's books have not the spiritual possibilities which could turn their material failure into tragedy. In ignoring the importance of the ideal faculty, Mr. Dreiser cuts off the half of life which gives all the meanings to the half he treats; which is perhaps why all the passions of his books seem so perfunctory.

But this is farther than we need go to suggest his insufficiency. It is enough to point out that he belongs to nothing in the present; by which we mean, not that he is in advance of his age, but that he has stood still while his age was going somewhere. His most recent contacts are with Zola and with the George

Moore of *Esther Waters;* all he has done to modernize these influences is to exaggerate them. He writes with the French outspokenness but not with the French skill; he has the Russian savageness of portrayal without the Russian interpretative unity. He goes to an international school, learns carefully the opposites of all the things that are taught there nowadays, plumes himself on the tolerant breadth of his world-citizenship, his truly modern acquisitiveness—and comes out the complete Prussian. He commits the Prussian fallacy of transferring the war of different species to different individuals of the same species; and, unmindful of the drift toward fraternity, he is equally unmindful of the novel's self-development toward symmetry and organic design. While the Russian novel criticises life by penetrating to the truths which lie at the center of it, the novels of Mr. Dreiser continue to select and present life in series of loosely strung illustrations of a theory; and even if we admit that the abhorrent theory may be true, we can at the same time protest that the art is not only bad, but a bad anachronism.

While Mr. Dreiser is making a whole world out of the predatory individualism which ruled in our commerce twenty years ago,—and now rules less crudely even there, we must admit if we are honest,—a remarkably homogeneous group of writers, realists and humanists all, is spreading its far broader criticism of life on a much narrower canvas. Mr. Dreiser deals narrowly with all civilization. Gilbert Cannan, Compton Mackenzie, W. L. George, J. D. Beresford, and to a certain extent Hugh Walpole and D. H. Lawrence—these have dealt broadly with two allied subjects. One of them is the British middle-class family, and through it the inescapable tragedy of family life: the gap between generations in taste, in ideas, in ways of living—the sheer inability of the elder generation to change, and of the younger to conform. The other and closely related subject is the effort of individualistic youth to break away from the inhibitions in its environment and, through education, work, art, science, politics, or it may be simply love, find its own place and make its own terms with life. The sudden accession of interest in youth and youth's struggle to stand on its own feet is shown in a large group of biographical novels dealing with the lives of young men through adolescence to the edge of maturity. Mr. Beresford's trilogy of Jacob Stahl is such a work about an exceptional person; *Youth's Encounter* and *Sinister Street*, by Mr. Mackenzie, form the greater part of another such about an average person. In these the favorite theme of Mr. Galsworthy is divorced from his exquisite fragility of method and joined to the lavish and exhaustive method of Arnold Bennett. The treatment is full enough to re-create life whole, and the purpose is critical enough to control and centralize the mass of details.

Typical as we find the novels just named, they are not so typical as those which join the theme of youth and its lonely adventure with the history of average families—such novels as *These Lynnekers* by Mr. Beresford, or *Round the Corner* and *Three Sons and a Mother* by Mr. Cannan. Mr. Cannan's novels in particular seem extraordinarily full and readable footnotes to *The Way of All Flesh,* Samuel Butler's more and more influential satire of the tyranny, dullness, and narrow obscurantism which so often go with domestic respectability. Especially since the beginning of the war, the domestic life of the ante-bellum world, the very basis of Western civilization, has begun to receive such an overhauling as the artist has never before tried to give it. The task of the serious-minded social historian is to show us, in that strangely remote past which could not decipher its own oracles, the thousand obscure hints of what was to be. The whole English-speaking world is open, as in modern times it has not been, to the experience denoted by the fine old theological phrase "conviction of sin." A great deal of our realistic fiction is conceived in some such mood as that of Mr. Britling—the mood of self-examination and penitence—without Mr. Britling's too fluent readiness to forget everything and take a fresh start. In these novels of the younger generation we see humane and searching criticism of society linking for the first time a treatment as full as that of a Thackeray novel and an effect as single as that of an Ibsen play.

V

We run the risk of losing, not our main point but the obviousness of its application, when we turn from these Butleresque novels of the family to the works of a writer who has wrought, by comparison, in hardy isolation, and whose more palpable contacts are with things past. Where the humor of Cannan, Beresford, Mackenzie, and the others is weighted with satire, the humor of Miss Ethel Sidgwick is lightened with whimsicality. Where they criticise certain provincial institutions from the outside, after an intellectual effort to escape, Miss Sidgwick shows how institutions are criticised by the best in themselves. If, as we suspect, the work of the men just named is as perishable as it is skilful, the reason is to be sought in the transience of the conditions with which it deals—usages and forms of intercourse that may pass and be forgotten. But if there is any threat of mortality in the stories of Miss Sidgwick, it is comparatively a trifle that betrays it: a mere fashion of speaking, the urbane slang in which most of her characters express themselves. The essence of her work is human nature, which is still much as it was when Fielding composed the "bill of fare to the feast" which prefaces *Tom Jones*. Picturing life where it is to be found at its finest, and admitting into her pictures the fewest possible of the colors that time and fashion can tarnish, she works in a medium to the center of which few since Jane Austen have preceded her—the timeless and indestructible medium of high comedy.

And yet there is more to Miss Sidgwick than her richly traditioned provincialism, her familiarity with the country aristocracy of Britain, her search for perfection of intercourse in a limited social stratum; there is more to her internationalism than her racily intuitive understanding of Ireland and the Irish. Very subtly and impalpably, without a badge or a formula, she is a modernist and an international critic of life—subtly and impalpably because, although she has nerves responsive to the best that is abroad in the world, she is deeply enough rooted in her own soil not to be shaken by every wind from every quarter. She assimilates and Anglicizes in a way to make one wonder whether the rest of us have not been too eagerly enslaved to things exotic, too quick to reap where we have not sown. Her way of respecting national identities is to stop at the incommunicable element in them. But that is very different from the Victorian way of ignoring their existence; and it is certainly, if not quite definably, modern.

The most recent available illustration is Miss Sidgwick's novel *Hatchways*, an unpretentious social comedy of eight or nine unforgettable people introduced to us at a country estate which gives its name to the book. One of them, M. Gilbert du Frettay, is the embodied fineness of French civilization, as certain of the others are of English. In his appreciation of Hatchways and its mistress,—both the place and the woman being coolness and quietude, taste and useful beauty, havens of all the perfections,—in their appreciation of him, and in the intuitive understanding between him and the two young Englishmen of the story, Miss Sidgwick seems to be saying to us that the finest is the finest, wherever one finds it. She shows us the best of England and the best of France flashing out like lightning to accept and embrace each other, in the time before the war. *Hatchways* received on its publication a stupid semi-official Tory frown for having noth-

INDEX

ing to do with the war. Well, in one sense a rainbow has nothing to do with a thunder-shower; but even the staidest Tory critic, reading *Hatchways,* should know that he is in the presence of a book which has, so to speak, *swallowed* the war, gulped it down at whatever cost, got outside it with never a thought of evasion. Every chapter has the tremulous and noble beauty of a face which, having once known and conquered the uttermost of sorrow, can thereafter smile—and wait.

This is thoroughly typical of Miss Sidgwick's process of assimilation everywhere. She seems to know everything and use everything, even to very small children and dumb animals; and ideas come to her naturally, make themselves at home in her presence. But one never finds her having convulsions over an idea, any more than one would have found Ernestine Redgate going into cheap raptures over a guest. Beside this effortless art, the work of most of Miss Sidgwick's contemporaries seems self-conscious, violent, orgastic. Miss Sidgwick says of one of her most adorable young women, Bess Ryeborn: " She never messed things, or dropped things, having the quick firm fingers of art." This sentence deserves to be reaimed at Miss Sidgwick herself. It perfectly describes the impression we were enabled to form through *Promise, Le Gentleman,* and *Herself,* three novels published almost simultaneously in this country after their author had won some recognition abroad; and that impression is more than sustained by the later novels, which have lost nothing in delicacy to compromise their gain in power.

If there is creative genius of the first order at work upon the novel in this younger generation of its practitioners, it is surely here that we must look for it, in a writer who, while as soundly local and realistic as we need wish, holds out in addition a gift of serene and timeless beauty. At the poorest estimate, we must reckon her one among many valuable evidences that the novel is still renewing itself out of the tissues of modern life; that its development, in both shape and substance, is an endless story of which some of the most absorbing chapters belong to the future.

Meanwhile, it remains as true as ever that the great persons are those who have both something to teach their age and an endless capacity to learn from it. They must be ahead of it, but they must also be in the line of it; they must lead it, but only to where it is going. Such greatness as we can discover in the fiction of to-day seems but the echoed hope of the whole race; a hope expressed long ago in the words of an old cry, since muffled sometimes by the uproar of irrelevant things, but only to ring out again, above all the tumult of our waste and war, the cry of "Liberty, Equality, Fraternity." There is room for faith that the newest books of our younger generation shall presently be the oldest books of our younger world.

INDEX